The Invention of Pornography

The Invention of Pornography

Obscenity and the Origins of Modernity, 1500–1800

Edited by Lynn Hunt

ZONE BOOKS · NEW YORK

1993

© 1993 Lynn Hunt

ZONE BOOKS

611 Broadway, Suite 608

New York, NY 10012

Printed in the United States of America.

Distributed by The MIT Press,
Cambridge, Massachusetts, and London, England

Library of Congress Cataloging in Publication Data

The Invention of pornography: obscenity and the
origins of modernity, 1500–1800 /
[edited by] Lynn Hunt.
    p.   cm.
    Includes bibliographical references
    ISBN 0-942299-68-X (hard): $26.95
    1. Pornography—Europe—History. 2. Social
History—Modern, 1500- . 1. Hunt, Lynn Avery.
HQ472.E85158   1993
363.4'7'09—dc20   92-42237
                                     CIP

Contents

Acknowledgments

The essays in this volume were all presented publicly at a conference on "The Invention of Pornography" held at the University of Pennsylvania in October 1991. The School of Arts and Sciences and the Annenberg Fund of the History Department funded the conference. Victoria Thompson, Jeffrey Horn and David Smith, graduate students in the History Department, helped to organize the conference and ensure its smooth functioning. We are grateful to them and to the participants at the conference who helped improve the papers with their comments and questions.

Introduction: Obscenity and the Origins of Modernity, 1500–1800

Lynn Hunt

Pornography Has a History

Pornography still provokes intense debate, but in Western countries it is now generally available to adult consumers and scholars alike. When you make your way to the Reserve Room of the Bibliothèque Nationale in Paris, for instance, there are only a few reminders of the secrecy formerly shrouding the famous Collection de l'Enfer. As late as 1992 you still had to fill out a form explaining your "precise reason for request." The asterisk on the front of the form referred you to the back where it said, "general or vague terms ('scientific research,' 'documentation,' 'personal research') will not be accepted." When you read those words of warning it is hard not to think of prim, worried librarians trying to keep dirty books out of the hands of the wrong people, most likely aging men in fraying suit jackets who would occupy their seats in search of something other than scholarship. It is a measure of the changing times that no one ever questions your responses any more.

The very existence of the Collection de l'Enfer or its English counterpart, the Private Case of the British Library, gives a sense of definition and clarity to pornography that it has not always had. Pornography did not constitute a wholly separate and distinct category of written or visual representation before the early nineteenth century. If we take pornography to be the explicit depiction of sexual organs and sexual practices with the aim of arousing sexual feelings, then pornography was almost always an adjunct to something else until the middle or end of the eighteenth century. In early modern Europe, that is, between 1500 and 1800, pornography was most often a vehicle for using the shock of sex to criticize religious and political authorities. Pornography nevertheless slowly emerged as a distinct category in the centuries between the Renaissance and the French Revolution thanks, in part, to the spread of print culture itself. Pornography developed out of the messy, two-way, push and pull between the intention of authors, artists and engravers to test the boundaries of the "decent" and the aim of the ecclesiastical and secular police to regulate it.

Although desire, sensuality, eroticism and even the explicit depiction of sexual organs can be found in many, if not all, times and places, pornography as a legal and artistic category seems to be an especially Western idea with a specific chronology and geography. As a term in the modern sense, pornography came into widespread use only in the nineteenth century. For some commentators, consequently, the late eighteenth and early nineteenth centuries were critical in the development of a modern notion of pornography. But the main lines of the modern pornographic tradition and its censorship can be traced back to sixteenth-century Italy and seventeenth- and eighteenth-century France and England (albeit with important antecedents in ancient Greece and Rome). Thus, the essays that follow shall focus on this time period and these places.

Pornography came into existence, both as a literary and visual practice and as a category of understanding, at the same time as – and concomitantly with – the long-term emergence of Western modernity. It has links to most of the major moments in that emergence: the Renaissance, the Scientific Revolution, the Enlightenment and the French Revolution. Writers and engravers of pornography came out of the demimonde of heretics, freethinkers and libertines who made up the underside of those formative Western developments. For this reason, a historical perspective is crucial to understanding the place and function of pornography in modern culture. Pornography was not a given; it was defined over time and by the conflicts between writers, artists and engravers on the one side and spies, policemen, clergymen and state officials on the other. Its political and cultural meanings cannot be separated from its emergence as a category of thinking, representation and regulation.

Early modern pornography reveals some of the most important nascent characteristics of modern culture. It was linked to freethinking and heresy, to science and natural philosophy, and to attacks on absolutist political authority. It was especially revealing about the gender differentiations being developed within the culture of modernity. Although no judgment is offered here on the value of modern pornography, understanding its history is an essential element in understanding the current debates.

The need for a historical perspective was recognized in the 1986 Meese Commission report on pornography, which complained that "the history of pornography still remains to be written."[2] The 1,960-page final report included only sixteen pages on the history of pornography in all times and all places (that is, less than one percent of the total report) and another forty-nine pages on the history of the regulation of pornography. This disproportion between the history of the practice and the history of its regulation is significant, since pornography has always been defined in part by the efforts undertaken to regulate it.

The Commission's brief historical overview was, however, sur-

11

prisingly good. It argued that the control of written and printed works in Europe from medieval times through the seventeenth century was undertaken primarily in the name of religion and politics, rather than in the name of decency, and it showed that modern obscenity laws only took shape in the early nineteenth century. The first conviction in the United States for the common law crime of obscene libel, for instance, took place in 1815 in Pennsylvania, in the case of *Commonwealth* v. *Sharpless*. As the Meese Commission report shows, while regulation of pornography was not invented in modern times, regulation in the early nineteenth century marked a clear departure from earlier concerns.[3]

In *The Secret Museum*, Walter Kendrick traced the origins of modern attitudes toward pornography with more precision. Kendrick attributed the invention of pornography to the conjunction of two very different events at the end of the eighteenth and during the early decades of the nineteenth century: the creation of "secret museums" for objects classified as pornographic and the growing volume of writing about prostitution. Kendrick situated the secret museum (whether in the form of locked rooms or uncataloged holdings) in the long-term context of the careful regulation of the consumption of the obscene so as to exclude the lower classes and women. With the rise of literacy and the spread of education, expurgation of the classics was required; this practice, insofar as English-language books are concerned, began in the early eighteenth century, flourished throughout the nineteenth, and came to an abrupt though incomplete end at the time of World War I. Thus, the prospect of the promiscuity of representations of the obscene — "when it began to seem possible that anything at all might be shown to anybody"[4] — engendered the desire for barriers, for catalogs, for new classifications and hygienic censoring.

In other words, pornography as a regulatory category was invented in response to the perceived menace of the democratization of culture. As the Meese Commission itself noted, albeit with a somewhat loose sense of chronology and a penchant for understatement, "until the last several hundred years, almost all written, drawn, or printed material was restricted largely to a small segment of the population that undoubtedly constituted the social elite."[5] It was only when print culture opened the possibility of the masses gaining access to writing and pictures that pornography began to emerge as a separate genre of representation.

As Kendrick argued, the concept of pornography was historically shaped, and its development as a category was always one of conflict and change. Pornography was the name for a cultural battle zone: " 'pornography' names an argument, not a thing." Obscenity has existed just as long as the distinction between private and public behavior, yet around the middle of the nineteenth century, according to Kendrick, something changed in the balance between obscenity and decency, private and public, and pornography emerged as a distinct governmental concern.[6]

The middle of the nineteenth century was certainly crucial in linguistic terms. The word *pornography* appeared for the first time in the *Oxford English Dictionary* in 1857, and most of the English variations on the word (*pornographer* and *pornographic*) date from the middle or the end of the nineteenth century. The words emerged in French a little sooner. According to the *Trésor de la langue française*, *pornographe* surfaced first in Restif de la Bretonne's treatise of 1769 titled *Le Pornographe* to refer to writing about prostitution, and *pornographique*, *pornographe* and *pornographie* in the sense of obscene writing or images dated from the 1830s and 1840s.[7] The Collection de l'Enfer of the Bibliothèque Nationale was apparently set up in 1836, though the idea had been in the air since the Napoleonic regime and perhaps even earlier.[8] Thus, in the decades just before and just after the French

Revolution, the term begins to gain consistency, a fact that is far from accidental.

The earliest modern usage of the term *pornography* that I have been able to find is in Etienne-Gabriel Peignot's *Dictionnaire critique, littéraire et bibliographique des principaux livres condamnés au feu, supprimés ou censurés*, published in Paris in 1806. Peignot was interested in cataloging not only the books but the reasons for censoring them. In his preface, he established three classes of reasons: religious, political and moral. Included in the moral class were those books that disturbed the social order and contravened good morals. This class of suppressed books was further subdivided: books that, though not obscene, were filled with "bizarre and dangerous opinions," such as Rousseau's *Emile* and the works of Helvétius; immoral books written in prose which "one calls *sotadique* or pornographic"; and works of the same kind written in verse. Pornography is here clearly associated with immorality and with the need to protect society.[9]

Peignot was trained as a lawyer and worked as a librarian and school inspector. As a consequence, he was no doubt especially alert to the concerns characteristic of modern discussions of pornography: legal regulation, library classification and consideration of the effect on morals. Peignot began his dictionary in ways reminiscent of all the early catalogers of pornography and of much current commentary, that is, with assurances that he recognized the "delicacy" of his subject: "I did my best to treat it decorously, that is, in a fashion designed not to shock any opinion but to inspire horror for these debaucheries of the spirit which have justly provoked the severity of the laws." Yet, again like his successors, he insisted on the need to pursue such investigations rigorously and evenhandedly. Some books have been unjustly censored, he argued, and many writers and booksellers were punished too severely when all that was required was the simple suppression of publication. Peignot was grappling with the problem of print in a supposedly modern society; books should not be suppressed just because religious and political authorities do not like them but rather because they offend some basic shared sense of the social order.[10]

Peignot recognized the contradiction implicit in openly discussing pornographic literature: If you write about the loathsome, don't you give it the very publicity that a good moral order would try to suppress? To get around this problem, Peignot announced that he had cited very few pornographic works even though they were "unfortunately all too numerous." He gave two reasons for his reticence: it would be dangerous to make the books known, and few of them had been publicly condemned. The police, he claimed, ordinarily took these books away in secret. He then gave a representative list of the most abhorrent and included several, though not all, of them in his dictionary. Peignot thus placed himself exactly on the crucial battleground identified by Kendrick: on the border between the zones of darkness and light, the secret and the revealed, the hidden and the accessible. Peignot was extending the zone of light by compiling his dictionary even while supposedly condemning certain books to darkness.[11]

From the way Peignot tossed off his list of the most repugnant, immoral books, it is clear that a kind of galaxy of the most explicit pornographic writing was already in place in the minds of connoisseurs at the beginning of the nineteenth century. At the top of Peignot's list of prose works was the *P—des Ch—*; *Th—ph—*, and the *A—des d—*. Since the author of the first was listed as well as the "translator" of the last, it is clear that Peignot expected to fool no one by failing to list the full titles: *Histoire de Dom Bougre, portier des Chartreux* (1741), *Thérèse philosophe* (1748) and *L'Académie des dames* (1660). He included in the same category the libertine works of both Fromaget (author of *Le Cousin* de *Mahomet*, 1742) and Crébillon fils; *Les Bijoux indiscrets*, *Jacques le fataliste* and *La Religieuse* of Diderot; *Les Liaisons dangereuses* of Laclos; *Le Poëte* (Pierre-Jean-Baptiste Desforges, 1798); and the *Veillées conjugales* and the *Galerie des six femmes* of Desf— (presumably *Galerie des femmes* by Victor-Joseph-Etienne de Jouy, 1799). He listed several works in verse as examples of that genre, including the *Pucelle d'Orléans* of Voltaire (1755), *Chandelle d'Arras* of Dulaurent (1765), the *Ode à Priape* of Piron (1710) and the *Epigrammes* of Jean-Baptiste Rousseau, in circulation since the early eighteenth century (figure I.1).[12]

Peignot reserved his only extensive commentary in the preface for the one work – seized by the police – that "includes all that the most depraved, cruelest, and most abominable imagination can offer in the way of horror and infamy": *Justine*. His reference to the two editions, to the engravings, and to the initials of the author (M.D.S—) again make clear that Peignot expected many if not most of his readers to be familiar with this work of Sade's. However, Sade does not appear in the dictionary itself, for, as Peignot insists, we should "penetrate no further into the sewers of literature."[13]

Thus, by 1806 at the very latest, a French pornographic tradition had been identified. In the main body of his dictionary, however, Peignot listed suppressed books only in alphabetical order, with no distinction made between pornography, heresy, political subversion and philosophic radicalism. Aretino's sonnets (1527) and *L'Ecole des filles* (1655) are listed along with La Mettrie's materialist tract *L'Homme machine* (1748) without much discussion of their differences. If, as Peter Wagner has argued, pornography "becomes an aim in itself" sometime after the middle of the eighteenth century, rather than merely an adjunct to other forms of criticism of church and state, the distinction was still not widely understood.[14] Robert Darnton has demonstrated that the

FIGURE I.I. The Pornographic Author. Frontispiece to *Histoire de Dom B—,*
portier des Chartreux (Frankfurt edition, 1748).

French government of the ancien régime prohibited all books that threatened religion, the state or good morals, and all these were indiscriminately labeled "philosophical books," whether they were politically motivated scandal sheets, metaphysical treatises, anticlerical satires or pornographic stories.[15] By the time of Napoleon's empire, critics such as Peignot were beginning to think of pornography as a separate category of bad books, but the separation was still far from complete.

The Pornographic Tradition

In September 1800, Paris police commissioner Louis-Nicolas Violette was ordered to search a bookstore on the Pont Neuf for licentious books. He found a large cache, which he duly listed for his superiors. Some of the books were beautifully bound with gold bindings; others were more cheaply stitched. After confiscating the books, he went to the home of the bookseller, where he found three more sets of forbidden books. In the same apartment building he located a woman who worked as a bookbinder and who had in her possession 200 unbound copies of Piron's *Oeuvres badines*, a collection of eighteenth-century erotic poetry that had been republished in 1796 with pornographic engravings.

Commissioner Violette's list is not identical to Peignot's dictionary entries of only six years later, but it overlaps in many important respects: *Thérèse philosophe*, *L'Académie des dames* and the poetry of Piron were included, as well as *La Philosophie dans le boudoir* of Sade. Not surprisingly, works published during the revolutionary decade were especially prominent: *Julie philosophe* (1791), *Le Portefeuille des fouteurs* (1793), *Etrennes aux fouteurs* (1793) and the novels of André-Robert Andréa de Nerciat (*Félicia*, 1775, and its sequel *Monrose*, 1792). The police knew what they were looking for.[16] Like the librarians, the police clearly had their own lists, lists which resembled, indeed shaped, those of the librarians. By the late 1790s, the French police had a special Morals Division which devoted some of its energies to the discovery and confiscation of "licentious works."[17]

As this example from 1800 shows, the policing of pornography seems to have been directed at a mixture of pornographic classics and more ephemeral types of literature. In 1718, nearly a century earlier, the Paris police reported a cache of bad books typical of that earlier time. At the top of the list were copies of *L'Académie des dames* and *L'Ecole des filles*, the leading seventeenth-century classics. The list was filled out with political pornography, anticlerical obscene works and potentially subversive but nonpornographic political pamphlets as well. Listed alongside the well-known classics of the pornographic genre were pamphlets defending the powers of the courts against the crown or detailing the loves of the recently deceased Louis XIV or other high-ranking courtiers.[18]

Pornography was a category constituted by both the regulation of and the market for printed works. On the one hand, the efforts of religious and political authorities to regulate, censor and prohibit works contributed to their definition. On the other, the desire of readers to buy certain books and of authors to produce them also contributed to the construction of a category of the pornographic. The readers' desire was heightened by the prohibition, but the prohibition alone does not explain which books readers sought out, because some prohibited books sold much better than others regardless of the level of censorship. That readers ordered the same books again and again and that authors made constant references to their predecessors show that information about pornographic books and engravings was quite readily available, at least to upper-class, educated men.

Readers knew which products were "hot" and which were not, as Darnton demonstrated in his study of the best-selling books offered by the Société typographique de Neuchâtel in the last decades of the ancien régime. Prominent on Darnton's lists are many books that are also cited by Peignot in his preface. *Histoire de Dom Bougre, portier des Chartreux*, *Pucelle d'Orléans* and *Chandelle d'Arras* are on Darnton's list of the ten best-selling impious or obscene religious works, and *Thérèse philosophe* and *L'Académie des dames* rate among the top ten best-selling books in Darnton's category of pornography.[19]

Darnton's work has told us much more about French readers of pornography in the eighteenth century than we know about readers of pornography in other places and times. The frequently cited case of Samuel Pepys in England is unfortunately the exception that proves the rule of general silence on these matters. Unlike most diarists, journalists or memoir writers of the seventeenth and eighteenth centuries, Pepys actually described buying *L'Ecole des filles* in his *Diary* in 1668:

> Thence away to the Strand to my bookseller's, and there stayed an hour and bought that idle, roguish book, *L'escholle des Filles*; which I have bought in plain binding (avoiding the buying of it better bound) because I resolve, as soon as I have read it, to burn it, that it may not stand in the list of books, nor among them, to disgrace them if it should be found.

A few days later, Pepys recounted in a kind of code language his masturbation while reading the book. It was a "mighty lewd book," Pepys insisted, "but it did hazer my prick para stand all the while, and una vez to decharger." Afterwards he burned it as promised, had supper and went to bed.[20] Respectable men (not to mention women) did not collect works known as "mighty lewd" in their libraries, though they often did seek them out for their own private pleasures.

It is not surprising that Pepys bought a French book, because the French pornographic tradition was central to European consumption. The French were not the only source, however. English writers contributed some important elements to the pornographic tradition in the seventeenth and especially the eighteenth century; the French translation of John Cleland's *Memoirs of a Woman of Pleasure* (popularly, *Fanny Hill*, 1748–1749) was the best-selling pornographic work in the catalogs of the Société typographique de Neuchâtel.[21] *Fanny Hill* may be the single most read pornographic novel of all time (figure I.2). It was translated into many other languages during the nineteenth century – German translations were published in 1792, 1863, 1876 and 1906, for instance – but it took its place alongside many translations from the French. *L'Ecole des filles*, *Histoire de Dom Bougre*, *Thérèse philosophe*, and, later, the novels of Sade appeared in German, Spanish and other European languages throughout the nineteenth and twentieth centuries. Translations from the English and especially the French pornographic classics constituted the core of available pornography in Spain, Germany and the Dutch Republic, as well as other European countries, and these translations were of course supplemented by works in the original French and English.[22]

Some measure, however imperfect, of the predominance of English and French titles can be found in the catalog of the Private Case of the British Library. The overwhelming majority of the 1,920 titles are either English or French. Those two languages are followed by German (127 titles, twenty-eight of which were translations from French or English); Italian (thirty-eight titles); Latin (thirty-two titles); Spanish (nine titles); Dutch (eight titles) and so on to Hungarian (two titles) and Finnish (one title). Moreover, hardly any of the non-English or French titles, and even the translations from those languages, were published before 1800. There are three titles in German, all from the 1790s; one in Dutch

FIGURE I.2. French translation of *Fanny Hill*. *La Fille de joie, ou Mémoires de Miss Fanny* (French edition, 1786).

(a collection of prints); and none in Spanish, for example. Until at least the middle of the nineteenth century, French and English publications overwhelmingly dominated European pornography.

Although the catalog of the Private Case is no doubt biased against non-English and French publications, it is the best source for establishing a crude international chronology of pornography. Of the 127 German titles, three were published before 1850 (all in the 1790s); twenty-nine were printed between 1850 and 1899; forty-six between 1900 and 1918; and thirty-two between 1919 and 1933.[23] Although more pornography was published in French, the first half of the nineteenth century seems to mark a similar lull in publication of new works. The standard work on nineteenth-century erotic French prose, Louis Perceau's *Bibliographie du roman érotique au XIXe siècle* (1930), lists only twenty-six new works for the period of 1800–1850, but lists seven times as many being published in 1850–1900.[24] The pace of publication picked up again almost everywhere in the last decades of the nineteenth century and the first decades of the twentieth. Significantly, it was only in the decades of the emergence of mass politics – the 1880s and afterward – that most countries began to produce their own indigenous pornography, a fact again suggestive of the link between pornography and democracy.

The relative weakness of national pornographic traditions outside France and England is clearly evident in the recently studied example of eighteenth-century Russian pornography.[25] The largest private Russian library in Catherine the Great's time included much of the well-known French and English pornography. Not only was little indigenous pornography produced in Russia, but nonpornographic novels were also under fire. Even nonpornographic foreign novels were often only available as handwritten translations commissioned by high-ranking nobles. Production of both novels and pornography seem to be related, and countries that did not produce novels did not produce much pornography either.

The one Russian writer who, in the eighteenth century, produced something close to pornography was Ivan S. Barkov. His name became a code word for illicit writing: *barkovscina* became the word for pornography in Russian. In his short and tumultuous life, Barkov wrote odes, tragedies, fables, satires, idylls, songs, epitaphs, epigrams, riddles and couplets (but, significantly, no novels), most of which circulated only in *samizdat* manuscripts. Barkov combined the classical forms he had learned from such works as Piron's *Ode à Priape* with elements of Russian folklore. One collection was titled *The Maiden's Plaything*, a reference to the male member that he glorified in all of his pornographic writing. Although Barkov's writing was quite tame compared to Western models, it continued to exercise an influence in the Russian literary underground until well into the nineteenth century. When questioned about the source of his freethinking ideas, one man arrested in the Decembrist conspiracy of the 1820s replied, "various compositions (who does not know them?) of Barkov."[26]

Although French works formed the core of the pornographic tradition in the seventeenth and the eighteenth century, the first modern source cited by every expert on pornography – and by many of his would-be successors – is the sixteenth-century Italian writer, Pietro Aretino. Aretino made two contributions to the tradition, one in prose and the other in sonnet form. His *Ragionamenti* (1534–1536) became the prototype of seventeenth-century pornographic prose. In the *Ragionamenti*, Aretino developed the device of realistic and satirical dialogues between an older, experienced woman and a younger, innocent one. This dialogue form had a long life; it completely dominated seventeenth-century pornography in every language, and it still appears, for example, in Sade's *La Philosophie dans le boudoir* (1795), 250 years later. The most influential section of the *Ragionamenti* was the dialogue in the first part, which deals with the lives of whores. Soon, this section alone was widely circulated in Spanish, Latin, German, Dutch, French and English.[27]

Aretino also composed a series of sonnets, known as the *Sonnetti lussuriosi* (listed in Peignot's *Dictionnaire*), to accompany a series of erotic engravings in which the various positions for lovemaking were graphically depicted. The engravings had been published without text in 1524 and suppressed by order of the pope. Aretino's name was quickly associated with the illustrations as well, even though they did not come from his hand, and "Aretino's postures" became the name commonly given to the entire collection of imitations and variations supposedly drawn from the sixteenth-century original. References to Aretino's postures abound in seventeenth-century English drama, for instance, and especially in works of pornography.[28] When an English translation of *L'Ecole des filles* was advertised in a London newpaper in 1744, the advertisement described the book as adorned with twenty-four curious prints, "after the Manner of Aratine [*sic*]."[29]

In the minds of his successors, Aretino stood for the basic pornographic intention. The name *Aretino* represented what Peter Wagner has defined as pornography: "the written or visual presentation in a realistic form of any genital or sexual behavior with a deliberate violation of existing and widely accepted moral and social taboos."[30] Aretino seemed to take this role on himself. In a letter of dedication he defended his action as countering hypocrisy and celebrating bodily pleasures:

> I renounce the bad judgment and dirty habit which forbid the eyes to see what pleases them most.... It seems to me that the you-know-what given us by nature for the preservation of the species should be worn as a pendant round our necks or as a badge in our caps, since it is the spring that pours out the flood of humanity.[31]

Aretino brought together several crucial elements to form the basis of the pornographic tradition: the explicit representation of sexual activity, the form of the dialogue between women, the discussion of the behavior of prostitutes and the challenge to moral conventions of the day.

In this book's opening essay, Paula Findlen sets Aretino in the context of sixteenth-century Renaissance culture and the creation of a new marketplace for the obscene. Aretino was only one of many authors and engravers who produced forbidden works on the fringes of the new print culture. Images of amorous encounters, which had been previously confined to humanist circles and were often in the form of high art, now circulated in cheap reproductions designed for a more popular audience. Sixteenth-century pornography relied heavily on classical models, including the revival of Roman poems to the god Priapus, which circulated in manuscript form during the fifteenth century. In its reliance on classical themes, pornography in the sixteenth century was not especially innovative. Rather, it was the diffusion through print culture that marked a significant new departure.

Sixteenth-century humanists also wrote a kind of "academy pornography," designed for limited distribution to an educated elite, in which local politics were dissected in sexual terms. Findlen analyzes one of them, Vignali's *La Cazzaria* (1525–1526), which depicts Sienese factional struggles in terms of competition between Pricks, Cunts, Balls and Asses. Such works provided the prototypes for seventeenth- and eighteenth-century political pornography. In the sixteenth-century versions of pornography, sodomites and prostitutes were already depicted as privileged observers and critics of the established order, thanks to their membership in the "third sex." Aretino and his peers, when compared to those who wrote in the pre-sixteenth-century literary forms, can be seen to have inaugurated a literary tradition which was new in two respects: it appealed to a broader audience thanks to the use of printing, and it employed political satire, which would play an increasingly important role in the next two centuries.

Works inspired by Aretino appeared immediately, beginning with the pseudo-Aretine *La Puttana errante* (1531). The next major moment in the establishment of a pornographic tradition came a century later in France, in the late 1650s, with the publication of *L'Ecole des filles* and *L'Académie des dames* (published originally in Latin as *Aloisiae Sigaeae Toletanae Satyra Sotadica de arcanis Amoris et Veneris...* in 1659 or 1660, figure I.3). The last professed to be a translation, by a Dutch philologist, from a work originally composed in Spanish by a woman, Luisa Sigea. It was, in fact, written by a French lawyer, Nicolas Chorier. This convoluted story shows how the pornographic tradition was almost immediately imagined, both by authors and readers, to be European rather than narrowly national.

The publication of *L'Académie des dames* in Latin was probably designed to evade prosecution rather than to ensure an international audience, but the internationalization of the tradition can be seen in the diversity of places of publication for such books (figure I.4). Experts disagree, for example, about whether *L'Académie des dames* was first published in Lyon, Grenoble, or the Dutch Republic, the final being a well-established haven for publishers of forbidden books. These books were immediately available in England. Pepys bought his copy of *L'Ecole des filles* in 1668, and another English diarist records knowledge of the Latin edition of *L'Académie des dames* in 1676 (the French edition appeared in 1680). An English translation of *L'Académie des dames* appeared in 1684.[32] Likewise, in the eighteenth century English pornography was quickly translated into French; the French translation of Cleland's book appeared only two years after its English publication.

JOANNIS MEURSII
ELEGANTIÆ
LATINI SERMONIS
SEU
ALOISIA
SIGÆA TOLETANA
De arcanis Amoris & Veneris
Adjunctis Fragmentis quibusdam Eroticis.
PARS PRIMA.

LUGD. BATAVORUM,
EX TYPIS ELZEVIRIANIS.
cIↄ Iↄcc LVII.

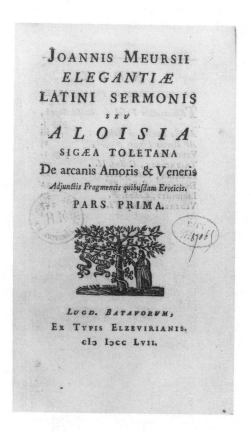

FIGURE I.3. (above) Title page to one of the Latin versions of *L'Académie des dames* (1678).

FIGURE I.4. (right) Title page to a nineteenth-century French reprint edition of *L'Académie des dames* (despite its claims to being published in Venice by Aretino – long since dead – it was published in Grenoble, 1680). This engraving may have been added in the nineteenth century.

David Foxon has claimed that "pornography seems to have been born and grown to maturity in a brief period in the middle of the seventeenth century."[33] At that time sex became intellectualized, particularly in the two books just cited. One sign of this new experience of sex was the use of what are now called *sex aids*, with the reading of pornography being a prime example. In the 1660s, imported Italian dildos, as well as condoms, first became available in London.[34] Almost all the themes of later prose pornography were present by 1660: the self-conscious aim of arousing sexual desire in the reader, the juxtaposition of the material truth of sex against the hypocritical conventions of society and the rulings of the church, and, new in the seventeenth century, the cataloging of "perversions" as so many variations on a self-justified, amoral gratification of the senses (even when some of these perversions were supposedly condemned). These aspects, as well as the emergence of libertinism as a mode of thought and action, were related to the new emphasis on the value of nature and the senses as sources of authority.[35] From the beginning, pornography had close ties to the new science as well as to political criticism.

Because pornography first emerged in the sixteenth century, and developed concomitantly with print culture, it is hardly surprising that its next big step forward in the seventeenth century was closely related to the development of the novel, which was the most important new genre of that culture. The publication of *L'Ecole des filles* and *L'Académie des dames* signaled the displacement of the center of pornographic writing from Italy to France, and this shift occurred just when French novels were increasingly being differentiated from the romance as a genre. Marie-Madeleine Pioche de Lavergne, countess de Lafayette, for example, published her influential novels between 1662 and 1678.

Just how the development of the novel and pornography were related in the seventeenth century is far from clear, however, and it is a topic that bears further investigation. As Joan DeJean shows in her essay, the pornographic originality of *L'Ecole des filles* was exaggerated by contemporaries and later literary historians because it was included in the repression of texts linked to the Fronde (1648–1653), the internal civil war of nobles and magistrates against the crown and its ministers. *L'Ecole des filles* was linked to the novelist Paul Scarron and his wife, Françoise d'Aubigné, the future Madame de Maintenon and mistress of Louis XIV, and to Louis's disgraced minister of finances, Nicolas Fouquet, who had in his possession one of the few surviving copies. DeJean speculates that the authors of *L'Ecole des filles*, whomever they were, were experimenting with various forms of prose fiction at a moment when the novel as a genre was far from fixed or settled. Both *L'Ecole des filles* and *L'Académie des dames* show traces of the effort to combine Aretino's dialogue between women with many of the elements of the emerging novel.

Between the publication of these two works in the middle of the seventeenth century and the next major recasting of pornographic writing in the 1740s, pornography stagnated as a genre.[36] Pornography, however, continued to be published in this period, and much of it was explicitly related to political issues, as is shown in the essay by Rachel Weil on English Restoration political pornography. During the Fronde in France, pornographic pamphlets had attacked the Regent, Queen Mother Anne of Austria, and her presumed lover and adviser, Cardinal Mazarin. Libertine and libelous pamphlets were also published against Queen Christina of Sweden after her conversion to Catholicism in 1654.[37] Despite the continuing flow of pornographic pamphlets, no new major works emerged to join the classics of the tradition.

Then, in the 1740s, pornographic writing took off with the rapid-fire publication of a series of new and influential works: *Histoire de Dom Bougre, portier des Chartreux* (1741); *Le Sopha* by

Crébillon fils (published 1742, written 1737); *Les Bijoux indiscrets* by Diderot (1748); *Thérèse philosophe* (1748); and Cleland's *Fanny Hill* (1748–1749), to name only the best-known works. These classics of the genre appeared in a very short period of time, all of them now utilizing the extended novel form rather than the previous Aretinian model of a dialogue between two women. Did pornographers, as some have suggested, have to await the development of the novel in its eighteenth-century form – Richardson's *Pamela* was published in 1740 – before they could advance their own prose efforts? And if so, how was the new novelistic form of writing so quickly assimilated into the pornographic tradition?

The link between pornography and the novel in the eighteenth and nineteenth centuries has been commented on by many. Steven Marcus has argued, for example, that "the growth of pornography is inseparable from and dependent upon the growth of the novel." Yet his analysis is very general and, therefore, vague. He attributes both pornography and the novel to the "vast social processes which brought about the modern world": the growth of cities and with them of an audience of literate readers; the development of new kinds of experience, especially privatization; and the splitting off of sexuality from the rest of life in an urban, capitalist, industrial and middle-class world. Pornography, for Marcus, is "a mad parody" of the new, private experience set up by these social changes.[38]

Such a broad analysis, though not without merit, fails to explain the timing of the major bursts in pornography and especially the differences among countries. If pornography reflects (and reflects upon) the growth of cities, literacy and privatization, then why don't the writers of the Dutch Republic – arguably the most urban, middle-class, literate and privatized country – specialize in the genre? Much early modern pornography was published in the Dutch Republic, but little was written originally in

Dutch, as Wijnand W. Mijnhardt's essay on politics and pornography demonstrates. Although Dutch writers produced a few home grown pornographic novels in the last decades of the seventeenth century, sometimes as direct imitations of Aretino, the increased pornographic output the French and English experienced in the 1740s passed by the Dutch almost unnoticed. Instead, as Mijnhardt argues, the Dutch turned away from their previous openness about the public discussion of sexuality, which was so evident in the numerous sexual and erotic manuals published in the late seventeenth century, and removed all sexual references from the public sphere, whether in brothels, paintings or pornographic books.

It hardly seems coincidental that the rise in pornographic publications in the 1740s also marked the beginning of the high period of the Enlightenment as well as a period of general crisis in European society and politics. The year 1748, so rich in pornographic publications, was also the year of publication of Montesquieu's *L'Esprit des lois* and La Mettrie's *L'Homme machine*. Darnton has shown that pornography was often enlisted in the attack on the ancien régime, but he describes such politically motivated pornographic writing as the underside or lowlife of Enlightenment literature.[39]

Others have postulated a closer relationship between pornography and the Enlightenment's stinging criticism of clerical rigidity, police censorship and the narrowness and prejudices of conventional mores. Aram Vartanian argues that eroticism in general played an important, if neglected, role in providing creative energy to the Enlightenment as a movement. His exemplary philosophe, Diderot, wrote pornography (and was imprisoned for it in 1749), and, according to Vartanian, the Enlightenment provided a climate favorable to the progress of "literary sexology," which began with pornography. He attributes the resurgence of

33

the erotic in literature and painting in the eighteenth century to the Enlightenment's understanding of nature: sexual appetite was natural; repression of sexual appetite was artificial and pointless; and the passions might have a beneficial influence in making humans happy in this world. Sexual enlightenment was consequently a part of the Enlightenment itself.[40]

Margaret C. Jacob's essay on the philosophical and social content of pornography in the seventeenth and eighteenth centuries traces this radical side of the Enlightenment. She shows that pornography was first naturalist and then profoundly materialist in inspiration. Eighteenth-century pornography was Lockeian and La Mettrian in philosophy, and a large part of its shock value rested on its materialist underpinnings. Materialist thinkers such as La Mettrie seemed to be drawn inexorably from their writings on the soul's subordination by physical influences toward efforts to theorize pleasure, as with La Mettrie's own *L'Art de jouir*. Diderot, also a materialist, wrote pornographic novels along with his more conventional, philosophical, yet nonetheless threatening, works. As Diderot remarked in one of his letters, "There is a bit of testicle at the bottom of our most sublime feelings and our purest tenderness."[41]

The burst of publication in the 1740s may have been related, in addition, as Jacob suggests, to a more general crisis in the French state caused by the unsuccessful prosecution of the War of Austrian Succession. The war ended in 1748 in a stalemate that carried with it the prospect of continuing decline in influence for the French. Materialist philosophy and pornography were both ways of criticizing the status quo at a time when the status quo was weakening.

By the end of the 1740s, the pornographic tradition was becoming well established and was clearly linked to the novel in form. By then, French publications predominated in the genre, despite the remarkable international influence of *Fanny Hill*. Between the 1740s and the 1790s French pornography turned increasingly political. As criticism of the monarchy grew more strident, pornographic pamphlets attacked the clergy, the court, and, in the case of Louis XV, the king himself.

In the 1790s, the French Revolution let loose another cascade of pornographic pamphlets directly linked to political conflicts and, at the same time, the early modern pornographic tradition culminated in the writings of the Marquis de Sade. Virtually all of the themes of modern pornography were rehearsed by Sade; indeed, he specialized in the cataloging of pornographic effects. Rape, incest, parricide, sacrilege, sodomy and tribadism, pedophilia and all the most horrible forms of torture and murder were associated with sexual arousal in the writings of Sade. No one has ever been able to top Sade because he had, in effect, explored the ultimate logical possibility of pornography: the annihiliation of the body, the very seat of pleasure, in the name of desire. This ultimate reductio ad absurdum of pornography would not have been possible without the prior establishment of a pornographic tradition. By the early nineteenth century, when efforts at regulation for moral purposes expanded dramatically, the police, the writers, the printers and the readers all knew what the models were.

Pornography as Politics and Social Commentary

From the days of Aretino in the sixteenth century, pornography was closely linked with political and religious subversion. Aretino decided to write sonnets to accompany obscene engravings when he heard of the arrest of the engraver of the original sixteen postures. The identification between pornography and political subversion could also work in reverse: *L'Ecole des filles* was assumed to be wildly pornographic because it was the subject of a determined

35

political repression. As Rachel Weil argues, however, political pornography was continuous with other forms of political commentary and not always easily separated out as a genre. Charles II's potential tyranny was often represented in sexual terms, but the argument that despotic kings resembled Eastern tyrants could be found in more formal political works as well. The link between debauchery and tyranny or despotism could be found throughout the seventeenth and eighteenth centuries. It culminates in the flood of pamphlets attacking Marie Antoinette and other leading figures of the French court after 1789, which I discuss in my essay on pornography during the French Revolution.

Pornography's relationship to the novel as a form of narration heightened its reputation as an oppositional genre, because the novel itself was under severe attack through the eighteenth century. Jean Marie Goulemot has shown that pornography engaged the same paradoxes of imagination and reality as the novel, and novels were also regularly condemned for their capacity to incite desire. Some pornography, then, is simply a specialized version of the novel; it plays upon the imagination of the reader to create the effect of real sexual activity, all the while, of course, being purely imaginary. But there seems to be an important gender differentiation that Goulemot misses in his analysis: women were thought especially susceptible to the imaginative effects of the novel, while men were usually assumed – rightly or wrongly – to be the primary audience for pornographic writing, at least until the end of the eighteenth century.[42] If pornography is just a subset of the novel, why is it imagined to be so different in its gender audience and effects?

Pornography, like the novel, was often associated with libertinism.[43] Libertinism followed the same trajectory as pornography; under the influence, in part, of the new science, it took shape in the seventeenth century as an upper-class male revolt

36

against conventional morality and religious orthodoxy, and then spread more broadly in the eighteenth century into the artisanal and lower middle-class circles of many Western countries, especially England and France. Libertines were imagined to be freethinkers who were open to sexual, and literary, experimentation. By the definition of their adversaries in church and state, libertines were the propagators of and audience for pornography. As a consequence, the thread of libertinism weaves through many of the following essays.

Pornographic novelists explored realist techniques of writing, which became increasingly important in the eighteenth century. In *La Philosophie dans le boudoir*, for example, Sade parodied the interminable scenes of seduction found in novels such as Richardson's *Pamela*. This truth-telling trope of pornography went back to Aretino. "Speak plainly," the prostitute Antonia insists in the *Ragionamenti*, "and say 'fuck,' 'prick,' 'cunt' and 'ass'. . . ." Similarly, in *Histoire de Dom Bougre* a libertine nun explains the true meaning of the expression "to be in love": "When one says, the Gentleman . . . is in love with the Lady . . . it is the same thing as saying, the Gentleman . . . saw the Lady . . . the sight of her excited his desire, and he is dying to put his Prick into her Cunt. That's truly what it means."[44]

In her essay on the obscene word, Lucienne Frappier-Mazur explores the significance of the language of transgression. The obscene word played on the contrast between different social registers of language – crude and elegant, lower and upper class, masculine and feminine – in order to achieve its effect. To enact social transgression and a kind of hyperrealism, obscene language fetishizes certain words related to sex; the obscene word substitutes for the body part in question but, in the process, acquires the status of a fetish. As a consequence, the original emphasis on realism paradoxically devolves into a form of the grotesque, where penises are always huge, vaginas multiply in number and sexual coupling takes place in a kind of frenzy that is hardly "realistic." This results in pornography that is imaginary and at times fantastic even though its effects on its readers are very real.

One of the most striking characteristics of early modern pornography is the preponderance of female narrators. Frappier-Mazur emphasizes the structures of voyeurism and eavesdropping that are established by female narrators, which turn the male readers of such works into complicit third parties. Both Margaret C. Jacob and Kathryn Norberg address the issue of the female narrator, but with a different focus. They emphasize the potential for social and philosophical subversion in female narration. Materialist philosophy, for example, required that women be materially or sexually equivalent to men; otherwise, all bodies in nature would not be equally mechanical. Randolph Trumbach argues in his essay on eighteenth-century England that male sexuality was codified before female sexuality to eliminate the legitimacy of male homosexual relationships, with the result that men were less likely than women to be represented as sexually polymorphous. (Sade's male characters are the exception in this respect rather than the rule.) Thus the issue of the female narrator and her transgression of expected female roles goes to the heart of questions of sexual difference.

In her essay on the pornographic whore, Norberg focuses on the privileged figure of early modern pornographic literature, the prostitute. From Aretino's dialogues onward, the female narrator is often a prostitute by occupation. The pornographic whore, such as Margot (the stocking mender who is the main character of *Margot la ravaudeuse*, 1750), is most often portrayed as independent, determined, financially successful and scornful of the new ideals of female virtue and domesticity. Such texts, written by men, consequently elide the very sexual difference that was increasingly coming into vogue in medical tracts and domestic manuals.

Margot and the other prostitute narrators in the pornographic novel were always astute social observers, and they saw much of the social world because of their unique position. They resemble in many respects the foundlings and bastards who are the staple of the early realist novel. Both the pornographic and the realist novel endeavored to reimagine and represent the social world during the eighteenth century. The pornographic novel in the eighteenth century was a kind of reductio ad absurdum of the realist novel, and, as such, it is immensely revealing of the social concerns of the time. Margot and characters like her are usually born poor and see much of the underside of life, but they also make their way to the opera, to the world of the salons and to the highest levels of church and government, thanks to their profession.

This is not to say, however, that the pornographic novel transparently represented the social. As Stephen Marcus has asserted, the "governing tendency" of pornography "is toward the elimination of external or social reality." In *pornotopia*, Marcus's term for the utopian fantasy implicit in pornography, space and time only measure the repetition of sexual encounters, and bodies are reduced to sexual parts and to the endless possibilities of their variation and combination (a materialist vision if there ever was one). As a result, pornography "regularly moves toward independence of time, space, history, and even language itself."[45] In a similar vein, Angela Carter argues that pornography reinforces by its very nature the tendency to think in universals:

> So pornography reinforces the false universals of sexual archetypes
> because it denies, or doesn't have time for, or can't find room for,
> or, because its underlying ideology ignores, the social context in

which sexual activity takes place.... Therefore pornography must always have the false simplicity of fable.[46]

The ultimate in this tendency toward erasure of the standard coordinates of time, space and social reality can be found in Sade's underground caverns, forest lairs and solitary castles, all of which are so many versions of the ideal brothel.

Yet pornography also invariably engaged the social, whether in its efforts to give realistic descriptions of characters or in more abstractly coded ways. Carter insists that "sexual relations between men and women always render explicit the nature of social relations in the society in which they take place and, if described explicitly, will form a critique of those relations, even if that is not and never has been the intention of the pornographer."[47] In the early modern period, it often was the intention of the pornographer to criticize existing social and sexual relations. Accounts of conversations about whores or between them were perhaps the favorite devices of early modern pornography, and they were frequently used to reveal the hypocrisy of conventional morals. Descriptions of brothels were used to attack leading aristocrats, clergymen, and, in France, even Marie Antoinette. The pornographic pamphlet *Les Bordels de Paris, avec les noms, demeures et prix...* (1790), for instance, was devoted to denouncing the queen's own brothel and was filled with detailed descriptions of her orgies with various aristocrats and clergymen. The prostitute, moreover, was the public woman par excellence and hence an essential figure for discussing the roles of women, the supposedly excessive powers of some politically active women and the general commercialization of social relationships.

As Trumbach demonstrates, the social context for the consumption of pornography was most often a masculine one. It was men who sang obscene songs in the street, cited gross verses at

male gatherings and socialized at brothels, even though pornographic prints seemed to have been aimed at women and men
alike. Male sexuality, paradoxically, is one of the obscure areas
in much pornography. Although early modern pornography was
written by men for a presumably male audience, it focused almost
single-mindedly on the depiction of female sexuality, as if male
sexuality were too threatening to contemplate. Implicit in much
early modern pornography is the question of sodomy: Were men
(except for the Catholic clergy, who were depicted as capable of
anything) to be imagined as sexually ambidextrous and polymorphous, that is, like women, or not?

Trumbach explores this question by focusing on the sexual ideology of John Cleland, author of *Fanny Hill*, and his presumed
readers. Cleland and others like him were attracted to the religions and sexual representations of ancient Greece, Rome and
India. They may have dreamed of inaugurating a new deistic, libertine religion of their own that included homoerotic rituals. A
fraternity of this sort was established by Sir Francis Dashwood at
Medmenham Abbey in the 1750s, although those who participated, including the notorious John Wilkes, insisted on its heterosexuality. Similar notions were taken up later in the century
by Richard Payne Knight, who wrote extensively about the cult of
Priapus as an alternative stamped out by the arrival of Christianity.
Sodomy seems to be linked in various ways with these cults, and
Trumbach suggests that Cleland and Payne Knight might well have
been sodomites themselves. From the time of Aretino forward,
pornography and sodomy were intertwined in various ways, not
least in the minds of the police. Sade's exaltation of sodomy in
his works in the 1790s grew out of and reinforced this connection.

A major turning point in the social and political functions
of pornography seems to have been reached sometime between
the 1790s and the 1830s, depending on the country (earlier in

France, later in Britain). Until the end of the 1790s, explicit sexual description almost always had explicitly subversive qualities. At the end of the 1790s, pornography began to lose its political connotations and became instead a commercial, "hard-core" business. At this point, which Wagner attributes too narrowly to the novels of Restif de la Bretonne and Andréa de Nerciat, "nothing remains to be said on the ideological level...sexual pleasure is the only aim left."[48]

Obscenity continued to serve political purposes in England until the early 1800s. Iain McCalman has shown, for instance, how "obscene populism" animated radical printers during the Queen Caroline Affair in the early 1820s, but by the 1830s, he claims, the purpose of sexual arousal had replaced radical populist and libertine elements in underworld publishing. As a consequence, the social character of the audience for pornography was also transformed, or perhaps merely reverted to an older configuration. After the 1820s, pornography for sexual arousal was bought by male aristocrats, professionals and clerks but not by the working classes. Printers of the new pornography left or were chased from radical political circles.[49]

There is less known about parallel developments in France, although their turning point seems to have come earlier, during the revolution of 1789. During the decade of revolution, as I argue in my essay, pornography reached a wider audience in France, both in social terms and in numbers, than it had ever touched under the ancien régime. Kathryn Norberg demonstrates the similar ways in which the image of the whore changed in the 1790s. The whore comes down off her social pedestal and is available to all men; even the pornographic prostitute is democratized. By 1795, perhaps as an ironic result of this democratization, explicitly political pornography began to die a slow death in the country of revolution. Despite some revivals of political pornography at the end of the 1790s, most pornographic works thereafter were, as Wagner argues, entirely devoted to sexual arousal. The police still found these works dangerous, as the determined harassment of Sade shows, but the danger was perceived as moral and social rather than political. The shock of the French Revolution helped galvanize the policing of pornography everywhere in Europe. As a consequence, censorship for exclusively moral reasons got under way just when pornography stopped being social and political criticism.

Thus, pornography has a peculiar, even paradoxical relationship to democracy. In the sixteenth and seventeenth centuries, pornography was written for an elite male audience that was largely urban, aristocratic and libertine in nature. In the eighteenth century, the audience broadened as pornographic themes entered populist discourses, a development given even greater impetus by the French Revolution. But the democratization of pornography was not a straight, one-way street. David Underdown has shown how, during the English Civil War, a royalist newspaper could use sexual slander to attack the revolutionary government, accusing it of being composed of cuckolds and fornicators who allegedly used words like "freedom" and "liberty" as passwords for entering brothels.[50] Similarly, in the first years of the French Revolution of 1789, royalist papers and pamphlets used scatological and sexual insults to attack the new constitutional monarchy and, in particular, its more democratic supporters. Pornography was not a left-wing preserve. Moreover, pornography had much less appeal, it appears, in the Dutch Republic, where there were no kings, no effective courts, no entrenched privileged nobility and no established church. Pornography seems not to have been just a tactic of democratic propaganda, but a variable arm of criticism whose use was shaped by local circumstances.

Pornography developed democratic implications because of its

43

association with print culture, with the new materialist philosophies of science and nature and with political attacks on the powers of the established regimes. If all bodies were interchangeable – a dominant trope in pornographic writing – then social and gender (and perhaps even racial) differences would effectively lose their meaning. Early modern pornographers were not intentionally feminists *avant la lettre*, but their portrayal of women, at least until the 1790s, often valorized female sexual activity and determination much more than did the prevailing medical texts. *Thérèse philosophe*, *Margot la ravaudeuse* and *Julie philosophe* had much more control over their destinies than was apparent in other representations of women during that time.

Yet there was another side to this picture, which became more apparent toward the end of the eighteenth century. In the novels of Sade, determined, libertine women were the minority among the legions of female victims. Women's bodies might be imagined as equally accessible to all men, whether in Restif de la Bretonne's tract, *Le Pornographe*, which advocated the establishment of giant houses of prostitution, or in Sade's proposal of mammoth Temples of Venus in *La Philosophie dans le boudoir*. The point of such establishments was not the liberation of women but the community of women to service men. In this period, ranging from the sixteenth to the eighteenth century, pornography as a structure of literary and visual representation most often offered women's bodies as a focus of male bonding. Men wrote about sex for other male readers. For their own sexual arousal, men read about women having sex with other women or with multiple partners. The new fraternity created by these complex intersections of voyeurism and objectification may have been democratic in the sense of social leveling, but in the end it was almost always a leveling for men.

The male-bonding effect of most pornography no doubt ac-

44

counted for its total incompatibility with the new ideals of domesticity that were developing in the eighteenth and nineteenth centuries.[51] The ideology of a separate, private sphere for women depended on a reassertion of fundamental male and female sexual (and, therefore, social and political) difference. Pornography, in contrast, always intentionally transgressed the boundaries establishing difference. As Mijnhardt demonstrates in his essay on the Dutch Republic, the Dutch were among the first in Europe to actively celebrate the private and domestic spheres of life, and this may account, in part, for the Dutch rejection of pornography in the eighteenth century. As new biological and moral standards for sexual difference evolved, pornography seemed to become even more exotic and dangerous. It had to be stamped out. Much – though certainly not all – of our modern concern with pornography follows from that conviction.

PART ONE

Early Political and
Cultural Meanings

FIGURE 1.1. Pietro Liberi, *Man Fallen by Vice* (ca. 1650).

CHAPTER ONE

Humanism, Politics and Pornography

in Renaissance Italy

Paula Findlen

> Neither for all this will I affirm that this solitarinesse
> of place is chosen of all, to bestow them selves in
> laudable studies, and commendable speculations, for
> that there are some who having in their handes all day
> long bookes full of naughtinesse and leude examples,
> roote and inure them selves in this doctrine, and make
> an ordinarie practice of it: insomuch that these ill
> disposed persons may well say that they have learned
> more naughtinesse beeing by them selves, then they
> should have done beeing always in companie in
> publick and frequented places.
> – Stefano Guazzo, *Civil Conversation* (1574)

The seventeenth-century artist Pietro Liberi in his painting *Man
Fallen by Vice* effectively portrayed the tensions between the virtues of humanism and its attendant vices (figure 1.1). In the fore-
ground, a man covers his head in shame and in self-defense, his
body arching backward as he falls. Above him stand the Vices,
whose actions precipitate his unsavory end. To the right, a voluptuous woman, the embodiment of lust, gracefully balances her
right foot on her chosen victim. It is uncertain whether she is

contributing to his fall or attempting to anchor him to the marble portico in order to slow his departure. To the left, a Bacchanalian figure leans over the precipice, allowing the juice of his handful of grapes to drip onto the falling man. In the center, a dwarf precipitates the visual action of this scene of castigation: his foot, firmly planted in the victim's groin, sends the man reeling over the edge. What does the dwarf, situated between the twin poles of Lust and Excess, represent? Clad in courtly attire, holding a book aloft, he links the fallibility of mankind with the culture of the Renaissance courts. As the embodiment of all the social vices and textual excesses that characterized the practices of Renaissance elites, the diminutive but learned courtier alerts us that Liberi has chosen to depict the Humanist Fall.

Shaping his image over a century after the Renaissance proper had come to a close, Liberi had ample opportunity to reflect on the impact of this political and cultural movement on his society. His visual critique of humanism as a form of excess, a destabilizing force, cannot be considered unique. Rather, his painting was the expression of the conflicting emotions that his engagement with the past produced. Humanist learning, as Liberi reminded his viewers, was a product of a specific social and political environment whose leisurely ethos was suspiciously pagan in its origins as well as its goals. The deck of cards, waved high above the falling protagonist and an emblem of the forces that combined to force man into the abyss below, recalled the vice-ridden nature of the activities that defined humanist culture. While not a canonical expression of learning, it nonetheless was a talisman of the leisurely forms of knowledge that circulated within the upper classes. Learning, produced by courtly creatures, who were comfortable with the behavior of Bacchanalian drunkards and charming seductresses, was not simply a by-product of this moral unraveling; it was *the source.*

Let us imagine, instead, that the hand of the dwarf held a book rather than a deck of cards, for this would have been an equally appropriate expression of the "fall." While we can do no more than speculate on exactly which book Liberi would have chosen to put in the hands of his dwarf, if he were like many of his contemporaries, or the late nineteenth- and twentieth-century historians who invented the Renaissance as a moral artifact, he would not have found the writings of Pietro Aretino (1492-1556) to be an inappropriate selection. Writing about Aretino, John Addington Symonds remarked, "The man himself incarnated the dissolution of Italian culture."[1] Aretino is best known for two famous pieces of pornography, the *Sonnetti lussuriosi* (1527) and the *Ragionamenti* (1534-1536), though he authored many popular religious tracts, plays and pasquinades and published a famous collection of his letters as well.[2] Frequentor of the Gonzaga and papal courts and a resident of the Republic of Venice from 1527 until his death in 1556, Aretino was one of the first writers to make a living from his pen. Shortly after his arrival in Venice, he established a circle of friends that included painter Titian, art critic Ludovico Dolce, sculptor Jacopo Sansovino and numerous printers, and his presence served as a magnet for aspiring writers like Niccolò Franco, Lorenzo Venier and Anton Francesco Doni, who helped to transform Aretino's literary works from singular productions into a well-recognized genre.

Because his pen spared no one, Aretino attracted many epithets during his lifetime: "Scourge of Princes," "Teller of Truth" and "The Divine Aretino."[3] Others described him in less than glowing terms. For disciples like Franco and Doni, who eventually severed their ties to Aretino, he became "the scourge of pricks" and "Peter, writer of the vices of others," possessor of "the most horrible, vituperous and ribald tongue ever born."[4] In the 1540s, Doni had praised Aretino's skill as a *poligrafo* – a writer

of many genres – commenting, "your wisdom knew how to distinguish the tongue in which we should discuss Christ...from
that of the Dialogues on the state of women...."[5] By the 1550s,
he had joined the ranks of critics who shaped Aretino's image as
the most infamous writer of a reputedly infamous and immoral
age. It is these characterizations that earned Aretino the retro-
spective label as the creator of a genre of representation that we
call pornography.[6]

Pornography, if we follow Jacob Burckhardt's classic account
in *The Civilization of the Renaissance in Italy* (1860), was the inevitable epilogue to a glorious but problematic age. While humanists
initially soared to great spiritual and intellectual heights, their
full-scale embrace of antiquity ultimately, in Burckhardt's schema,
resulted in a new form of paganism: "the misleading influence
of antiquity...undermined their morality," he wrote.[7] "Antiquity"
encompassed not only the works of "respectable" and edifying
writers such as Cicero and Virgil, but the lusty tales of Ovid,
Lucian and Petronius, the obscenities of Martial, Juvenal and
Catullus, and a host of other writers who offered their Renaissance readers no succor against the temptation to sin. It also
included a host of disturbing visual images: "diminutive Pans,
naked girls, drunken satyrs, and erections exposed in pictures,"
as Johannes Molanus, a sixteenth-century critic and official censor for Philip II of the Netherlands, put it.[8] Like the eighteenth-
century boys who had been diagnosed as victims of onanism,
humanists, too, had turned their seed sour by masturbating once
too often with the classics. The proud lineage of scholarship,
stretching from Petrarch to Erasmus, ultimately produced Pietro
Aretino, the most famous of the pornographers of the Renaissance,
and – not coincidentally – the Reformation, in its final hour.

How might the Renaissance have facilitated the emergence of
pornography in Western Europe? All cultures produce some form

of sexually explicit art and literature. But not every culture distinguishes the erotic from the pornographic, nor is pornography defined in the same way in every instance. Pornography, a repository of multiple meanings with constantly shifting boundaries, emerged from the literature and imagery that purported to recount the lives of prostitutes, a genre that traced its origins to Lucian's *Dialogues of the Courtesans*. This genre flourished in the erotic and obscene writings of sixteenth-century authors such as Pietro Aretino, Francisco Delicado, Lorenzo Venier and Niccolò Franco, whose work contemporaries like Tommaso Garzoni judged "dirty and immoral."[9] More generally, Aline Rouselle's definition of *porneia* – "any manifestation of desire for another's body.... a measure of human weakness in the service of God" – reminds us of the Christian roots of this concept.[10] As it emerged in the early modern period, pornography, among its many other functions, charted the collision between competing representations of desire and virtue.

While acknowledging that it is impossible to be sure exactly *what* is defined *as* pornography when writing its history, nonetheless it is a history that needs to be written, particularly because its undefinability suggests that it is at once everywhere and nowhere. If we begin by identifying some of the matrices most relevant to the subject, we quickly amass a formidably heterodox list. The history of pornography charts changing attitudes toward male and female bodies, sexual practices and their respective representations. It tells us something about the persistence of manuscript culture, the impact of printing, the nature of authorship, the diffusion of literacy and the process by which words and images circulated. In addition, early modern pornography was a medium used frequently to convey the image of a "world turned upside down," and its strongly satirical components make it a sensitive measure of shifting social hierarchies and the vicissitudes

53

of intellectual and political culture in the complex network of republics and courts that composed Renaissance Italy. Rather than consigning pornography to the margins of the early modern world, treating it as the product of an emerging subculture, let us put it at the center.[11] To define Renaissance pornography is, in an essential sense, to define the intersections of sexuality, politics and learning – the constitutive elements of the culture itself. In the pages of books like Aretino's *Ragionamenti*, the moral fabric of Renaissance society was laid bare for all to see. From this perspective, an inquiry into Renaissance pornography is an attempt, first, to understand the sexual underpinnings of sixteenth-century Italian society, and, second, to understand the sexual and moral meanings of Renaissance cultural production.

Entering the Marketplace of the Obscene

At the end of the fifteenth century, Western Europe was a society that had only recently acquired some of the tools necessary for the development of a pornographic culture. The advent of printing not only offered scholars the opportunity to disseminate their learning with greater speed to a larger audience, but, subsequently, generated subsidiary industries that capitalized on the formation of an urban reading public, and on the power of reproducible images.[12] The private circulation of manuscripts now competed with the less regulated public marketplace of printed goods; engravings by Marcantonio Raimondi and Agostino Carracci turned what had been unique artistic productions into popular and accessible commodities. While Titian's erotic paintings, which hung in the Escorial of Philip II, were hidden behind a curtain and shown only to visitors of the monarch's choosing, popular prints and books were available in bookstores in most urban centers.[13] The reactions of various authorities to the appearance of erotic and obscene materials in print reflected the uneasy transition of a society from one in which access to knowledge was restricted to the social and intellectual elite to one that divulged its secrets daily and indiscriminately.[14] The widespread circulation of political, sexual and scientific secrets by the mid-sixteenth century represented the fulfillment of the most dire prophecies of learned men, who argued that the formation of a "marketplace of ideas" would lead society to inevitable ruin. Printing, as the formation of a new medium of exchange, had subverted the implicit pact of the *letterati* that confined the circulation of words and images to a circumscribed elite.

One method of dealing with the unchecked passage of morally dangerous and improper materials from the restricted world of the humanists to the wider public was to formulate mechanisms of censorship that essentially defined the boundaries between licit and illicit. While the Index of Forbidden Books, most comprehensively established by Paul IV in 1559, was primarily designed to excise from the Catholic world heretical works and the writings of Protestants, it tangentially addressed the moral content of art and literature. The *Canons and Decrees of the Council of Trent* (1563) outlined the official view on this matter:

> Books which professedly deal with, narrate or teach things lascivious or obscene are absolutely prohibited, since not only the matter of faith but also that of morals, which are usually easily corrupted through the reading of such books, must be taken into consideration, and those who possess them are to be severely punished by the bishops. Ancient books written by the heathens may by reason of their elegance and quality of style be permitted, but by no means read to children.[15]

By 1558, Aretino's work took its place alongside that of Machiavelli and the expurgated editions of Boccaccio, and his work remained on the Index throughout the early modern period. Under pressure from the Church authorities, civic governments increasingly allowed ecclesiastical officials to inspect bookstores unannounced, where they discovered numerous copies of prohibited and unexpurgated books. These books were particularly plentiful in the Republic of Venice, where attempts to curtail the freedom of the printing industry met with considerable resistance.[16] While castigating the works of contemporaries that violated this injunction, church officials were decidedly more ambivalent about the censorship of the classics. The "elegance and quality of style" that deterred officials from a wholesale condemnation of the writings of the ancients effectively made the humanist virtue of eloquence an excuse for licentiousness. Thus, the Tridentine characterization of "things lascivious or obscene" implicitly defined the classics as works neither produced nor appreciated by humanists. It was left up to those who acted upon this decree to put this classification into practice.

By the end of the sixteenth century, literate Europeans had developed a common understanding of the effects of the Index on the circulation of prohibited literature. In Torriano's *Piazza universale*, an Italian phrasebook for Englishmen, the forty-second dialogue, entitled "Stranger in Conversation with a Roman Bookseller," offered the following example of a model conversation in an Italian bookstore:

"I am seeking the works of A[retino]," says the Stranger.

"You may seek them from one end of the Row to the other, and not find them," replies the bookseller.

"And why?"

"Because they are forbidden, both the *Postures* and *Discourses*, that imbracing [sic] of men and women together in unusual manners, begets a scandal, and the Inquisition permits no such matters, it con-

demns all such sordid things, nay not so much, but the Amorous
Adventures in Romances it condemns."[17]

Rather than eradicating this sort of literature, the efforts of the
Inquisition and the Index gave it a special status by making it difficult to acquire. In the back rooms of bookstores, printers made
available a burgeoning erotic literature to an eager audience, as
exemplified by a Venetian in late sixteenth-century Paris who
claimed to have sold more than fifty copies of Aretino in less
than a year.[18]

The same printers who produced the works of Aretino and his
imitators on the sly also contributed to the growing market for
erotic prints. The decrees of the Council of Trent had said little
about the restriction of images, though the proceedings of the
twenty-fifth session (December 3–4, 1563) advised that "all lasciviousness should be avoided, so that images shall not be painted
and adorned with a seductive charm, or the celebration of saints
and the visitation of relics be perverted..."[19] By the 1580s, reforming archbishops like Gabriele Paleotti in Bologna and Federico
Borromeo in Milan took it upon themselves to inspect the content
of paintings and sculptures and to pass judgment upon the appro-
priateness of the modes of portrayal chosen by artists. Even laymen
like Ludovico Dolce clamored for greater regulation of images.
"The laws prohibit the printing of immodest books," he wrote
in his *Dialogo della pittura intitolato l'Aretino* (1557), "how much
more should they prohibit such pictures?"[20] Pagan imagery and
nudity, except where Holy Writ dictated, was systematically cen-
sured; the nudes in Michelangelo's *Last Judgement*, which Aretino
claimed to find more obscene than his own writings, gradually
were garbed with wisps of fabric, and a program of sanitized ico-
nography was encouraged, though never successfully imple-
mented. As Paleotti wrote in his *Discorso intorno alle immagini*

sacre e profani (1586), "for that which concerns obscenities, painted in a lascivious and provocative manner, or showing unseemly limbs, one should impede even their private possession. In the future, whoever dares to paint and sculpt them will be severely punished as a corrupter of manners."[21] The visual scandals of Giulio Romano, Marcantonio Raimondi and Titian, novel in the 1530s, had been transformed into the "obscenities" of the Carracci brothers by the 1580s.

In response, an illicit culture arose, which thrived on these restrictions. In late sixteenth- and seventeenth-century Venice, one could buy manuscript copies of Aretino and other forbidden works, such as Lorenzo Venier's *La Puttana errante* (1531) and the anonymous *Tariffa delle puttane* (1535).[22] Printers in less regulated cities like London and Amsterdam profited from the misfortunes of their Italian counterparts, while operating under the watchful eye of the Inquisition. Englishmen traveling to Italy in the late sixteenth century no doubt would have been surprised to discover that their treasured copies of Aretino, usually bought in Venice, were actually published in London by John Wolfe.[23] Copies of the infamous Aretine postures – Marcantonio Raimondi's engravings of sixteen sexual positions, originally conceived by Giulio Romano and later accompanied by Aretino's sonnets – also continued their tenuous existence on the margins of print culture and thrived in manuscript form.

It is in this widened circuit of popular printed goods and private manuscript erotica that the beginnings of a pornographic culture arose. Nanna, the famed protagonist of Aretino's *Ragionamenti*, who lived and thrived in the anti-humanist environment in which her creator's works were produced, was a self-described "market bitch."[24] At the hands of Aretino and his followers, Mikhail Bakhtin's teeming, Rabelaisian marketplace was endowed with yet another feature: the ability to create and sustain a pornographic culture.[25] By appropriating the site of popular culture, which was inhabited by grotesque rather than courtly bodies, Renaissance pornographers destabilized the site of artistic and literary production by purporting to dissolve the boundaries between "high" and "low." In doing so, they also defined the conditions of authorship as ambiguous at best, and problematic at worst. What identity was left to writers who straddled the worlds of both the marketplace and the court? In the language of Renaissance pornography, authors, as well as whores and sodomites, were classified as members of the "third sex" and in the forging of their identities, all the constitutive elements of the culture intersected and collided.

Eroticizing the Senses

While pornography was partly defined by the impact of print culture, with subsequent redefinitions of the nature of authorship and readership, it also was the result of certain artistic and philosophical trends that conditioned the act of seeing. The erotic and obscene literature of the Renaissance developed an elaborate visual currency integral to the formation of pornography. Once again, such techniques were not particular to a special genre delimited by the term *pornography*, but permeated the humanist discourse of the arts. As Edgar Wind and more recently Leonard Barkan have observed, Renaissance Platonism recuperated the erotic.[26] One aspect of this revival was the diffusion of representational strategies that we might characterize as voyeuristic. The seductive and arousing powers of images had long been noted by guardians of morals such as Clement of Alexandria (second century A.D.), who admonished the Greeks for defiling their ears and prostituting their eyes with profane images.[27] The appearance of printing, in conjunction with the revival of classical culture, produced an unforeseen and largely uncontrollable "enrichment of the erotic imagination."[28]

From the 1520s onward, vast quantities of prints and paintings depicting the amorous encounters of gods and men poured
forth from the workshops of Raphael, Giulio Romano, Titian and
the Carracci, were reproduced by engravers such as Marcantonio
Raimondi, Giulio Bocasone and Agostino Carracci, and were then
printed for popular consumption. Semi-pornographic prints, like
the popular images of courtesans that were sold on the streets,
allowed viewers to undress them with their hands, revealing the
male underwear which these women (scandalously) wore and leaving in doubt the gender of the sex beneath (figure 1.2). Sequences
of engravings such as Agostino Carracci's *lascivie* (ca. 1590–1595)
took viewers from the moment of discovery, in which a satyr
came upon a sleeping nymph, to her eventual "awakening" and
"embracing," depicted in the fashion of Raimondi's *modi* (figure
1.3).[29] The availability of cheap reproductions made public, for
the first time, a series of images formerly confined to humanist
circles and the inner recesses of the courts, and popularized an
erotic discourse initially designed for an elite audience.

Renaissance writers and artists strove to replicate the effects
of such tales as that of a young man who copulated with the statue
of Venus in Cnidos, "leaving behind actual traces of his lust," or
Terence's more well-known story of a Roman depiction of Jove
coupling with Danaë in a shower of golden rain.[30] Girolamo
Morlini's pornographic *Novellae* (1520), for example, recounted
the story of a woman who was so moved by the sight of a statue
with an erect penis (*erectus ille priapus*) in a public square, that
she conceived of the desire to kiss it. When flesh touched stone,
she succumbed to the temptation to copulate, enjoying the pleasures of the statue until dawn.[31] Morlini's fantasy that images
could so move their viewers had a realistic counterpart when, in
the 1630s, several Venetian patricians were brought to trial for
allegedly copulating with a statue of Christ.[32] While the sixteenth

FIGURE 1.2. Anonymous engraving of a Venetian courtesan (ca. 1590).

FIGURE 1.3. Agostino Carracci, *A Satyr Approaching a Sleeping Nymph* (ca. 1590–1595).

century had placed such images within the discourse of the arts, the seventeenth century understood them to be potentially blasphemous. Morlini's playful tale, an object of Renaissance mirth, was now a matter of public morality.

By the sixteenth century, Renaissance artists and humanists had constructed an image of the senses that increased the potential for danger. Writing to Federico Gonzaga in 1527, Aretino commented on the anticipated pleasures of a statue commissioned for the duke from Aretino's friend Sansovino: "I understand that the most rare Messer Jacopo Sansovino is about to embellish your bedchamber with a statue of Venus so true to life and so living that it will fill with lustful thoughts the mind of anyone who looks at it."[33] In Aretino's world, all forms of representation harbored an erotic potential. This potential lay, not so much in the medium, as in the gaze of the beholder who could no longer contain his emotional reaction to the viewing of provocative imagery.

Pietro Bembo, in a famous passage in Castiglione's *Book of the Courtier* (1528), described the follies of young men whose reason was depleted by the "unchaste desires" of the senses. "[I]f the soul allows itself to be guided by the judgement of the senses, it falls into very grave errors and judges that the body in which this beauty is seen is the chief cause thereof," admonished Castiglione, "and hence, in order to enjoy that beauty, it deems it necessary to join itself as closely to that body as it can...."[34] Castiglione's neoplatonic discourse was one of many texts that laid the theoretical groundwork for the Renaissance eroticization of the senses. In this fashion, artists, writers and patrons constructed an image of the senses that, Galatea-like, harbored the possibility that stone might turn to flesh and painted surfaces might come to life. Viewing a potentially erotic image, let alone enjoying physical contact with it, was considered an intimate and therefore unstable act, capable of transforming both the viewer and the object of contemplation. Certainly we need to distinguish the "proper" site for "lustful thoughts" – that is, the bedchamber of a duke – from the impropriety of having such thoughts in public, let alone performing obscene acts on a statue of Christ versus a statue of Venus. Nonetheless, Morlini's tale, Aretino's description of Sansovino's statue and the accusation against the Venetian libertines all indicated the perceived power of images to move their audience.

Enhancing this tradition were images and descriptions of famous couplings like that of Jove and Danaë, Venus and Adonis, and Leda and the Swan. These were the "metamorphic lies" lampooned by writers like Niccolò Franco, who felt that the images proliferated "in order to say that one fucks even in heaven."[35] They filled the canvases of most of the major Renaissance and Mannerist painters, and they were popularized in prints like Raimondi's version of *Leda and the Swan*, in which the sexual explicitness is unmistakable (figure 1.4). It is tempting for modern viewers to distinguish high cultural productions like Titian's *Danaë* and *Venus and Adonis* (figure 1.5), from scruffy pornographic prints like Bocasone's version of the Danaë tale, in which Danaë's legs are an open window on the scene (figure 1.6). However, we need to take into account descriptions from contemporary viewers, who themselves did not necessarily distinguish Titian's eroticism – produced for courtiers and humanists – from popular pornography.[36] As Anne Hollander aptly puts it, we are unable to fully place ourselves in the position of the Renaissance viewer because, to our eyes, the images are "wearing" the Renaissance nude.[37] All the more reason to inspect the words of contemporaries carefully, to better understand what effects the words of Aretino and the images of Titian or Raimondi could produce.

Writing to Alessandro Contarini in the 1550s, Ludovico Dolce described his encounter with Titian's *Venus and Adonis*. Praising the image for its virtuosity – "in her intimate parts we recognize the creases on the flesh caused by her seated position" – Dolce recounted how seeing the painting had caused "a warming, a softening, a stirring of the blood." Recalling classical descriptions of the effect of a statue of Venus, he concluded, "if a marble statue could by the stimuli of its beauty so penetrate to the marrow of a young man, that he stained himself, then, what must she do who is of flesh, who is beauty personified and appears to be breathing?"[38] While Dolce's assessment of Titian's paintings built upon the imagery present in both Aretino's assessment of Sansovino's sculpture and in the writings of Castiglione, and left open to interpretation whether he described the effect of the painting's eroticism or its artistry, the statements of Counter-Reformation critics about similar images were unambiguous in their condemnation. By the 1570s, art critic Pirro Ligorio described any nude image of Venus as "a filthy, obscene thing." His contemporary, Molanus, exclaimed, "What is disgraceful to name is freely painted and presented to the eyes. These subjects stand forth in public, in the taverns and marketplace, and are willy-nilly thrust on our view."[39] The fear of "things lascivious and obscene," formalized by the Tridentine decrees, now encompassed the presentation of the erotic in the visual arts.

Erotic imagery that played with the techniques of seeing was not relegated only to the domain of the visual arts, but also was developed in great detail in the writings of Aretino. Beginning with the sonnets that he attached to Raimondi's engravings of Giulio Romano's sixteen *modi*, Aretino constructed a world regulated by the logic of the gaze. In the first sonnet, the male lover's testicles are described as "witnesses of every fucking pleasure," the only anatomical part with a privileged view of all sexual secrets (figure 1.7). Two other sonnets dealt ironically with Ovidian themes by debasing them. In sonnet 11 (figure 1.8), the dynamic between the two participants is described in the following terms:

65

FIGURE 1.4. (above) Marcantonio Raimondi, *Leda and the Swan* (early 1500s).

FIGURE 1.5. (above right) Titian, *Danaë* (1553–1554).

FIGURE 1.6. (below right) Giulio Bocasone, *Danaë* (mid-sixteenth century).

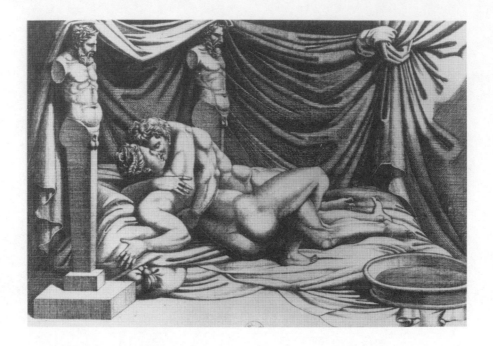

FIGURE 1.7. Reproduction of Aretino's first posture from the original engraving by Marcantonio Raimondi (1524).

Open your thighs so I can look straight
>
> At your beautiful ass and cunt in my face,
> An ass equal to paradise in its enjoyment,
> A cunt that melts hearts through the kidneys.

While I compare these things,

> Suddenly I long to kiss you,
> And I seem to myself more handsome than Narcissus
> In the mirror that keeps my prick erect.

Similarly, the male in sonnet 14 exclaims, "I mirror myself in your ass..." (figure 1.9).[40] In Aretino's language, the genitals were a window to the soul. In contrast to Castiglione's purified image of the soul – which resisted such debasement – Aretino suggested that seeing was an act of (male) sexual power. Like the pool of water into which Narcissus gazed, falling in love with his own reflection, the coupling of men and women in the *modi* became an opportunity for Aretino to meditate upon the way in which all forms of sexual experience were self-referential. By playing with mirror imagery, Aretino connected his verses to the more sanitized images of courtesans, whose erotic gaze also turned inward (figure 1.10), or to the tale of Susanna, whose nakedness was unsuspectingly revealed to the Elders as she gazed into a mirror (figure 1.11).[41] Aretino's *Sonnetti lussuriosi* firmly associated voyeurism with pornographic imagery, from the internal dialogue of the senses that the different positions produced to the external dialogue between the sonnets and the reader:

Just as people toss pepper or other spices
Up a nose to make them sneeze very suddenly
Thus by the smell of clamorous fucking you are corrupted.
Feel between your legs if you don't believe it.[42]

Apri le coscie, accio ch'io ueggia bene
  Il tuo bel culo, e ia tua potta in uiso,
Culo da compire un pare un paradiso,
Potta, ch'i cori stilla per le rene;
Mentre, ch'io uagheggio, egli mi uiene
  Capriccio di basciarui a l'improuiso,
E mi par esser piu bel, che Narciso
  Nel specchio, che'l mio cazzo allegro tiene;
Ahi ribalda, ahi ribaldo, in terra, & in letto
  Io ti ueggio puttana, e t'apparecchia
  Ch'io ti rompa due costole del petto;
Io te n'incaco franciosata uecchia,
  Che per questo piacer plusquamperfetto
  Entrarci in un pozzo senza secchia,
                              E non si troua pecchia
Ghiotta d'i fior com'io, d'un nobil cazzo,
E no'i prouo ancho, e per mirarlo sguazzo;

FIGURE 1.8. Aretino's eleventh posture (1527).

Non tirar futtutelo di Cupido
    La carriola, firmati bifmulo
Ch'io uó fotter in potta, e non in culo
Coftei, che mi to'l cazzo, e me ne ridoz
E ne le braccia, e ne le gambe mi fido,
    E fi difconcio fto, e non t'adulo,
    Che ci morrebbe a ftarçi un'hora un mulo,
    E però tanto co'l cul foffio e gridoz
E fe uoi Beatrice ftentar faccio
    Perdonar mi douete, perch'io moftro
    Che fottendo a difsaggio mi disfaccio,
E fe non, ch'io mi fpecchio nel cul uoftro
    Stando fofpefo in l'uno e'nl'altro braccio
    Mai non fi fruirebbe il fatto noftro,
                O, cul di latte, e d'oftro
Se non ch'io fon per mirarti di uena,
Non mi ftarebbe il cazzo dritto à penaz

FIGURE 1.9. Aretino's fourteenth posture (1527).

FIGURE 1.10. Giovanni Bellini, *Young Woman at Her Toilet* (1540).

FIGURE 1.11. Tintoretto, *Susannah* (ca. 1560).

As Aretino told Battista Zatti in 1537, Raimondi's images had produced this effect on him, and he envisioned his poems as the conduit through which he could convey this sensation to others. More than any other writer of this period, Aretino reinforced the dangerous powers of the senses through his repeated textualization of them in his pornographic writings.

The manipulation of the senses was refined and extended to an even greater degree in his *Ragionamenti*. Divided into two parts, with each part comprising three days of conversations, Aretino's dialogues made full use of erotic visual currencies. The first part, as Giulio Ferroni observes, was significantly more voyeuristic than the second.[43] This voyeuristic theme was particularly true of the first day, in which Nanna recounted her experience as a nun. Finding herself in a room that was a veritable erotic panopticon, the then innocent Nanna is initiated into the pleasures of sex by observing the different images of couplings decorating the walls of the monastery and by watching others through various peepholes. After Nanna has recounted what she has seen at length, her friend Antonia interrupts:

> *Antonia.* How could you control your desire for a man after seeing all that fucking?
> *Nanna.* I was all alather with lust.

Nanna's senses are bombarded throughout her early adventures. A lover gives her a book which, though "crammed with pictures of people amusing themselves in the modes and postures performed by learned nuns," is disguised as a prayer book; she devours it. She is constantly "[o]vercome by the scent of...pleasure...."[44] During the period before she becomes a prostitute, Nanna represents Aretino's ideal reader, susceptible to every sight, sound and smell she encounters. While it could be concluded that Aretino's imagined audience is female, Nanna's gender is not unambiguously "female." Because she is identified most frequently with the author of the text she remains, in a sense, outside the sexual circuit of the dialogues. Her early persona – not unlike Aretino's before he arrived in Venice – is best described as courtly, and as feminine without necessarily being female.

After experiencing the disappointments of the convent and the marriage bed, Nanna chooses whoredom as the best profession for a woman and transforms herself from a consumer of erotica into a creator and manipulator of the pornographic gaze.[45] Both Antonia and Nanna's daughter, Pippa, comment on her ability to arouse them with words. After hearing Nanna's story about a book of obscene postures, Antonia tells her:

> *Antonia.* Do you know, Nanna, what happens to me when I hear you talk?
> *Nanna.* No.
> *Antonia.* What happens to someone who smells a purge, and without even taking it, goes twice or three times to move her bowels.
> *Nanna.* Ha!
> *Antonia.* Yes, I tell you, your stories are so natural and vivid that you make me piss, though I have eaten neither truffles nor cardoon.

To the less experienced Pippa, who is initiated into the life of a prostitute in the second part of the *Ragionamenti*, the effect of Nanna's words is even more intoxicating:

> *Pippa.* Oh, you are a wonderful painter with words; and as I listened to you, I got all excited. I had the feeling that the hand you described touched my nipples and was just about to feel. . . . I won't say what.

Nanna. I saw the passion on your face, which changed completely, then blushed red while I was showing you what one does not see.[46]

In this fashion, Aretino challenged the Horatian commonplace that images were more vivid than words, drawing heavily upon the artistic vocabulary of the day to do so.

In a passage near the end of the dialogues, Aretino identified the social and political matrix out of which the pornographic gaze emerged. Describing the foibles of nobles, Nanna warns Pippa, "Sometimes they get a huge mirror, undress us and make us go about completely naked, and then they force us to hold the most obscene postures and positions that the human fantasy can concoct. They gaze longingly at our faces, breasts, nipples, shoulders, loins, cunts, and thighs, nor could I possibly tell you how that satiates their lust and the pleasure they get from looking."[47] These aristocratic whims are contrasted to the practices of "ordinary folk" who do not "dislocate your bones...."[48]

While Tridentine reformers would fret about the public diffusion of lewd and improper images to the illiterate masses, to which engravers like Raimondi and Carracci materially contributed with their *modi* and *lascivie*,[49] the complex emotions associated with the refinement of the senses continued to be the domain of the upper classes throughout the sixteenth century. Within twenty-five years of the publication of Aretino's *Sonnetti lussuriosi*, Brantôme could describe a noblewoman at the French court who "kept a figure of Aretino in her room... [for] 'books and other devices had served her well.'"[50] For men of learning, as well as for men and women of high social standing, the eroticization of the senses was accomplished through the viewing of these images and the reading of such books.

Masturbating with the Classics

The very bookishness of early modern pornography, replete with sly allusions to Ovid's *Metamorphoses* and other classical works, returns us to another central feature of this genre: its indebtedness to the past. While writers like Aretino delighted in telling their readers that they despised the classics, equating novelty with iconoclasm, they nonetheless drew heavily upon ancient erotica to create an essentially new literary genre. The tensions between the desire to both emulate the past while celebrating the virtues – or the vices – of the present met in the semantic field of "pornography."

Renaissance pornographers often presented their work as the end of metaphor, a negation of the eloquence and erudition that defined humanist culture. They loudly proclaimed that their works laid bare the truth, stripped of all the metaphorical witticisms and allegories that characterized the contemporary culture of learning. "But because the subject is somewhat immodest, I want you to approve of the fact that I will call everything by its name," Zoppino tells Ludovico before he launches into a description of the practices of Roman courtesans, in the anonymously written *Ragionamento del Zoppino* (1539).[51] Most famous, of course, is the statement of the prostitute Antonia during her conversation with Nanna in Aretino's *Ragionamenti*:

> Oh, I meant to tell you and then I forgot: Speak plainly and say 'fuck,' 'prick,' 'cunt' and 'ass' if you want anyone except the scholars at the University of Rome to understand you ... why don't you say it straight out and stop going about on tiptoes? Why don't you say yes when you mean yes and no when you mean no – or else keep it to yourself?[52]

Pornography purported to unveil "the thing" itself, and, in doing so, it participated in the strong current of anti-classicism present in sixteenth-century thought. Renaissance pornographers were not the first to react strongly to a perceived canon. As the *Priapeia* made fun of Roman intellectuals whose pretensions led them to substitute Greek words for Latin, and as the medieval fabliaux attacked troubadour lyrics for being too allegorical, writers like Aretino lampooned the pretensions of a Latinate culture in an increasingly vernacular world. Pornography, as he portrayed it, was a new literature for a new age. Freed from the constraints of subject and the dictates of style that made the mills of the humanists grind ever so slowly, writers like Aretino purported to shock their audience into the present.

Without denying that there is some truth to this view, Renaissance pornography can also be portrayed as a product of rather than a reaction to ancient canons. Aretino partially relied on Ovid and Boccaccio for the material in his *Ragionamenti*, and he surely must have been familiar with the Italian translations of Lucian then in circulation. While Aretino attacked the humanists at every opportunity, he no doubt took some satisfaction that he, like Ovid, had been forced to leave Rome for *carmen et error* – a poem and an indiscretion. Even the novelty of Romano's *modi* recently has been thrown in doubt, since they bear a striking resemblance to the Roman *Spintriae*, a series of chits used as a form of payment in brothels and illustrated with similar couplings. Romano, who fancied himself a collector of antiquities, may have owned a set.[53] Renaissance writers and artists drew heavily upon all forms of classical imagery, so it should hardly be surprising that pornographers drew inspiration from ancient erotic codes.

Yet pornographers and their audience did not interpret these codes in quite the same way as the Romans. In a sense, Burckhardt was right: for a Christian audience raised on the prohibitive writings of Saint Augustine and the Church Fathers, two of the most alluring and disturbing aspects of pre-Christian culture were its

attitudes toward and portrayals of sexuality. In attempting to create a culture modeled on antiquity, humanists had to come to
terms with all of its values and practices, however antithetical
those might be to the goals of a Christian society. Forays into
the monastic libraries of Europe revealed not only the lost letters of Cicero, but also a widespread documentation of an openly
erotic culture that depicted acts best left unseen and honored
practices later defined as *contra naturam*. Like the nineteenth-
century archeologists whose unearthing of Pompeii revealed
incontrovertible proof of the "scandals" of the ancients, humanists were forced to reevaluate their commitment to the restoration of antiquity *in toto*, when their own "excavations" yielded
such disturbing fruit as the cult of Priapus, the ever-erect god
whose statues were ubiquitous in ancient Rome (figure 1.12), or
explicit images of Leda and the swan, whose coupling inspired
several generations of Renaissance artists.

Humanism was hardly a monolithic enterprise. It allowed room
for scholars who preferred their editions of *Ovide moralisé*, with
the understanding that pagan mysteries were best seen through
the veil of religion, as well as for editors and translators of the
unexpurgated Ovid, like Aretino's friend Ludovico Dolce, who
argued that textual purity took precedence over content, and who
preferred to embellish upon the spicier tales.[54] The fortunes of
the *Carmina Priapeia* are a good case in point.[55] The *Priapeia*, a
series of playfully erotic and obscene poems dedicated to the god
Priapus, circulated widely in manuscript form during the fifteenth
century; the earliest surviving version was copied by Giovanni
Boccaccio.[56] All seventy-five extant manuscript versions date from
the early Renaissance and their presence during that period, when
compared to their absence in previous centuries, certainly testifies to the widening definition of "appropriate subjects" for
scholars to pursue. By 1517, twenty-two editions of the *Priapeia*

FIGURE 1.12. Attic bowl (470 B.C.). Pan chasing a shepherd with a statue of Priapus.

had appeared in print, signaling their immediate popularity during the transition from manuscript to print culture.[57]

The *Priapeia*, initially attributed to Virgil, first appeared as part of his complete works, which were published in Rome in 1469. They were subsequently issued by numerous presses throughout Europe, most frequently by the most important humanist press in Italy, the Aldine Press of Venice.[58] Quite often, this section of the Virgilian corpus was torn out. Readers were either ashamed to have it associated with Virgil or preferred not to display their copies openly, saving the "Virgilian Appendix" for more private uses. Having established Virgil as a poet of no inconsiderable virtue, critics were loath to drag his reputation through the mud – "For what could be more wanton than these poems?" exclaimed Pomponio Leto[59] – and searched for clues that the poems had been authored by writers of uneasy reputation, such as Ovid and Martial. By the late sixteenth century, the *Priapeia* had attracted no less a commentator than Joseph Scaliger, that "bottomless pit of erudition," who took time away from his many other textual exercises to establish the multiauthorship of the poems and to debate the significance of a particularly problematic line about a young homosexual who curled his hair: *num tandem prior es puella, quaeso, / quam sunt, mentula quos habet, capilli?*[60] Did this mean, Scaliger wondered, that the boy had plucked out his pubic hairs to appear girlish, or was it simply an acknowledgment that anatomy would always give one away? He also found one of the *Priapeia* – a poem about an impotent man unable to achieve an erection in the arms of a young boy – so delightful that he translated it into Greek iambics.[61]

While men like Scaliger, who were committed to a widescale program of restoring the literature of antiquity, viewed their editions of erotic and obscene writings as another exercise in textual purification and were quick to condemn the 1606 edition by

Gaspar Schioppius when the commentary appeared too obscene, they nonetheless made this literature accessible to a wider audience that appreciated the content more than the grammatical twists and turns. Rereading Giovanni di Pagolo Morelli's advice to his son about reading Virgil alone in the study – "he will never say no to you...and will give you pleasure and consolation"[62] – it is easy to imagine a double entendre, not so much present in Morelli's own words, but in the way later writers would define this act of solitude. The garden of Priapus, more accessible than Eden, was a tempting paradise that humanists entered over and over again. By the sixteenth century, priapic images abounded in art and literature. Giulio Romano painted them on the walls of the Palazzo del Te in Mantua, while the engraver Marcantonio Raimondi churned out images of a satyr attempting to couple with a priapic herm in his "Bacchanal" and surrounded the couple in the first Aretine posture with priapic herms (see figure 1.7). Pacifico Massimo invoked "holy Priapus" in his *Hecatelegium* (1489), an elegy to his penis, and many of the humanist sexual encomia were composed in the garden of Priapus.

Prominent humanists like Pietro Bembo and more popular writers like Niccolò Franco, Aretino's protégé in Venice, dubbed their own sonnets *Priapea*; Franco even made Aretino the "gardener" of this sexual paradise. "What do you think of poets?" leered Franco in *Le Pistole vulgari* (1542), "[d]o you believe that they could sleep nude (*senza braghe*) with their Priapea?"[63] The transition of the image of Priapus from a witty household god into an object of textual interest, and, finally, into a euphemism for obscene and pornographic writing, indicates the ambivalence with which humanists viewed their engagement with the past. While Scaliger could maintain that proper scholarly detachment lent decorum to the reading and writing of priapeia, writers like Franco undermined these efforts by reinforcing the idea that it

was the subject, as much as the mode of presentation, that mat-
tered. Rather than muting the relationship between humanist
textuality and Renaissance sexuality, writers like Aretino and
Franco strove to reveal their common origins. Literary production, as satirists like Ariosto proclaimed, was a profoundly sexual
act, the product of a male humanistic culture. Recalling Franco's
joke about sleeping poets, Ariosto remarked to Pietro Bembo,
"The vulgar laugh when they hear of someone who possesses a
vein of poetry, and then they say, 'It is a great peril to turn your
back if you sleep next to him.' "[64]

The most famous of the Renaissance priapeia was Antonio
Beccadelli's *Hermaphroditus* (1425). Unlike Scaliger, who dis-
tanced himself from the production of such literature through his
role as commentator, Beccadelli chose to follow the time-honored
tradition of *imitatio* by authoring his own priapic poem. Initially
praised by such prominent humanists as Guarino da Verona and
Poggio Bracciolini and such patrons as Cosimo de' Medici and
Gian Francesco Gonzaga, the *Hermaphroditus* became a cause célèbre within a year. Copies of it were publicly burned in Bologna,
Ferrara and Mantua, after it was attacked by preacher Bernardino
da Siena and condemned by Eugenius IV and influential scholars
such as Francesco Filelfo, Pier Candido Decembrio, Lorenzo Valla
and Leonardo Bruni. Even early supporters began to recant.[65] By
1435, "Il Panormita" found himself apologizing to Cosimo for
being so presumptuous as to dedicate this obscenity to him: "If
memory serves, Cosimo, I dedicated a little book with the base
title of *Hermaphroditus* to you. In that little book I described many
obscenities and vices against nature.... Now that renowned men
judge it base, forgive me. Oh yes, even I acknowledge my guilt
with a partial retraction."[66] What had led Beccadelli from success to scandal?

In his dedication, Beccadelli directed Cosimo to "disregard

the common herd and read this little book, despite its lasciviousness, with a serene mind...."[67] Throughout the book, Beccadelli
reaffirmed the classical roots of the poem, while continuing to
draw on contemporary experience. Beccadelli, responding to an
imagined critic, chastised him for not knowing the ancients thor-
oughly. "Odo surely has not read the tender Catullus, nor caught
a glimpse of your penis, phallic Priapus. Why should anything that
was permissible to the [Romans]...brand me as morally corrupt?"
Elsewhere, he affirmed, "I simply follow in the footsteps of the
Ovids and Virgils of this world,"[68] and he urged his patron Cosimo
to do the same.

Situated squarely in the priapic tradition, the poem was divided
into two parts, a textual hermaphrodite that "has both a penis and
a vagina."[69] As in the original *Priapeia*, matrons and virgins were
advised to shun the text because it contained *verba impudica*, or
unseemly words. In some seventy verses, Beccadelli highlighted
the places into which Priapus led him, among them the "gaping
ass" of a young boy, the "voracious vagina[s]" of several prostitutes, and the libraries of prominent manuscript collectors like
Giovanni Aurispa, Beccadelli's former teacher, who loaned him
precious copies of Martial and Catullus to fuel his fantasies.[70]
Poetry, in Beccadelli's terms, was the ultimate foreplay, and
a good poet was defined as an "expert at getting the last drop
out of penises." Erotic response was the ultimate test of literary
power, something Niccolò Franco also understood when he made
his penis his "pen."

Although the hermaphrodite wandered into the schoolrooms
of former teachers, commenting on their pederasty, and paused
in the workshops of several humanists to gaze at the secrets hidden in Greek and Roman manuscripts, its final resting place was
a Florentine brothel. Beccadelli concluded that there, surrounded
by prostitutes, "You can say smutty things and do naughty things

with them and you won't meet with a refusal that makes you blush for shame. How and as you please, you can do there what you want, you, dear book, who have long been used to fucking and being fucked."[71] With this witty epilogue, Beccadelli summarized the prostitution of all authors who passed their texts from hand to hand in search of patronage and recognition.

In a letter to Giovanni Lanola, Guarino da Verona described his initial delight in Beccadelli's eloquence, despite the questionable subject of the poem: "Nor would I modify my approval because of its playfulness, lasciviousness and impudence. Would you praise Apelles, Fabius and other painters any less because they painted those parts of the body that should remain covered, for propriety's sake?" It was, he affirmed, approved by "serious, continent Christians who do not abstain when the subject demands the use of very free language."[72]

Both the production of and reaction to the *Hermaphroditus* tell us something about the paradoxes of classical culture in a Christian society. As early as the fifteenth century, leading intellectuals had begun to puzzle over the extent to which the terrain mapped out by the ancients might also be made their own, even when religious prudence dictated otherwise. Humanists like Beccadelli struggled with the proscriptions of a learned culture that, tied closely to the Church, was uneasy with any discussion of sexuality, let alone the problematic subject of homosexuality.[73] The initial praise and subsequent condemnation Beccadelli received, at times from the same people, amply reflected the tensions of a society that had not come to terms with its perception of the past, and the past as revealed through its artifacts and documents. Nor had they reconciled the chasm between their own sexual practices and official pronouncements on normative sexual behavior. Was Beccadelli's work pornographic? By our standards, probably not. And yet it was condemned, burned and largely forgotten.

Certainly the fortunes of the *Hermaphroditus* provide some insight into the less publicized aspects of humanist culture, in which homosocial bonds were often imperceptible from homosexual relationships, and the playful relationship between textuality and sexuality was not simply noted but celebrated. What Beccadelli had done, in making his textual genitalia tell the "truth," was to expose the sexual foundations of humanist culture, and this was unforgivable to Christian humanists like Valla, author of the famous exposé of the Donation of Constantine. The erotics of humanism, as Leonard Barkan has observed, were profoundly homosexual, tied more to the exaltation of Jupiter's possession of Ganymede than to equivalent heterosexual myths.[74] From a private joke, read aloud to dinner guests at the Palazzo Medici, to a public scandal that eventually caused Beccadelli to return south – where he enjoyed the patronage of the king of Naples until Beccadelli's death in 1471 – the *Hermaphroditus* signaled the beginnings of a pornographic culture that both celebrated and reviled the classics, and commented on the masculine and humanist culture that reinvented the sexual, political and intellectual traditions of antiquity.

The Prattling Pricks of Siena

Beccadelli's *Hermaphroditus* was soon replaced by even more elaborate displays of the juxtaposition of humanist erudition and pornographic imagination. The smutty conversations that Beccadelli had deemed appropriate for Medici banquets gave way to the more formal discourses conducted in the academies and courts of late Renaissance Italy, where humanists produced the erotic *Ficheide*, in imitation of Homer's *Iliad*, and cleric Giovanni Della Casa composed his *In laudem sodomiae*.[75] While Aretino and other *poligrafi* were responsible for a great portion of erotic and obscene literature, the literary academies also contributed their fair share.

In sixteenth-century Siena, members of the Accademia degli Intronati produced such works as Antonio Vignali's *La Cazzaria* (1525–1526) and Alessandro Piccolomini's *La Raffaella* (1539). In seventeenth-century Veneto, the Accademia degli Incogniti had among its ranks Francesco Pona, Ferrante Pallavicino and Antonio Rocco, authors of *La Lucerna* (1625), *La Rettorica della puttana* (1642) and *L'Alcibiade fanciullo a scola* (1652) respectively.[76] If anything, the academies made visible the association between humanism and libertinism to those not privileged to participate in this social world. Filled with men who occupied their leisure time writing about prostitutes and sodomy, and – even worse – invited prominent courtesans like Veronica Franco to join their literary conversations,[77] the academies seemed to bear out the idea that young men, left to their own devices, would do no good. Implicit in this evaluation was the idea that they would read and produce literature that was potentially "uncanonical."

Illuminating the essential features of academy pornography is an analysis of Antonio Vignali's *La Cazzaria*.[78] Founder of the Intronati and member of a Sienese patrician family, Vignali (1501–1559) lived there until 1530, when he left Siena during its period of political unrest. It is quite likely that the libelous content of *La Cazzaria*, which portrayed Siena as a literal "phallontocracy" run by a party of tyrannical and aristocratic Pricks, as he dubbed the supporters of the recently fallen signorial government, led to his exile.[79] Writing under his academy name of Arsiccio Intronato, Vignali fabricated a series of conversations among academicians about sex, philosophy and politics in Siena during the final days of its last republic.

The story began as a conversation between Bizzarro (Marcello Landucci) and Moscone (Giovan Francesco Franceschi), who were actual members of the Intronati. One evening, Bizzarro found himself in Arsiccio's library, waiting for a street whore to arrive so that he could experience the pleasure of "true fucking." To pass the time, he browsed through "certain bad books" and discovered the manuscript of *La Cazzaria*, "the greatest tangle of pricks that there [ever] was."[80] Aroused by what he read, Bizzarro thought immediately of his friend Moscone, and he purloined the manuscript so that they could share its pleasures together. Significantly, the woman he awaited never came to mind. The unspecified textual pleasures were subsequently revealed as those masculine delights that join "males together in various sorts of friendship," as Gian Paolo Lomazzo would later put it[81] – in short, the forms of exchange that were the stuff of academy life.

From the start, Vignali painted a vivid portrait of the humanist and libertine culture to which pornography appealed. Arsiccio's library, filled with illicit works, is a veritable "secret museum" – to borrow Walter Kendrick's phrase – teeming with sexual and philological secrets. The *studio*, traditionally a site of contemplation and devotion, turns out to be nothing more than a pornographer's den in which humanists read, collect and create further obscenities. "Friends take each other in[to] the study," proclaimed the protagonist of Antonio Rocco's *L'Alcibiade fanciullo a scola*, suggesting the pervasiveness of the image of a space in which secret learning and secret pleasures intertwined.[82] In *La Cazzaria*, the textual gaze of humanists has become a pornographic one. Arsiccio's friends, also connoisseurs of this material, are the voyeurs whose viewing of the hidden manuscript places it in circulation. And there is the promise of more to come. Fearful that Arsiccio might discover his transgression, Bizzarro swears Moscone to secrecy; he does not wish to be "deprived of the ability to see several other beautiful things, or little works, that he mentions in this dialogue, which I have seen and partially read."[83]

La Cazzaria is a dialogue between Arsiccio and a young academician, Sodo (Marc' Antonio Piccolomini), who, except for a cursory reading of Aretino, is relatively innocent in the ways of the world.[84] Their dynamic might be imagined as a textual parallel to Giulio Romano's image of Apollo with a young lover, in which the god fondles the boy's genitals.[85] Arsiccio initiates Sodo by presenting sexual knowledge as the core of natural philosophy. Someone who aspires to "knowledge of natural things" must be versed in "the most natural things" to claim any philosophical competence. Wouldn't you be ashamed, Arsiccio asks Sodo, to find yourself unable to participate in the discourse of learned men, due to ignorance? Sodo's reply – "[M]y philosophy does not deal with pricks or asses, and I am not ashamed to not know them since my studies are founded upon neither the ass nor the cunt, but in more perfect things..." – does not satisfy Arsiccio at all. "[M]aking yourself touch your prick with your hand is one of the first things one should learn in philosophy...," he replies, adding that "Then, from the mixing of the cunt, prick and ass, knowledge of fucking and buggery follows, and thus *scientia* is enlarged."[86]

Arsiccio gives a lengthy paean on the male organ as the most perfect of all creations, adding a characteristically humanist reminiscence about the Golden Age before Babel, when providential design ensured that each man was made to fit each woman perfectly. He then develops an Aristotelian justification for male homosexual practices, in which the "fit" of the different anatomical parts justifies the variety of non-procreative sexual practices. Sodo, who has already confessed his experiences with his priest, is aroused by Arsiccio's logic ("Arsiccio, tu mi tocchi i lombi con questo tuo ragionare"), and the conversation moves to a bedroom where, in the tradition of Sade, pornography and philosophy happily intermingle.[87] "Scholars..." – as Arsiccio constantly reminds Sodo – "know many secrets."[88] This is a theme underlying the entire work.

Vignali justifies the language and subject of *La Cazzaria* by underscoring the need for decorum "with women and men of some gravity," but notes the need for the absence of this constraint on conversation among young men of similar social standing ("un ritrovo di giovani a te e per età e per esercizio conformi"). With young men, he tells Sodo, it is "licit to discuss all those things that come to mind" [ci venivano a bocca].[89] This defense is borne out by the nature of his imagined conversations with Sodo in bed. As an exchange for Sodo's succumbing to his advances, Arsiccio reveals the plan of his *opus eroticum*. It entails a tripartite work under the rubric of the *Lumen pudendorum*, a parody of a popular religious genre, and is composed of *De la genealogia e battesimo del cazzo, De la natività e opera de la potta* and *De la vita e passione del culo*. It is written in Latin "in order to preserve the honesty of women" and also to quiet ignorant pedants who saw no danger in learned obscenities:

> And thus when I say *priapum, mentulam, nervum*, reading these [words], they will not believe that it means "prick." Likewise, when they see *vulvam* and *cunnum* written, they will not know the names for cunt, and thus they will be quiet.[90]

While Arsiccio and Sodo do laugh at the pedants, who are incapable of naming "the thing itself" when they see it, they also wish to protect this form of knowledge from outside encroachments. The humanist reading of texts is more transparent than its scholastic counterpart, but it still maintains the boundary between learned and unlearned discourse. Vignali's protagonists castigate the "traitors" who vulgarize the classics so that even porters, whores and blacksmiths can have "all of Pliny, Livy, Ovid, Apuleius and many other excellent authors on the tip of their tongue."[91] For them, erotic and obscene dialogue is a closed circuit that includes only the men of wit, honor and social prominence who are capable of flirting with dangerous subjects without contributing to public vice.

As soon as Arsiccio has sated his passion, he recounts the fable of a fallen government dominated by a tyrannical Big Prick (*Il Cazzone*) and composed of four competing parties: the patrician Pricks and Cunts, the aristocratic Balls and the plebeian Asses. After the Little Pricks and Ugly Cunts, with the help of the Asses, overthrow the Big Prick and Pretty Cunts who are his followers, they debate the best form of government. The more conservative Pricks are concerned that the participation of the Cunts and the Balls in the governance of the city will lower their status. For their betrayal of the other factions, the Balls are assigned a subsidiary role to the Pricks and the Cunts and that is why, Arsiccio concludes, returning to a theme that figured prominently in Aretino's sonnets, "the balls never enter the ass..."[92]

The story, of course, was no fable, but a thinly veiled retelling of the events in Siena that led to the overthrow of the signorial government of the Petrucci family by members of the four *Monti* – the Noveschi, Libertini, Riformatori and Gentilhuomini – in September of 1524.[93] The subsequent struggles between the Noveschi, former supporters of the Petrucci who were generally in favor of an oligarchical government, and the Libertini, the people's representatives in favor of a communal government, culminated in the ascendence of the latter by 1527.[94] Vignali's family had belonged to the sector of the Noveschi that had switched allegiance from the Petrucci family to the Libertini. The debates about the proper form of representative government, so effectively satirized by Vignali, soon became irrelevant as Siena eventually fell victim to the Medici's expansionist policies for the Tuscan state. In Vignali's tale, the body becomes a moral map onto which the sexual and political divisions of the day are grafted. Written in a world of shifting and unstable political allegiances, *La*

Cazzaria is the prototype of the political pornography that appeared with increasing frequency in the mid-seventeenth and eighteenth centuries.

Like other scurrilous works, *La Cazzaria* circulated first in manuscript among Sienese notables and then in surreptitious printings, like the one that appeared in Venice in 1531.[95] Vignali had written it as a form of private entertainment for his fellow Intronati, and he probably had little to do with its later circulation. By 1541, however, it was a centerpiece of Niccolò Franco's attack on Aretino in his *Priapea*:

> Priapus, I am Arsiccio Arcintronato
> And in enthroning the greatest [person],
> Who today brings you perfumed honor
> I have brought you my little book as a gift.
>   Here there are pricks of every kind,
> Cheap pricks, valuable pricks,
> Widow's pricks, nun's pricks,
> Pricks for the *Granmaestro* and the Prelate,
>   Pricks one touches only with gloves....[96]

Franco's allusion to *La Cazzaria* in his own poem, in which he proposed to castigate Aretino with language more obscene than Aretino's, suggests how quickly the work had traveled from the academy to the marketplace. While not intended for the reading public, as Aretino's *Ragionamenti* would be, it nonetheless took its place in the pornographic canon of the sixteenth century.

In characterizing *La Cazzaria* as "a map of sixteenth-century libertinism," Nino Borsellino interprets the work as both a product of and a critique of humanist practices.[97] In Vignali's text, sexual and social hierarchies collide. Patrician politics are linked to patrician sexual practices, and sodomy is presented as the logical expression of nobility and learning. For different reasons this was reaffirmed by Aretino, who has Nanna tell Antonia: "The really frightful things occur among the great ladies and gentlemen." Nanna also advises Pippa to dress like a boy to entice noblemen.[98] In his *Sonnetti lussuriosi*, sodomy is portrayed as something "important people" (*i grandi*) do. Men insist upon anal intercourse in several sonnets, crying out that "He who is not a buggerer, is not a man," and "May my lineage die out with me!"[99]

Clearly, Aretino's parody of the practices of nobles was the antithesis of Vignali's affirmation of the virtue of these actions. And yet both served to undermine the social and political foundations of the humanist culture that had made them possible. Vignali's portrayal of the humanists who fostered the academies and governments of Renaissance Italy as nothing but a "bunch of pricks" was ultimately as subversive as any message that later writers such as La Mettrie and Sade imparted about the sexual networks buttressing the political and intellectual culture of the ancien régime. If republics were the place in which pricks, cunts and asses could form indiscriminate alliances, as Vignali's political allegory suggested, then the republic's decline was inevitable. In contrast, the aristocratic culture, which preferred either the fruitful union of "big pricks" and "pretty cunts" or the hierarchical coupling of pricks and asses, was bound to thrive. While Vignali's work cannot be said to have had the same impact as Aretino's – like Beccadelli's *Hermaphroditus* it was successfully obscured in its own time – it nonetheless sheds light on the uses of the erotic as a medium for philosophical and political expression among the Renaissance elite, and, once again, reaffirms the strong ties between humanism and the emergence of a pornographic culture.

The allusions from Boccaccio – evident in the statement *pedagogus ergo sodomiticus* – that the teaching of grammar will lead to sodomitic practices are amply borne out in the writings of Vignali and his seventeenth-century follower, Antonio Rocco.[100] Eloquence, as Rocco has his pedagogue Filotimo instruct his pupil Alcibiade, arises from the mixing of tongues. Such actions are a decisively male prerogative. With women, Filotimo warns Alcibiades, echoing Leon Battista Alberti's admonishments about the necessity of separating the affairs of men from those of women, "one must leave behind serious affairs and lose oneself."[101] Identity, in the humanist sexual universe first articulated in print by Vignali, is also a profoundly masculine prerogative. To spend too much time in the company of women is to "lose oneself." For these reasons, in the rhetoric of Italian Renaissance pornography, sexual initiation must accompany instruction, "thrusting knowledge up the ass," as Rocco inelegantly puts it. The path to erudition and the proclamations of friendship that accompany intellectual affinities must begin with a sexual transfer of "virtue" from master to pupil in order that a scholar be turned out "perfectly learned."[102] Most importantly, the emulation of the past must begin with sexual imitation. Only after one has established the sexual foundations of a society can its political and cultural life be articulated. What Vignali did explicitly for Siena, Rocco did implicitly for Venice, both uncomfortably reminding their readers that the alignment of politics and learning that shaped Renaissance society could not be divested from its sexual practices.

"Whorish Hierarchies"

While idle academicians animated penises to discover what truths they might tell, Aretino and the Venetian *poligrafi* constructed a world of chattering cunts that revealed an equally shocking, and competing, set of secrets. Like sodomites, prostitutes were considered a "third sex," and this ambiguity enabled them to gaze dispassionately at society, as did the pornographer or, later,

94

Montesquieu's Persians. [103] While Beccadelli restricted the circulation of his obscene poems to a select circle of patrons and learned friends – a practice followed by many other academy pornographers like Vignali – Aretino made this type of literature accessible to a wider reading public and altered its content to meet the demands of his perceived audience.

Aretino's first foray into the world of pornography came about by accident. In 1524, Marcantonio Raimondi published sixteen engravings depicting various sexual positions (see figures 1.7 through 1.9). The originals had been done by Giulio Romano who, conveniently, was working for the Gonzaga in Mantua when the scandal broke. As Vasari notes, "[S]ome of these sheets were found in places where they were least expected," presumably at the papal court. [104] At the urging of the papal datary, that "clown of religion" [105] Gian Matteo Giberti (later known for his role as a model reforming bishop in Verona), Clement VII had Raimondi thrown in prison. There he languished for almost a year until the efforts of Aretino, sculptor Baccio Bandinelli and Cardinal Ippolito de' Medici gained his release; in return, Raimondi promised to burn the prints and destroy the plates from which the prints had been made. [106] However, Aretino's involvement in Raimondi's affairs made him curious to see the pictures that were the talk of Rome. As he recounted in a letter to the Battista Zatti:

> No sooner had I obtained from Pope Clement the release of Marcantonio of Bologna, who was imprisoned for having engraved on copper the *Sixteen Positions*, etc., than I desired to see those pictures which had caused the complaining Giberti and his followers to cry out that the worthy artist ought to be crucified. As soon as I gazed at them, I was touched by the same spirit that had moved Giulio Romano to draw them. And since poets and sculptors, both ancient and modern, in order to amuse themselves, have often written or

carved lascivious objects such as the marble satyr in the Chigi Palace attempting to rape a boy, I tossed out the sonnets at the foot [of each figure]. With all due respect to hypocrites, I dedicate these lustful pieces to you, heedless of the scurvy strictures and asinine laws which forbid the eyes to see the very things which delight them most.

What wrong is there in seeing a man mount a woman? Should beasts be free-er than we are? It would seem to me that that thing which is given to us by nature for the preservation of the species should be worn around the neck as a pendant, or as a medal on the hat, for it is the spring from which all the rivers of people gush forth, and the ambrosia which the world drinks on feast days. It made you, one of the greatest living surgeons. It created me, and I am better than bread. It produced the Bembos, Molzas, Fortunios, Varchis, Ugolin Martellis, Lorenzo Lenzis, Dolcis, Fra Sebastianos, Sansovinos, Titians and Michelangelos, and after them the popes, emperors and kings. It generated handsome boys, and the most beautiful women with their "holy of holies." Hence one should order holidays, vigils and feasts in its honor, and not shut it up in a bit of cloth or silk.[107]

By 1527, Aretino had printed "the book of sonnets and the lustful figures" which he promptly sent to patrons like the Genoese noble Cesare Fregoso. Even before their official publication, members of the Accademia degli Intronati in Siena had acquired a copy. By 1528, they were sufficiently well known outside Rome that Ludovico Ariosto could, in a play written for the d'Este court at Ferrara, make a casual joke about the "diverse acts, forms and various postures . . . that in our day are revived in holy Rome, printed more beautifully than honestly so that all the world may have a copy."[108] More maliciously, the barbed tongue of Franco suggested that Priapus should try all the positions in "this little

book Pietro Aretino presents to you" with Aretino's sister, because she reputedly knew them all.[109]

The book's assault on the senses was judged by contemporaries
to be more complete than that of any previous work. In the opening lines of the sonnets, Aretino loudly proclaimed their novelty
of intent as well as form:

> This is not a book of sonnets...
> But here there are indescribable pricks
> And the cunt and the ass that place them
> Just like candy in a box.
>   Here there are people who fuck and are fucked
> And anatomies of cunts and pricks
> And asses filled with many lost souls.
>   Here one fucks in more lovely ways,
> Than were ever seen
> Within any whorish hierarchies.
>   In the end only fools
> Are disgusted at such tasty morsels
> And God forgive anyone who does not fuck in the ass.

Variations of this stanza appeared in the introductions to well-
known licentious works like the *Tariffa delle puttane* and the
Dialogo di Maddalena e Giulia, suggesting the extent to which
the "novel" content of pornography had become associated with
a certain literary novelty soon after the appearance of Aretino's
sonnets.[110] Echoing the indignant words of Clement of Alexandria
to the Greeks, artist and art critic Giorgio Vasari later wrote, "I
know not which was the greater, the offense to the eye from the
drawings of Giulio, or the outrage to the ear from the words of
Aretino."[111] Despite their origins in the artistic work of Romano
and Raimondi, the sixteen plates, now printed with the sonnets

97

beneath them, were subsequently known as "Aretino's postures" by connoisseurs of erotica all over Europe.

Shortly after their appearance, a plethora of imitations sprang up that were often attributed to Aretino but that had been written by his disciples. The *Tariffa delle puttane*, for example, was advertised as a work "not unworthy perhaps of the pen of Aretino." On the altar that Aretino created, numerous aspiring pornographers made their "sacrifice to Saint Fuck."[112] Within a decade, the number of sexual positions had swelled as other writers competed with Aretino in the chronicling of every conceivable position for intercourse. A 1531 edition of the pseudo-Aretine *Dialogo di Maddalena e Giulia*, also known as *La Puttana errante* (a title taken from the poem of the same name by Lorenzo Venier), counted forty-four positions, although other versions restricted themselves to a modest thirty-five.[113] In *La Rettorica della puttana* (1642), Ferrante Pallavicino suggested that "the figures of Aretino are exemplary, and whenever someone becomes infatuated with caprices (*stravagenze*), he imitates the model."[114]

The themes introduced by Aretino in the *Sonnetti lussuriosi* were expanded further in his *Ragionamenti*. The famous dialogues on the best professions for women – nun, wife or prostitute – brought together the sexual imagery of the sonnets and the scathing criticisms of the social practices and political culture of Renaissance Italy, themes first put forth by Aretino in *La Cortigiana* (1525) and in his pasquinades, and further developed in the *Ragionamento delle corti* (1538). From the beginning of the work, Aretino further flaunted convention by dedicating the first book to his pet monkey and refusing to cite any classical precedent (while liberally scattering classical allusions throughout). "[I]f you were without taste, as princes were," he informed his monkey, "I would try to excuse the licentious speech in this work...by mentioning in its behalf Virgil's *Prispea* [*sic*] and all those salacious works which were written by Ovid, Juvenal, and Martial."[115] Rather than drawing on the stock of old images, as humanist pornographers like Beccadelli had done, Aretino claimed to take his portraits directly from the streets of the *Roma lasciva* that he knew well.

Highly anticlerical, like most early modern pornography, Aretino's work vividly portrayed a world in which the courtiers were whores, the whores courtiers and the clergy sodomites. Making a joke out of the linguistic relationship between *cortigiano* and *cortigiana*, courtier and courtesan, Aretino suggested that the relationship between words revealed even stronger affinities between the groups they described. "So courtesans are even as great sinners as courtiers?" asked Aretino's Pippa. "If they gave us their name, it's in the cards that they also gave us their faces: *verbo et opere*, as the *Confiteor* says," responded Nanna.[116] While recounting the lives of prostitutes and the debauched practices of their clients, the *Ragionamenti* also purported to be a book of manners in the fashion of Castiglione's *Book of the Courtier* or Della Casa's *Galateo*. Pippa is instructed in all the social and sexual mannerisms of the nobility. "By my faith, yes, it needs something more to be a whore than lifting up your petticoat and crying: 'Go ahead and screw, I'm ready,' " Nanna warns her.[117] Imitating the practices of the most successful courtesans who cater to a humanist clientele, Pippa has filled a table with the works of Petrarch, Boccaccio and Ariosto – in short, the vernacular classics – in order to provide the "conversation" that humanists crave.

In the moral economy of Aretino's dialogues, a whore is the only honest creature. Scornful of the *cortigiane oneste* – like Matrema-non-vole and Veronica Franco, who belonged to the libertine culture of the courts through their knowledge of the classics, their writing of Petrarchan poetry and, ultimately, their willingness to engage in anal intercourse – Nanna represents a different sort of civility, *una civiltà puttanesca*. "We whores, even if we are sly, vicious, close-fisted, thieving, and faithless never leave the straight path of whoring," she affirms.[118] This unswerving sense of purpose stands in marked contrast to the slippery practices of nobles, who would "interrupt a conversation about the state...to be introduced to a bawd," and the "indulgence-scratchers" who "drink, sodomize, and whoremonger."[119] Through the creation of such taxonomies, Aretino reaffirmed the boundaries between humanist and nonhumanist culture, and between courts and republics, which other writers like Vignali had established for entirely different purposes.

Excepted from Aretino's criticisms are the Venetians, who, living in a republic known for its antagonism toward the institutional church and its antipathy toward Rome, engage in more "honest" practices; "with them you can put aside all your courtesan's tricks and gratify them with your own person...," Nanna advises Pippa. Undoubtedly this was the reason why, as Aretino would have described it, so many prostitutes and pornographers came to Venice in the sixteenth century.[120] The antithesis of courtly Rome, Venice rested on its reputation as a city of infinite possibilities and freedoms. In their respective mythical representations, the political liberties of Venice, which were grounded in the virtues of republicanism, competed with the moral "liberties" of Rome, which were the products of its paradoxical status as a city of Christian sanctity and pagan antiquity.

In Aretino's vision of the world, sex is not fueled by philosophy, but serves as its replacement. This anticlassicism stands in marked contrast to the juxtaposition of these two elements in humanist academy pornography. Nanna's genitals – elusive and mysterious – are the ultimate source of power in this sexual theater.[121] As she well knows, "a pair of luscious buttocks can accomplish more than all that the philosophers, astrologists, alchemists and necromancers have ever wrought." Nanna has no need to read because she possesses all the secrets of the world "between the legs."[122] The only book that she treasures is a "book of recipes," in which she has recorded all the secrets of maintaining and enhancing her beauty.[123] Not unlike the popular "books of secrets" then in circulation – for example, the Venetian Isabella Cortese's *Segreti* (1561) – it is the symbol of all the dangerous and subversive knowledge that springs not from reading the classics but from being a whore.

In an era when "pornography" was defined as much by the novelty of its message as by its graphic sexual content, Aretino's sonnets and dialogues represented the worst of all possible worlds to the authorities who banned them. By using pornography as a vehicle to attack everything from the humanist educational program to clerical piety to the vicissitudes of court life, Aretino exposed the vices of the upper classes to an indiscriminate readership. He further offended the upper-class sense of propriety by putting his pronouncements in the mouth of a whore. When the censor Johannes Molanus warned of the danger of images being placed "in the taverns and in the market place," he defined the parameters of Nanna's world. The "sorry affairs with Pippas, Nannas and filthy courtesans" that Aretino publicized were precisely what "certain masticators of Paternosters and hunters of Avemarias," the ecclesiastic censors singled out by Aretino's Protestant editor John Wolfe, most despised.[124] Subsequent attempts to quench the tide of pornographic writing that sprang first from Aretino's workshop in Venice and then expanded outward, threatening to envelop every corner of Europe, indicate just how dangerous an author who respected no social, moral or linguistic boundaries was perceived to be. In the eyes of the Tridentine authorities who banned his works, Aretino was more dangerous than all the erotically inclined artists and humanist pornographers put together, not because of his frank portrayals of sexual behavior but because of his refusal to restrict his audience to men of virtue who were allowed to read the erotic classics due to their "eloquence and quality of style." While Aretino's canonical status in the world of post-Renaissance pornography rested on the infamy and rarity of the sixteen *modi* and the accompanying sonnets, his contemporary reputation was a product of his desire to publicize, and therefore betray, the practices of the courtiers and humanists with whom he was intimately familiar.

Political Identity and Sexual Experience

Renaissance pornography emerged in two meaningful contexts: the private world of humanist eroticism and the public arena shaped by print culture. In the former, humanists and libertines like Antonio Vignali enjoyed smutty conversations with men of virtue and created the first pornographic museums, whose walls were lined with the writings and images of the past. In the latter, professional writers like Aretino capitalized on the demands of the marketplace, producing a genre of literature whose sheer repetitiveness over two centuries testifies that he understood his audience well. Certainly these two worlds cannot be completely separated; in fact, the Vignalis of Renaissance Italy were probably Aretino's best customers. And yet we cannot fully unite them. It is hardly coincidental that the patrician Vignali chose an eloquent male sodomite as his mouthpiece, while Aretino was represented by Nanna, "the wickedest and lewdest whore in all of Rome."[125] While the libertines of the Intronati are moved by words, Nanna is moved by images; they are the embodiment of humanist consumers of pornography, and she the emblem of the illiterate masses whose access to profane and immoral images so worried church reformers. Neither is disengaged from the other's affairs — Arsiccio tells us that he regularly enjoys a gutter girl as well as the attentions of his homosexual friends, while Nanna advises Pippa to act and dress as boy as well as girl for her clients. The interlocutors of *La Cazzaria* are, in the moral economy of late Renaissance pornography, *fottenti* (fuckers) and those of the *Ragionamenti, fottute* (fucked), to borrow Aretino's terms. Only in the imagined terrain of the *Sonnetti lussuriosi* could these two worlds come together.

While the "whorish hierarchies" of court and church divided the world ad infinitum, Renaissance pornographers offered their readers a simpler, less mutable division of society: those who had power and those who succumbed to it. At the same time, they played upon the humanist love of paradox by posing startling and revealing questions: What if the world were ruled by pricks? What if whores were the "women on top"? The contrasting images of a "world ruled by pricks" (*mondo incazzito*) and the "whorish monarchy" (*monarchia puttanesca*) defined the arena in which pornography, as a form of sociopolitical commentary, thrived.[126] "Fuck in the ass, flee the cunt," went one seventeenth-century pornographic poem. While knowledge of a woman was monarchical, in the sense that women would use their sexual power to "immediately acquire despotic and absolute rule, and if possible tyranny" over men, knowledge of another man was a form of prolonged republicanism.[127] From this perspective, it is hardly surprising that a number of the humanist academies, known for being subversive, should express their political allegiances in the more libertine writings of their members.

The relationship between sex, power and politics is perhaps best represented in medium different than those we have yet explored: the majolica of Francesco Xanto Avelli, employed by the duke of Urbino in the mid-sixteenth century. While Xanto Avelli introduced many motifs from the Aretine postures into his ceramic creations, none is more striking than the image reproduced on a 1534 plate depicting the defeat of the French king Francis I by the Holy Roman Emperor Charles V at the Battle of Pavia in 1525 (figure 1.13). On the bottom left lies Francis I who has fallen to the ground and who, in the act of falling, has dropped his scepter. Above, a figure on horseback represents Charles V's ascendency over the French king. To the left, a female standing atop a ball and leaning on a curled wooden staff represents the fortune that has favored the Emperor and led Francis I to devastating defeat.[128]

The resemblance between the position of Francis I and that of the female in the first posture is unquestionable (see figure 1.7). Lying on their sides, their left arms bent backward for support and their right legs almost doubled, both succumb to the advances of the stronger partner. In Xanto Avelli's interpretation of the outcome of Pavia, Charles V has "taken" Francis I just as a man would take a woman. With an image that recalled the opening lines of the first sonnet, "Let's fuck, my love, let's fuck quickly... the world would be just a prick without this [act],"[129] Xanto Avelli reminded his audience – most significantly the duke of Urbino who had a personal stake in the outcome of this battle – that political victory was a form of sexual conquest. Francis I, feminized by his defeat, is emasculated in the confrontation with Charles V. Like the whores and sodomites inhabiting the pornographic universe of the Renaissance, the French king succumbs to the superior force of a masculine power. On the back of the plate, an inscription indicates tersely: *1534. Cadette il Re Christia[no] sotto Pavia* [The Christian King Fell Beneath Pavia]. Xanto Avelli imagined that a courtly audience of the 1530s would be familiar enough with Aretino's postures to recognize the additional meaning of his depiction.

Juxtaposed to the visual allegories spun by Xanto Avelli, which paralleled the textual allegories of Vignali about early sixteenth-

FIGURE 1.13. Francesco Xanto Avelli, *The Christian King Fell Beneath Pavia* (1534).

century political life, were recurrent images of prominent urban centers whose moral well-being was also perceived to be indicative of the contemporary political climate. In the moral map of Renaissance Italy created in the writings of pornographers, Rome, as a result of its precipitous decline from the head of the world (*caput mundi*) to the tail of the world (*coda mundi*), had become whorish and sodomitic – a "city of women" (*terra da donne*) that Aretino said was ruled by "the cruelty of harlots" and "the insolence of Ganymedes."[130] Embodying all the social and political evils of Italy in the decades following the coming of Luther and the Sack of Rome in 1527, Rome was an easy target for lampoon.

The competing images of Siena and Venice in the works of Vignali and Aretino are more difficult to define. Siena, vacillating between republic and oligarchy in the early sixteenth century, appears as a world of divided choices in *La Cazzaria*. In contrast to Aretino's unequivocal praise for the republican culture of Venice – ironic given its firmly noble base[131] – Vignali's assessment of the Sienese republic is more guarded. While acknowledging that the world cannot be ruled by Pricks alone, he nonetheless questions the ability of the lesser parts – the Cunts and Asses – to work in tandem with the dominant social class, as well as the ability of nobles to change their ways. "[G]iven that we Pricks have been on top of Cunts and Asses from the earliest times," observed Vignali, it now was difficult, despite the changing political climate, "to lower ourselves so that we all may be equals."[132] Thus, pornographers, not unlike Machiavelli and Guicciardini, explored the problems of republican culture in a progressively aristocratic society, relating political identity to sexual experience.[133]

The use of homosexuals and prostitutes in pornographic writings, as emblems of social and political hierarchies, was not an idle choice. Both were the embodiment of vice and yet exhibited a certain detachment from the social hierarchies, due to their perceived marginality. They were competing dangers in the eyes of the urban magistrates who harshly condemned their influence. Homosexuals were publicly burned in cities like Venice, and the movements of prostitutes were increasingly restricted by officials who feared that their "many lascivious words," spoken in the wrong places, would throw into doubt the chastity of other women.[134] As Nanna succintly put it, "Whores are not women; they are whores."[135] Neither group had to answer for the procreative relations between men and women, but their omnipresence in pornography and everyday life threw into doubt the stability of the heterosexual regime. Their membership in the so-called third sex gave them a privileged view of the practices of others and, thus, empowered them to speak, quite literally to "authorize" a portrait of society. Their gaze, however, was not the pornographic one, though they existed to foster it. Instead, it was the critical gaze of the pornographer, who looked into the souls of men and told them what they least wanted to hear.

Before becoming a whore, Nanna was susceptible to the erotic impulses of Renaissance society; every purloined look, every image, every act moved her. However, her susceptibility to the powers of the senses alters dramatically with her final choice of profession. As she tells Antonia, "[l]ust is the least of the desires they [whores] have, because they are constantly thinking of ways and means to cut out men's hearts and feelings."[136] Like Aretino, whores are manipulators of the pornographic gaze. They have the power to move others, but do not succumb to temptation.

What does all this have to do with the invention of pornography? The erotic and obscene writings of the sixteenth century set the stage for the more widespread diffusion of pornography in the seventeenth and eighteenth centuries by charting the terrain in which pornography was formulated, and by setting the parameters of its subject and the techniques of presentation. Voyeuristic, subversive and highly philosophical, pornography quickly became the preferred medium through which to vent one's outrage about the ills of society while, at the same time, making a tidy profit. The technology of print made much of this possible. Printing effectively publicized a previously extant erotic culture and commodified it. Had Beccadelli written his *Hermaphroditus* only a century later and chosen to put it into print, it undoubtedly would have been a best-seller and featured even more prominently on the Index than the works of Aretino, since it dealt with a more controversial subject. Publicity was the key to the establishment of pornography. Printing, as the ecclesiastic reformers of the Counter-Reformation learned to their chagrin, not only edified a wider portion of the population, but had the potential to produce uncanonical and unstable images of society. While Ludovico Dolce praised Giulio Romano for keeping his paintings of the sixteen *modi* from the eyes of the public – he "did not expose it in the public squares or in the churches" – he condemned Marcantonio Raimondi, "who for his own profit engraved them...."[137] In the hands of the printers, engravers and Grub Street writers of Renaissance Italy, pornography first saw the light of day.

Acknowledgments
Many thanks to Cristelle Baskins, Michelle Fontaine, Laurie Nussdorfer, Catherine Kudlick, Randolph Starn, Wendy Stedman Sheard and members of the Wesleyan University Renaissance Seminar and the Stanford–Berkeley Italian Renaissance Reading Group for their helpful suggestions. Thanks to the audience at Pomona College – especially Pamela Smith, Richard Olson and Mary Terrell – for noticing a detail of the Liberi painting that I had neglected. A separate thanks to Katharine Park for convincing me, some years ago, that Aretino was at least worth an undergraduate thesis, and to Lynn Hunt, for reviving my interest in the subject.

CHAPTER TWO

The Politics of Pornography:

L'Ecole des Filles

Joan DeJean

Literary historians return obsessively to the notion of an absolute beginning, speaking, for example, of the "first" modern novel, or of the "origins" of modern tragedy. Sometimes these accepted beginnings have a reassuring stability. *La Princesse de Clèves* (1678) is always assigned the role of the first modern novel in the French tradition, and the parallel role for the English tradition is consistently played by *Robinson Crusoe* (1719). At other times, the notion of an origin is more problematic: numerous candidates, notably several of Racine's plays, have been designated the "first" modern tragedy. However, no amount of dissent has ever dimmed the desire to identify *the* "first" of every genre.

The quest for origins, moreover, is all-consuming, a goal unto itself; commentators never reflect upon the possible significance of the shape thereby given a national literary tradition. For example, the placement of *La Princesse de Clèves* as the origin of the French novel implies a trajectory for the genre vastly different from that which would have been suggested by the choice of another contemporary candidate, such as the *Lettres portugaises* (1669), or, more radically still, one of Sandras de Courtilz's homocentric memoir novels. Literary historians never suggest that literary history is a matter of choice and that the choice of original works might be other than innocent. They never discuss what the origins agreed upon might reveal about a tradition – or about its historians.

In France, at least, pornography appears to enjoy a privileged relation to beginnings. Those who have worked in this field will tell you without hesitation that *L'Ecole des filles* is *the* original work of pornography published in French. The title of the most recent study devoted to the genre, Jean-Marie Goulemot's *Ces Livres qu'on ne lit que d'une main*, indirectly confirms this idea. The title cites Rousseau's evocation, in Book One of the *Confessions*, of "those dangerous books that a beautiful woman of the world finds bothersome because, as she says, one can only read them with one hand [ces dangereux livres qu'une belle dame de par le monde trouve incommodes, en ce qu'on ne peut, dit-elle, les lire que d'une seule main]." To evoke "reading with one hand" is usually to evoke a founding image in the history of pornography at the same time. Many who hear the title, *L'Ecole des filles*, think of Samuel Pepys remembering a reading practice similar to that which horrified Rousseau's "belle dame."[1] The image of Pepys is important precisely because the book with which he associates the technique is that primal pornographic volume, *L'Ecole des filles*, which Pepys shuns as "the most bawdy, lewd book that ever I saw," even as he attempts to justify his passionate involvement with it.[2] It is, Pepys continues, "a mighty lewd book, but yet not amiss for a sober man once to read over to inform himself in the villainy of the world."[3]

But *L'Ecole des filles* plays an originating role for French pornography in more than just this historical sense. Scholars place it where Pepys did, at the beginning of what is generally considered the French literary innovation that French literary history would prefer to ignore – or that sober men would read only to keep themselves informed of textual villainy. Thus, Frédéric Lachèvre, who built his reputation by returning numerous suppressed texts and authors to French literary history, calls it "the first specimen of a deliberately obscene book written in French [le premier spécimen des livres délibérément obscènes écrits en français]."[4] However, Lachèvre goes on to admit, as do literary historians in general, that *L'Ecole des filles* is thought to have had an Italian model. He quickly tries to eliminate any doubt about its status as origin by mentioning that the alleged model has never been identified. He goes on to add that he has not even bothered to read the suggested candidates, including that candidate referred to as soon as *L'Ecole des filles* was published, Aretino.[5]

Lachèvre's ambivalence is emblematic of literary history's involvement with *L'Ecole des filles*. Pornography must have an origin. Because literary history would portray it as a quintessentially French genre — even when, following Lachèvre's lead, that portrayal is always coupled with a denial of its French birthright — that origin can still only be seen as French. Because of this bias, *L'Ecole des filles* has long seemed the only act in town. Why else would scholars all down the line have been willing to tolerate all the rumors that continue to put the work's primacy in question?

L'Ecole des filles is a dubious origin indeed. The work's strangely tantalizing status is immediately evident in Lachèvre's description, in which he simultaneously offers it as absolute origin even while he erodes the possibility of its originality. This ambivalence is fundamental to every discussion of the work's authorial status. If *L'Ecole des filles* is mentioned to those who have some knowledge of the text, they are likely to list the various authors whose names were quickly linked to it, particularly that unlikely duo, novelist Paul Scarron and his wife, Françoise d'Aubigné, the future Madame de Maintenon.[6] For, while it has long been relatively accepted that the two men who paid for the work's printing and who were put on trial and condemned for it — the otherwise virtually unknown Michel Millot and Jean L'Ange – were indeed its authors, the facts of their alleged authorship are not completely convincing. In particular, unlike the trial proceedings of other contemporary writers charged with obscenity or heresy – notably Théophile de Viau and Claude Le Petit – the dossier of the trial of Millot and L'Ange offers absolutely no insight into the creative process or what the alleged authors thought they were doing by creating this dangerously innovative work. In brief, during the rather extensive police interrogations that have come down to us, Millot and L'Ange never once spoke as though they were authors.[7] The only information they offered concerned the work's production and its distribution, from the press on which it was printed to the number of copies produced. Millot and L'Ange sound as if they had simply been fall guys for some figure or figures too important to be put on trial.

This hypothesis is reinforced by the punishments reserved for the putative authors. Théophile de Viau won an extended stay in prison for the mild blasphemy of his *Fragments d'une histoire comique*. Claude Le Petit was burned – not, for once, in effigy, but in actuality – for the flagrantly juvenile blasphemy of *Le Bordel des muses*. Compare those punishments with the sentences delivered at approximately the same period for the far more innovative scandal of *L'Ecole des filles*. The volume had just been printed, since only a few copies had been bound, when, on June 12, 1655, officers of justice seized all the copies they could find and began questioning suspects. After numerous interrogations, sentences were handed down on August 7. The symbolic hanging of Millot took place on August 9, and all known copies of the book were burned, along with his effigy. He was then released, after less than two months in prison. His possessions were to have been confiscated, but there is no record that this decree was carried out. L'Ange made an *amende honorable* (a public ceremony of confes sion), was given a small fine and banned from Paris for three years, though this last decree was certainly not enforced. (However, because of a mix-up involving the already traditional August vacation period, L'Ange did accidentally spend four months in prison.) Were their sentences so mild, literary historians over the centuries have wondered, because those really responsible for *L'Ecole des filles* were powerful enough to have arranged a form of limited immunity for them? Just who is alleged to have been behind this elaborately staged politico-legal charade?

The response suggests there is still another way in which *L'Ecole des filles* simultaneously invites and refuses its status as origin. The flames that consumed Millot's effigy also destroyed all known copies of the book – that is, with the exception of the eight or nine bound copies that, during interrogation, L'Ange admitted having given to "le Sieur Scarron" and "that he could have given to his friends [qu'il peut avoir donné à ses amis]."[8] The fate of only one of the copies distributed by Scarron is known: it resurfaced six years later, in the course of more celebrated legal proceedings, during the search that followed the arrest of Louis XIV's overly glorious minister of finances, Nicolas Fouquet. Fouquet had provided elaborate protection for the surviving copy. As Lachèvre notes, it was discovered "in the table of a secret room in a house with a hidden entrance, which the minister of finances had had furnished for his mistress [dans la table du cabinet secret d'une maison, avec entrée mystérieuse, que le surintendant des finances avait fait meubler pour sa maîtresse]."[9] On the fate of this painstakingly concealed exemplar there is no need to speculate. Of the remaining seven or eight copies slipped into circulation by Scarron, we know only that they must have provided the basis for subsequent editions, but that none, apparently, have survived. In other words, no trace remains of the original edition of pornography's alleged original work; the earliest editions available, those on which all modern editions have been based, date from 1667 and 1668.

The work thus elaborately concealed and tracked down for destruction with such vehemence hardly seems to merit either excess of precaution. To know a tradition's full history is, some-times, to lose the ability to gauge the impact of its initial mani-festations – in this case, to measure the potential for corruption that the slim volume was perceived to represent in the spring of 1655. Nevertheless, it is hard to believe that *L'Ecole des filles*, so elaborately concealed and diligently destroyed, deserved the reaction it provoked. Surely modern readers always come to it when they already have a certain familiarity with classic porno-graphic texts. To such readers, *L'Ecole des filles* might seem an ideal origin for the genre, for it reveals that pornography has always/already been predictable and has always/already been founded on repetition and enumeration.

The volume is composed of two dialogues between young cousins, the sixteen-year-old innocent, Fanchon, and the more experienced Susanne (figure 2.1). In the first dialogue, Fanchon asks the questions and Susanne lists the ways in which men can give her pleasure, if she would only let them. In the second dia-logue, they reverse roles: Susanne inquires about the progress made by her protégée, and Fanchon details the extensive experi-ence she has acquired, virtually overnight, with a certain Robinet. Throughout, the text's principal shock value results from the technique that the Vicomte de Valmont describes to the Marquise de Merteuil as the most visible sign of his corruption of Cécile Volanges in letter CX of *Les Liaisons dangereuses*: every body part that can be involved in their exertions is named, renamed, and, if possible, named again, with both its anatomical designation and as many vulgar ones as can be imagined.

On the basis of its content, *L'Ecole des filles* does not belong

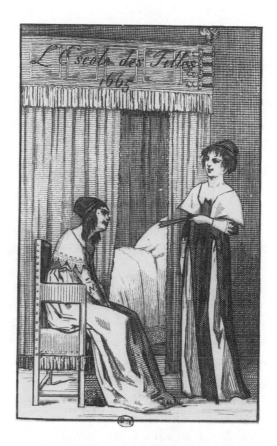

FIGURE 2.1. Frontispiece to *L'Escole des Filles* (Brussels, 1865). This is a reprint edition supposedly based on the Dutch original of 1668. Although it claims to reproduce the Dutch edition perfectly, it is not possible to verify the authenticity of the engraving. No trace remains of the frontispiece to the original French edition that was often alluded to in the trial proceedings.

to the classic tradition of French pornography, in which the dialogue form is the preferred vehicle for a blend of philosophical and sexual subversiveness. The dialogues hardly live up to the promise of the work's subtitle, *La Philosophie des dames*, for in them sexual explicitness is completely without philosophical implications. *L'Ecole des filles* is unrelieved by any signs of what modern readers would understand as truly threatening forms of corruption, subversion or perversion. There is no hint of blasphemy, for instance, nor is there any lack of political orthodoxy, nor any trace of sexuality other than hetero. Nor is there any violence in Susanne and Fanchon's boudoir philosophy; it remains strikingly good-natured and seems more a throwback to medieval and Renaissance ribaldry than a precursor of the darkness to come.

Yet, despite *L'Ecole des filles*'s all too evident lack of corruptive complexity or ambivalence, Lachèvre did not hesitate to name it as the "first work...written in French to elaborate directly on libertine morals, the territory of the culture of disbelief [premier ouvrage...écrit en français pour développer directement le libertinage des moeurs, terrain de culture de l'incrédulité]," and to argue that "it should have come out in 1755 and, thus, on time, to take its place among the most fundamentally perverse works that have seen or will see the light [il aurait dû paraître vers 1755 et serait alors venu à son heure, occupant sa place...dans la littérature la plus foncièrement perverse qui ait vu et verra le jour]."[10] Furthermore, the desire that Lachèvre demonstrates to link *L'Ecole des filles*'s obscenity with a more dangerous politico-religious subversiveness was also felt by the text's readers in the century following its initial publication, as is implied by the replacement title used when the work was illegally slipped into France in the eighteenth century. The book was discreetly hidden under cover sheets labeled *La Liturgie des Protestants en France*.

Almost from the beginning, in other words, all those involved

with either the dissemination or the suppression of *L'Ecole des filles*
have tenaciously promoted it as, in Lachèvre's phrase, "among the
most fundamentally perverse works that have seen or will see the
light." Almost from the beginning, everyone has wanted to believe
that *L'Ecole des filles* inaugurated the particularly French tradition of so-called philosophical books, whose existence Robert
Darnton has convincingly retraced in a series of fascinating studies. Darnton has demonstrated that, among the best-sellers of
eighteenth-century France, dangerous books all belonged to the
same category and were known as *livres philosophiques*. Works thus
classified were advertised in separate catalogs, ordered by means
of secret codes and smuggled into France after their pages had
been "married," that is, slipped between pages of inoffensive
titles. The category of philosophical books included volumes that,
using modern definitions, would be put into three distinct classifications: political, pornographic and philosophic.[11] The commercial bond forged and maintained during the Enlightenment
among works from these three categories has inspired Darnton
to return repeatedly to a central question: What link can be established between clandestine literature of all types and the political explosion that was the culmination of the Enlightenment? In
other words, is it possible to use the category of philosophical
books to help explain how the French were collectively able to
rise up in revolution?

Using the example of *L'Ecole des filles*, I would put a spin on
Darnton's question and ask if we might view the creation of the
category of philosophical books by eighteenth-century booksellers not only as an eventual cause of the Revolution, but also as the
effect of a primal force already evident for some time in France,
from the time of the mid-seventeenth-century political unrest that
prefigured the Revolution. From this perspective, the persistent
argument that *L'Ecole des filles* is the origin of pornography can

be explained by the work's association with the forces for change, even for revolt, that would eventually transform French society and the French nation. In addition, this positioning of *L'Ecole des filles* is evidence for the type of revolutionary change that Foucault terms the creation of an episteme.[12] Finally, we can see the placement of this dialogue as proof that, in France, the creation of pornography played an essential role in the formation of a new episteme and even as proof that the creation of both pornography and the myth of pornography was necessary to make the Revolution possible.

The forces of justice were able to take such swift action against L'Ange and Millot because the machinery for the suppression of books was well oiled by 1655. Until then, however, that machine had been set into action to silence political works. In particular, it had been in almost constant use during the years just prior to *L'Ecole des filles*'s publication to stem the flow of seditious texts produced during the Fronde (1648–1653), the civil war that had united Parliamentarians and nobles against the monarchy. Massive efforts had produced only mixed results, however, and numerous forbidden works continued to circulate so widely that, in 1655, the government was still trying to suppress them. This is evident from the interrogations of *L'Ecole des filles*'s alleged authors: each was questioned extensively about the types of forbidden books he owned; the only specific titles they were asked about were antigovernment satires and, in particular, *mazarinades* – pamphlets and plays mocking Prime Minister Cardinal Mazarin.[13]

This is not to suggest that the government's inquisitors were sensitive to a political content in *L'Ecole des filles* that we are no longer able to decode. What is interesting is that once *L'Ecole des filles* had been caught up – whether accidentally or not, it is unimportant to establish – in a trap laid for politically subversive works, that association remained glued to it. Furthermore, this must have occurred because those who made this association had a stake in its continued acceptance.

Those who prosecuted Millot and L'Ange in the manner reserved for authors of politically subversive works in effect transformed the obscene dialogues into a sort of *frondeur* manifesto. (Here the adjective is used as it was used from the mid-seventeenth century to the Revolution in its more general sense of antimonarchist activity.)[14] Fouquet probably took such elaborate precautions to conceal the book because he sensed that its obscenity had become a political threat; similarly, the letters from prominent women found in his famous *cassette* compromised their authors politically at least as much as they did socially. Also, in similar fashion, when the Fronde received its first overt literary inscription in *Le Tartuffe* (1664–1669), Molière deliberately kept the contents of Orgon's compromising *cassette* secret, the better to recreate the *frondeur* atmosphere in which the line between sexual and political subversiveness was never clearly drawn.

In her introduction, Lynn Hunt suggests that pornography developed out of a complicity between the desire of authors "to test the boundaries of the 'decent' " and the desire of the police and others to "regulate" those boundaries.[15] While this theory is amply demonstrated by pornography's history, it is less clear that these complicitous desires were the driving forces behind its initial formulation in France. The interpretive tradition that presents *L'Ecole des filles* as a politically subversive work begins in the eighteenth century. By then, many factors were already in place, most notably those that generated the Enlightenment, and those, often identical, that made possible the development of a pornographic *tradition*. Initially, however, when there was not yet a tradition, so to speak, but only the first of a few isolated examples, and, at a time just prior to the historical period in which Foucault initiates his history of modern sexuality, there is not enough evidence to permit an irrefutable interpretation of the intentions of either authors or regulators. *L'Ecole des filles* has been enshrined as a beginning, but it is important to remember that it is the product of a true transitional moment, a period entirely in process toward new ways of thought and expression, hence my reference to Foucault's theory of the episteme. *L'Ecole des filles* is one of those rare works in which one can sense the transition between world views. The one certain statement that can be made about its (unknown) authors' intentions is that they cannot have been clear. *L'Ecole des filles* is, above all, a work of experimentation, a work created to test "boundaries" – of "the decent," perhaps, but other boundaries as well.

This sense of work in process is evident in the form chosen for the initial French pornographic impulse. During the 1640s and 1650s, writers were actively experimenting with highly varied forms of prose fiction. It seems almost that authors somehow collectively sensed that the modern novel was about to emerge but were simply unable to tell which form it would take. One of these forms, historical fiction, eventually dominated the literary scene and, especially in its canonic manifestation, Lafayette's *La Princesse de Clèves*, became known as the modern novel par excellence. Variants, such as the pornographic novel, had no immediate future, but in this fate pornography was hardly alone. The form that eventually dominated the novel's eighteenth-century history, the epistolary novel, was experimented with several times at the same period, most famously in the *Lettres portugaises*. Each time, however, a tradition failed to develop, even though the *Lettres portugaises* in particular generated at least as much controversy as *L'Ecole des filles*. Still, the epistolary novel was placed on hold. Like the pornographic novel, the epistolary novel stagnated after this period of experimentation. It reappeared three quarters of a century later, at the same time the pornographic novel resurfaced.

Literary historians have posited a relation between the reemergence of pornography and the flowering of the eighteenth-century novel. I would argue that the link is more precise: pornography's history is bound up, not only with the development of the novel in general, but with that of the epistolary novel in particular. For, like pornography, the epistolary novel – from its earliest canonic manifestation in the *Lettres portugaises*, to Richardson's masterpieces, to *Les Liaisons dangereuses* – relied for its success on the (guilty) attraction to first-person narrative displays of female eroticism, which obviously exercised a powerful sway over the early novel's readers.[16] Pornography, in other words, may have originated as an (admittedly more extreme) manifestation of fictional strategies visible elsewhere on the contemporary literary horizon. During the Fronde, virtually no prose fiction was published. In the aftermath of the civil war, new forms exploded on the literary scene. *L'Ecole des filles* may have been, like other contemporary experiments, a translation into literary subversion of subversive contents that were intentionally left undefined. Initially, pornography might have been one attempt, among others, to rechannel within a literary context energy recently devoted to political sedition.

All involved in the repackaging of *L'Ecole des filles* as a work whose danger was purely political succeeded in giving French pornography the type of origin that came to define the specificity of the French tradition. The classic French pornographic tradition places pornographic literature at the intersection of sexual explicitness or obscenity and political dissidence. This is not to imply that the state began to treat sexuality as a political affair and, as Foucault analyzes in his history, to police it as such.[17] Rather, at the same time that this policing was being set in place, the use of sexuality to subvert such official control was also being developed. Classic French pornography was never sim-

ply solitary or homosocial male pleasure inspired by writing on or
across the female body. In early modern France, writing obscenity on the female body was always also writing the body politic.
It is the politics of pornography that, from the beginning, guar-
anteed the genre's importance – indeed, its centrality – for the
French tradition.

From this perspective, it is easy to see why, despite its annoy-
ing lack of original qualities, *L'Ecole des filles* would eventually be
enshrined as an origin for the French pornographic tradition. Was
it still another *mazarinade* by Scarron, a master of the genre, and,
therefore, the last gasp of the Fronde, that revolt against the monarchy by those often disturbingly close to the throne? Because the
last known original edition ended up in the hands of Louis XIV's
unruly minister of finances, could the work be linked to Fouquet's
subversive role? Or could this school for female sexual knowledge
be connected with Madame de Maintenon, the best-known seventeenth-century proponent of women's education, who established
a state-financed school for girls and who actually wrote dialogues
intended for female education?[18] Could the woman who allegedly obtained the revocation of the Edict of Nantes – that much
contested gesture defended as essential to the preservation of the
French nation's integrity – also have conspired in a plot against
the state? Most importantly, the original status that is maintained,
against all odds, for *L'Ecole des filles* reflects a desperate desire to
define pornography as a force for the political subversion of the
French tradition from within, from the very heart of that tradition. Without the policing of literature carried out in the wake of
the Fronde, would French pornography have come into existence?
Conversely, would the graphic literary inscription of sexuality
have been policed outside the climate of political unrest generated by nearly a decade of civil war? The creation of pornography
could, thus, be interpreted as a literary sign of the Revolution to

come, the unleashing of a force that would help redefine French society and the French nation.

The dossier of *L'Ecole des filles* reveals the strange case of a book which, throughout its history, has acquired importance because its judges – both those who condemn it and those who praise it – desperately wish to impose this status on the work. Literary historians could have chosen to ignore a book of such obviously dubious originality, enshrining instead as the first pornographic work Nicolas Chorier's *L'Académie des dames* (Latin version, 1660). However, the choice of *L'Ecole des filles* had one crucial advantage: it allowed the French pornographic tradition to be inaugurated just after the Fronde. It almost seems that, from the beginning, all had conspired to make *L'Ecole des filles* an origin and to make *L'Ecole des filles* political, thereby making pornography French and French pornography political. Pornography, rather than being the repressed of French literary history, may well be that genre which the French tradition most desires: the sign that, even as the great decades of French classicism were dawning, the seeds of that great tradition's eventual self-destruction had been sown. A group of collaborators gave the French tradition *L'Ecole des filles*. In so doing, they also made possible the tradition's first expression of its desire for the Marquis de Sade.

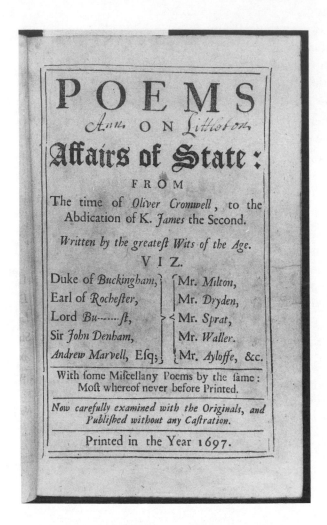

FIGURE 3.1. Title page to *Poems on Affairs of State* (1697).

CHAPTER THREE

Sometimes a Scepter is Only a Scepter:

Pornography and Politics in

Restoration England

Rachel Weil

In 1697, the publisher of *Poems on Affairs of State* printed, "without any castration," copies of poems that had circulated in manuscript during the reigns of Charles II and James II (figure 3.1). The volume contained some material that might be described as "purely political." It began, for example, with four panegyrics on Oliver Cromwell. It also contained many poems about Charles II's sex life, some of which contained graphic images of sexual acts. In one, Charles II's mistress, Nell Gwynn, is shown struggling to give the king an erection:

> This you'd believe, had I but time to tell ye
> The pains it cost to poor laborious Nelly
> While she employs hands, fingers, lips and thighs
> E'er she can raise the member she enjoys.[1]

Other poems in the collection were not as explicit about sexual acts, but were powerfully evocative of perversion and violence. Thus, in "Hodges's Vision from the Monument," the court was described with images of incest, priapic worship and cannibalism:

> Here parents their own offspring prostitute
> By such vile arts t'obtain a viler suit

125

Here blooming youth adore Priapus' shrine
And priests pronounce him sacred and divine
The Goatish god behold in his alcove
(the secret scene of damned incestuous love)
Melting in lust and drunk like Lot he lies
Betwixt two bright daughter divinities
Oh! that like Saturn he had eat his brood
and had been thus stained with their impious blood
He had in that less ill, more manhood shew'd.[2]

According to its editor, the purpose of printing these poems was
to encourage moral and political virtue. The poets were compared
to Catullus who, "in the midst of Caesar's triumphs attacked the
vices of that great man, and exposed 'em to lessen that popularity and power he was gaining among the Roman people, which he
saw would be turned to the destruction of the liberty of Rome."
The collection would "remove those pernicious principles which
lead us directly to slavery" by making available a "just account
of the true source of all our present mischiefs"; it constituted a
"just and secret history of the former times." Interestingly, the
slavery to be repudiated was imagined as a decrepit prostitute:
"Take off the gaudy veil of slavery, and she will appear so frightful and deformed that all would abhor her."[3]

The material in *Poems on Affairs of State* fits uneasily into
the history of pornography. While it has in common with pornography the fact that it contains "an expression or suggestion
of obscene or unchaste subjects,"[4] it doesn't necessarily meet the
more demanding definition, proposed by Angela Carter, that pornography is "propaganda for fucking."[5] The poems do not seem
to endorse the activity that they describe; they might, perhaps,
be better characterized as slander.

The exclusion of the poems in *Poems on Affairs of State* from the category of pornography would probably come as a relief to the book's editor. But this material is, in fact, more complex. The act of stripping away the "gaudy veil" of the whore, slavery, allows us to view her naked goods; the impulse to expose hitherto secret political truth is also an impulse toward voyeurism. Moreover, works that purport to reveal libertine sexual activity at court are actually inventing what they represent – they are imaginative exercises, not journalism. Slander may be more closely related to pornography than it at first appears.

The line between slander and pornography becomes even hazier if the inquiry is expanded to include material that the editors of *Poems on Affairs of State* didn't publish. A comparison of political poems existing in late seventeenth-century manuscript collections[6] with those published after 1688 suggests that the editors of the published collections, while not necessarily afraid to publish obscene material, were reluctant to publish works in which the political or moral intention was at all ambiguous.[7] They included only works in which the author's disapproval of the Restoration regime was explicit. This left out a large number of works in which the intention was imbedded in layers of irony, or in which the poet adopted a mock-heroic tone or a false persona.[8]

These were significant omissions. Some of the most effective satire of the period attacked the sexual libertinism at court by pretending to praise it, or by putting extravagant celebrations of libertine sexuality into the mouths of courtiers or Tories. In one work, the Tory speaker manically celebrates the new golden age:

> The parsons all keep whores
> In these most blessed times
> The sextons they sing bawdy songs
> And set them to their chimes

> The mayor of London town
> Is frigged by his two sheriffs
> The bishops bugger up and down
> And all beshite their sleeves[9]

A particulary effective and sustained example of this technique is John Oldham's "Sardanapalus," a poem probably written between 1676 and 1681. The poem's ostensible subject is the legendary Assyrian king whose notorious debauchery, according to classical authors, provoked his generals to rebel against him. Besieged in his capital city and perceiving that all was lost, Sardanapalus immolated himself on a huge funeral pyre, along with his concubines and vast amounts of gold and jewels. While classical writers, as John O'Neill points out, universally condemned Sardanapalus's debauchery and admired only the heroism of his suicide,[10] Oldham celebrates — or pretends to celebrate — the king's sexual achievements, which are described in the poem as if they were a legitimate affair of state, far more noble than the pursuit of mere honor and fame, certainly more pleasant and as worthy as the quest for empire:

> Methinks I see thee now in full Seraglio stand
> With Love's great sceptre in thy hand
> And over all its spacious realm thy power extend
> Ten thousand maids lie prostrate at thy feet
> Ready thy Pintle's high commands to meet
> All C—ts of honor, some of Queenly Breed
> That come to be anointed with thy royal seed
> Here eunuchs thy wise privy councellors debate
> In close cabals, Affairs of greatest weight
> Of Pego's conquests and its deep intrigues of state.
> Plenipotentiaries of great C—t, they here
> Ambassages of high importance bear

Far as wide as Nature spreads her thighs
Thy Tarse's vast dominion lies
All woman kind acknowledge its great sway
And to its large treasury their tribute pay
Pay custom of their unprohibited commodities
No glorious beauties which profess their Trade
Here find their noble services unpaid
Vast heaps of gold and piles of gems lie by
To recompense industrious lechery
One earns a province with an artful kiss
Another justly merits subsidies
At whose blest touch imperial Pego does vouchsafe to rise
But happy she, and most of all rewarded is
Who ever can invent new motions to advance your bliss.[11]

The king's death is not, as it was for ancient authors, the one different and redeeming feature of the king's life, but a logical extension of it: he is driven to suicide when "malicious rebels," urging "the impudent pretence of laws and liberties," try to abridge his "sovereign prick's prerogative" and "debar him from swiving." The funeral pyre is decorated to commemorate a lifetime of sexual triumph, as is evident in this portion of the description:

Atop a hundred golden beds were spread
All conscious marks of thy great prowess bore
All died a thousand times in maiden gore
Which thy victorious lance in many a fierce campaign had shed

Around the walls in distants arches placed
Stood statues of thy glorious punks diseased
In picture by, ye brave achievements of thy Tarse
Which poets had recorded in immortal verse

Lusts gaudy pageants, whose each lively scene
Showed the choice artists mastery and design
And far surpassed the wit of modern Aretine
And over all displayed and waving to ye sun
Thy royal arms, Priapus rampant was in triumph shown.[12]

The climax is a mass orgy. Ascending the pyre, the king encounters a "willing virgin" who "lay unbound / Ready from thy great stroke to meet the gentle wound." The other beds are populated by equally willing virgins provided for his nobles. The king outdoes his nobles in "swiving" the longest atop the pyre, and then, at the height of orgasm, orders the fire to be lit as a sacrifice to the god Priapus. The spectacular finale is worth quoting:

Here glowing C—t with flaming beard
Like blazing meteor appeared
There pintle squirting fiery streams
Like lighted flamboy spreading flames
Thus lechery's great martyr, revelling in fire
At every pore dripping out scalding lust
With all thy strength collected in one thrust
At [sic] gasping Thou didst give up thy mighty ghost
And midst a glorious heap of burning Cunts expire.[13]

An analysis of this poem shows how hard it is to draw a clear line between slander and pornography, or between attacks on the regime that are written from a sexually puritanical point of view and poems which themselves seem to express either a sexually libertine ethos or offer the reader the pleasures of pornography, or both. At one level, the poem should be read as a political attack on the regime. Oldham obliquely voices many of the complaints that had been made about Charles II at the time: that the king refused to stand up militarily against the burgeoning power of Louis XIV (and that this was done under the influence of his French mistress, the duchess of Portsmouth), that the country was being bankrupted because Charles spent extravagantly on his mistresses, that the king cared more for his pleasure than for the business of state. If the poem was written after 1679, one might read the king's suicide by fire as an allusion to Charles's reluctance to take seriously the warnings of Titus Oates that the Catholics planned to murder him and burn down London — or at least rekindle the Smithfield fires of Mary Tudor's days. Indeed, the fact that Charles is shown sacrificing to a pagan idol might suggest what many thought at the time, that Charles was himself a Catholic. It would have been obvious to a reader at the time that the poem was intended as political criticism of Charles's government.

At another level, "Sardanapalus" can work as pornography. It offers us a quasirealistic representation of sexual acts and has many of the elements that we would recognize in modern pornography: the huge and magnificent penises, the women literally dying to be penetrated, and, importantly, the equation of sex with power over and violence against women. Penises are imagined as lances dyed in "virgin gore," women lie prostrate, submit to "high commands" and are willing sacrifices. There is a vividness with which bodily secretions, ooze, slime and hot fluids are evoked that makes it difficult for the reader to remain aloof from the description. It isn't hard to imagine the poem being translated to the screen in any of New York's Forty-second Street movie theaters.

"Sardanapalus" calls attention to the problematic relationship between libertine literature and political opposition to Charles II's regime. It has often been suggested that political divisions in Restoration England were parallelled and reinforced by a cultural and sexual division, in which a sexually puritan "country" opposition confronted a sexually libertine and cavalier "court." This view is implicit in the preface to the 1697 *Poems on Affairs of State*. It is also present in more recent scholarship on Restoration political satire,[14] and it requires a closer look.

The cultural and sexual dimension to Restoration politics was complex, and the opposition was not made up exclusively of sexual puritans. For example, the second duke of Buckingham was a courtier often attacked for his alleged promiscuity and bisexuality, a member of the Cabal, and yet also a supporter of toleration for dissenters with ties to London radicals.[15] The lines between court and country, the regime and its opponents, and sexual puritanism and sexual libertinism were more hazy and complicated than the traditional stereotypes suggest.

Nonetheless, the notion that a sexually puritanical opposition confronted a libertine court is true in one significant sense. Even where the moral or erotic directions of political poems are ambiguous, the poems always associate the king himself with sexual libertinism, and no attempt is made to use sexual libertinism as the basis for an antiabsolutist political stance. In this respect, Restoration England seems different from eighteenth-century France, where, it has been argued, an explicit endorsement of sexual libertinism on philosophical grounds was connected to religious skepticism and irreverence for the monarchy.[16]

In late seventeenth-century England, by contrast, it was possible to attack sexual libertinism and religious skepticism by associating both with political tyranny and absolutism rather than with opposition to the monarchy. An extreme but revealing example is a narrative published in 1694 which purports to be Charles's posthumously discovered autobiography or political testament (figures 3.2 and 3.3).[17] In it, Charles's Catholicism, which he, of course, openly avows from the outset, is treated as a manifestation of both his religious skepticism *and* his absolutist ambition:

religion, he tells us, is merely a "trick of state," and he decided
to become a Catholic because, with its principle that "ignorance
is the mother of devotion," it is the religion "most agreeable to
a Prince who would...advance his prerogative."[18] The critique
of Christianity deepens when he finds himself lusting after his
own sister and recognizes his qualms about incest to be merely a
cultural construct:

> How happy are they in those parts of the world where they know
> no such restraints as we who are called Christians do labor under.
> There, Loves are promiscuous without offence, and they have no
> restraint on the appetites of nature, but satisfy all its desires to the
> full. Then why should I be scrupulous, or filled with horror, upon
> such a motion of the flesh as this? It's only the customs and tenets
> we imbibe, that make such impressions as these upon us.[19]

"From now on," he concludes, "I will worship no God, except
Priapus be one."[20] And he prays to Priapus to help him to debauch
his subjects so as to make them less rebellious.

In this context, it is possible to read Oldham's poem as a description of the rhetorical field in which writers of Restoration
political satire operated. The poem is not, in the end, so much a
pornographic work as it is a poem which contains representations
of pornographic works. Aretino's postures, or something like
them, are actually referred to in the poem as decorations on the
funeral pyre. Similarly, the speaker in the poem is a pornographer;
he appears in the poem as a character in his own right, a sort of
mad poet laureate. The poem's descriptive passages, while they
can – as argued above – function as pornography for the reader,
also function in dramatic terms as a monologue which reveals
the speaker's absurdly misplaced sense of what heroism is.[21] The
humor comes from the fact that the representations of sex – the

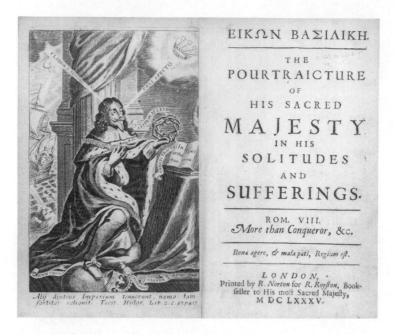

FIGURE 3.2. Frontispiece and title page to *Eikon Basilike. The Pourtraicture of His Sacred Majesty in his Solitudes and Sufferings* (1685). Purportedly written by King Charles I on the eve of his execution, and originally published in 1649, this popular work of royalist propaganda was reprinted many times in the seventeenth and eighteenth centuries. The image of the kneeling Charles I, eyes turned heavenward, casting aside his earthly crown and preparing to take up a crown of thorns, was reproduced in many editions.

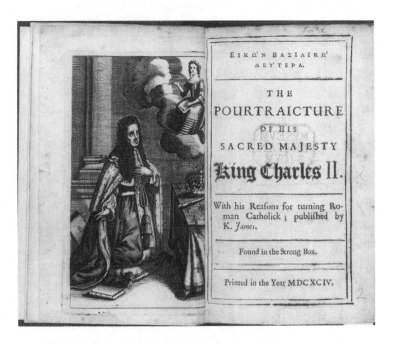

FIGURE 3.3. Frontispiece and title page of *Eikon Basilike Deutera. The Pourtraicture of His Sacred Majesty King Charles II* (1694). The illustration is clearly meant to allude to *Eikon Basilike*. Heaven is now occupied by a woman, who might be identified as one of the king's mistresses, his Catholic mother Henrietta Maria or the Virgin Mary.

pornography – inside the poem appear in totally inappropriate and unexpected contexts. We expect pornography to be read in secret and private places – recall Pepys's embarrassment at owning *L'Ecole des filles*. Here, it is proudly exposed as a decoration on a public monument. We expect pornographers to defy established authority; here, the speaker glorifies the king's deeds.

This presents an interesting conundrum. At one level, Oldham's poem seems to describe, in exaggerated form, a reality; that is, that one cannot embrace sexual libertinism and attack tyranny because libertinism is associated with tyranny. In that sense pornography is not, as it would have been in the eighteenth century, an appropriate weapon to use against Charles II. Oldham creates a situation within the poem in which pornography is neither illicit nor oppositional. Exposing the king's body in the act of copulation is, in some circumstances, a way of desacralizing it, but this exposure can't possibly be seditious when public sex has become a form of royal ceremonial. The poem tells us what we think we already know: that political opposition to the court in the Restoration had to be expressed in terms of sexual puritanism, the rejection of libertine sexual morality. Yet Oldham's poem also complicates that perception. Although he creates, inside the poem, an environment where pornography can be neither oppositional nor illicit, "Sardanapalus" itself *can* be considered oppositional, illicit and even pornographic. Thus, the poem transcends the situation it describes. Although it relies on and confirms a stereotype of Puritan killjoys attacking royal prerogative and royal sexuality (or, the royal "prerogative to swive"), it violates that stereotype by its own existence.

To explain the paradox of "Sardanapalus" it is necessary to understand the pattern of sexual stereotyping, of sexual attacks and counterattacks on political opponents, that dates back to the English civil war. In the political propaganda of the 1640s, Parliamentarians were portrayed as upright, orderly and pious by their friends, and as joyless, repressive and hypocritical by their enemies. Royalists, conversely, represented themselves as romantic and swashbuckling, while their opponents depicted them as drunken, disorderly and debauched. These stereotypes created expectations about the links between political and sexual behavior and shaped the strategies of legitimation deployed by the restored monarchy in 1660. Charles II was presented as having rescued England from a decade of repression; in effect, as having stolen Christmas back from the Grinch. The new regime associated itself in its own propaganda with fruitfulness, bounty and sensual pleasure.[22] At times, the relationship between the king and the people was likened to that of a lover and mistress, and the Restoration likened to a nuptial union between the bride, Britain, and her husband, the king.[23] It is important to emphasize that Charles II did not explicitly promote libertine sexuality. Royalists shared with Parliamentarians – and everyone else – an assumption that lewdness and debauchery were bad: the point of vulnerability in this strategy was that the fine distinction between pleasure and debauchery could easily be ignored for the sake of parody.

The language of blame directed against the crown exploited and played on the language that the regime used to praise itself. Where Charles presented himself as an amorous husband to the nation, satirists could treat him as its rapist or as an adulterous husband ignoring his marriage vows. The association of Charles with pleasure became the accusation that he "minded nothing but his pleasure." But these attacks, of course, provoked counterattacks, which again relied on the old stereotype of the Puritan as hypocrite. In "The City Painter," a royalist satire, a Whig alderman is shown masturbating while self-righteously watching a whore be whipped.[24]

From this perspective, it is evident how the rhetorical technique used by Oldham and other writers who purported to praise sexual libertinism functioned as a strategic response to the attempts by royalist propagandists to portray their opponents as hypocritical Puritans. By speaking in the voice of a libertine, by praising the king's prowess or the golden age of sexual liberty, or by using framing devices that rendered the moral direction of the poem ambiguous, writers could avoid being labeled as Puritans. Satirists like Oldham did, in fact, attack sexual libertinism and associate it – for reasons discussed below – with tyranny, but they put on a libertine mask and employed the techniques of pornography to do it. One might argue, then, that the polemical dynamics of the Restoration created a body of literature that was not truly pornographic, in the sense of endorsing libertine sexuality, but which nevertheless offered some of the pleasures that we might associate with reading pornography. The ambiguity was intentional and inevitable. If the line between pornography and slander is hard to draw when analyzing Restoration political poems, the difficulty is rooted in the political conditions of the period. None of this, however, answers a more fundamental question: Why sexuality? Were the objections to Charles II's regime sexual or political? And why were the two connected and expressed in terms of one another?

To begin answering these questions, the Restoration's rude poems could be placed in the context of a long-standing tradition of expressing fundamental political concerns and concepts in terms of the relationship between the king's two bodies: his mortal person and his eternal office, his private interests and the public welfare, his bedchamber and his council chamber.[25] It is important to note that there was no consensus about what that relationship was. In the civil war, for example, the Parliament, in declaring war on the king in the name of the king, implicitly asserted a distinction between the person and the office. Royalist propaganda, by contrast, often deliberately conflated the king's body with the body politic. Following the execution of Charles I, royalists represented the war-torn, bleeding and – to them – anarchic nation with the image of the bleeding, literally headless body of its king. Representations of the Restoration as a marriage between the king and the nation might be seen as a third option, a compromise that allowed a theoretical distinction between the king and the nation but that also emphasized the union between them, and the king's superior position as the "husband" within that union.

There was also no consensus about the proper relationship between the king's private pleasures and the public business of government. As David Starkey has reminded us, the ways in which monarchs combined or separated business and pleasure have always had significant political consequences because they decide such things as who controls access to the monarch and how offices get distributed.[26] Likewise, the problematic role of the "favorite" – that is, the person who is seen to serve the monarch's pleasure rather than the public good – was a theme in early modern English political discourse, from Elizabeth I's reign onward. The lament that the monarch was led astray by personal favorites was a convenient and long-standing way of criticizing the monarch's policies without appearing to attack the monarch's person. But favorites had their defenders, too. It could be argued that this was particularly the case for a regime which, like that of Charles II, tended to emphasize the value of friendship and love, as opposed to abstract duty, as elements of political obligation. The personal loyalty that had bound the cavaliers to the king in exile was idealized in Restoration literature. An attempt to scrutinize the monarch's friendships with men or women could be construed, at best, as Puritan meddlesomeness, and, at worst, as lèse-majesté, especially since the execution of the allegedly evil favorites, Strafford and Laud, had actually been a prelude to the regicide. Given the uncertainty about the proper stance to take toward the king's personal friends and pleasures, it isn't surprising that competing stories existed about their political significance. Did Clarendon fall, contemporaries wondered, because he was corrupt, or because the old minister had failed to share in the banter, games and intrigues of the royal bedchamber? Could one distinguish those mistresses who "ruled" the king from those who only pleased him? Should Charles II more closely imitate Louis XIV, who, as John Evelyn remarked to Samuel Pepys one evening, "hath his mistresses, but laughs at the foolery of our king, that makes his bastards princes and loses his revenues upon them – and makes his mistresses his masters."[27] Was Nell Gwynn to be tolerated, or even bemusedly praised as a Protestant or apolitical whore, interested, as one poem put it, in "scratching where it itches," or was the king's whoring itself the problem?[28]

There were, then, many conflicting and ambiguous attitudes toward the significance of the king's sexual behavior, and the relationship between his public and private bodies. The tendency to associate political positions with sexual styles, and the tendency to use images of and stories about the king's body for a variety of political purposes, make it hard to separate pornographic political poems from other kinds of political theory and commentary. There are a surprising number of sexual narratives embedded within otherwise straight political works. Sexual events were used to explain political events. It was widely rumored, for example, that Charles II had been induced to sign the secret Treaty of Dover in the course of an incestuous encounter with his sister, the duchess of Orleans.[29] Another common story concerned the duchess of Portsmouth, who, it was said, had plied the king with liquor and charmed him with the sight of three court ladies, who undressed before him in a reenactment of the judgment of Paris; when Charles, in return, offered to grant the duchess any wish, she ordered him to dissolve the Parliament.[30]

Political pornography was thus continuous with other forms of political theory and commentary, which is why it is hard to isolate it as a distinct genre. The manuscript books into which Restoration men and women copied items of current interest usually contained a mixture of sexual and "purely" political material, with no effort being made to create a distinction between them. A manuscript book belonging to William Haward, an undistinguished member of Parliament who also held a minor court office, contained in its more than 600 pages the following, which is a very partial list: a mock-pastoral by Charles Sedley entitled "In the Fields of Lincoln's Inn," in which "Phyllis who you know loves swiving / as earthly god loves pious prayers / lay most pensively contriving / how to fuck with pricks by pairs"; copies of speeches made in Parliament protesting the marriage of the duke of York to Mary of Modena; a fictitious answer from Charles's mistress, the countess of Castlemaine, to a petition from the "undone, poor, distressed company of whores" of London; a list of pensioners and placemen in Parliament, some of whom are described as "royal pimps," and some of whom are said to pimp for their own daughters; the seditious libel entitled "The True Englishman Speaking Plain English," which argued that Charles, though not a Catholic, was more tyrannical than his brother James; a catalog of "Goods" offered for sale at the Royal Coffeehouse, including "Twenty-four pieces of fine French gold-colored bribery of the treasurers.... Two whole pieces of the duke of Buckingham's religion.... Four ells of Nell Gwinn's virginity" and "the last royal clap of his royal highness...which cost the kingdom many thousands of pounds, but now may be bought by any man at an easy rate."[31]

This jumble suggests that stories about royal or court sexuality were a legitimate part of political discourse, not cordoned off into a separate category. Narratives about the king's body, its powers and vulnerabilities, its healthy and unhealthy states and its relationship to the body politic, provided writers with a way of dramatizing their deepest political concerns.

The focus here will be on only one of those concerns, although it is obviously connected to all the others: the fear of Charles's absolutist ambitions, which grew throughout the 1670s and culminated in the Exclusion Crisis and Charles's attempt thereafter to rule without Parliament. Charles's potential for tyranny was often represented in terms of his sexual excess. The fantasy that Charles had slept or wanted to sleep with every woman in the nation – encountered in "Sardanapalus" – was an emblem of his overweening power that worked on several levels. The cuckolding of male subjects is the quintessential tyrannical act, a deprivation of their property and manhood. (This is why, when Charles's ministers are attacked, it is often said that they are pimping for their own wives and daughters.) It was also an implicit parody of Robert Filmer's patriarchal justification of absolutism: the joke being that Charles was trying to become, literally, the father of his country.[32] Charles's promiscuity was also an emblem of his absolutist ambition because it made it possible to liken him to a Turkish sultan. Thus, many stories about Charles's sex life take place in Oriental settings.[33]

Finally, some writers linked debauchery to absolutism by suggesting that Charles was deliberately trying to debauch his people through his own example and thereby render them incapable of resistance. Algernon Sidney, in his *Discourses on Government*, argued that tyrants secure their power "by corrupting the youth, and seducing such as can be brought to lewdness and debauchery, [and thus] bring the people to such a pass, that they may neither care nor dare to exercise their rights."[34] Likewise, according to *The Secret History of the Reigns of K. Charles II and K. James II* (1690), Charles "set himself by his own persuasion and influence to withdraw both men and women from the laws of nature and morality, and to pollute and infect the people with all manner of debauchery and wickedness," in order to "weaken and make soft the military temper of the people by debauchery and effeminacy, which generally go hand in hand together."[35]

The connection between debauchery and absolutism was made startlingly literal in the frequent equation of Charles's scepter with his penis. In "Sodom," a mock court masque attributed to the earl of Rochester, the king declares that "my pintle shall my only sceptre be" and that "with my prick I'll govern all the land."[36] In "On the Duchess of Portsmouth," his "prick foams and swears he will be absolute."[37] As another lampoon put it, "Ah, reeling nation, well mayst thou be sick / Rex still pretends to rule thee with his prick."[38] Or, as Rochester wrote in the notorious "sceptre lampoon," "his pintle and his sceptre are of a length / and she may sway the one who plays with the other."[39]

Charles's excessive claims for royal prerogative were identified with insatiable sexual hunger. Sometimes the tone is humorous, as in Rochester's verse:

> His is the sauciest one that ere did swive
> The proudest and peremptoriest prick alive
> What e'er religion and his laws say on it
> He'll break through those to come to any cunt.[40]

Other writers more explicitly emphasized the violence implicit in Rochester's conceit. In "Brittania and Raleigh," Charles's relationship to his three kingdoms is portrayed, not as the marriage it was in the poems on his coronation, but as mass rape. Charles encounters a monstrous female figure representing French abso-

lutism, who is wearing a fleur-de-lis and carrying a sword engraved
with the word *Leviathan*. She urges him to

> Taste the delicious sweets of sovereign power
> Tis royal game whole kingdoms to deflower
> Three spotless virgins to your bed I'll bring
> A sacrifice to you their God and King
> As these grow stale we'll harrass human kind
> Rack nature, till new pleasures you shall find.[41]

Similarly, when a bound and naked female figure representing
Britain appears to Charles at the end of Marvell's "Last Instruc-
tions to a Painter," he cannot resist trying to rape her.[42]

Recall that the royalists during the civil war emphasized the
identity of the king's person and his office, and the ironic force of
the penis-as-scepter metaphor becomes clear. The poets parody
royalist rhetoric by literally equating the body (penis) and royal
prerogative (scepter). The result is a confusion between the pursuit of sexual pleasure and the exercise of the duties of kingship.
Evidently, this confusion was on the minds of contemporaries.
Samuel Pepys's *Diary* records numerous conversations with his
friends lamenting that "the king minds nothing but his pleasure" — meaning not, or not only, that the king paid no attention
to politics, but that policies were dictated by his need to maintain and increase his pleasures.[43] This meant acquiring enough
money to pay for his whores. The notion that the financial crisis
of the nation was caused by the king's extravagant expenditure
on his mistresses was a constant theme in satiric literature. The
author of "On the Duchess of Portsmouth," an attack on the
king's French Catholic mistress, fulminated:

> The nation must be taxed both land and gains
> Not to supply the public but his reins

And all the coin by harrassed subjects lent
Must through your conduit pipe of lust be spent[44]

This waste of revenues was, in turn, associated with the threat of absolutism. Specifically, Pepys and his friends speculated that, rather than risk a parliamentary inquiry into where the revenues were going, Charles would dissolve Parliament and resort to extra-parliamentary taxation or, worse, turn to Loius XIV for a subsidy, making England, in effect, a satellite of the French universal monarchy. It was this scenario that gave plausibility to the stories that Portsmouth had convinced Charles to prorogue Parliament, or – as Pepys and company heard rumored – that the countess of Castlemaine was urging the king to rule by a standing army.[45]

The king's debauchery was thus used to suggest that he had the potential to be a tyrant. But it can be further argued that debauchery did not only indicate a potential for tyranny, but also helped to describe the nature of tyranny. A closer analysis of how debauchery was used in rude poems can thus give a richer understanding of what Charles's critics thought tyranny was.

It was largely through narratives of sexual excess that satirists were able to establish an identity between absolutism and Catholicism. To understand why this is important, it is necessary to see that the equation of "popery and tyranny," although it was a commonplace of seventeenth-century political rhetoric, was artificial and constructed and, therefore, fragile. For example, it was as possible to identify popery with regicide as it was to identify it with absolutism; when convenient, the political connotations of popery could be reversed.[46] Even the claim that popery and absolutism were united in the threatening person of Louis XIV was unconvincing, as close examination would reveal that the French king's interests were hardly identical to those of the pope. Moreover, while one could establish a connection between popery and tyranny on

the grounds that Charles II had attempted to use royal prerogative to establish toleration for Catholics against the wishes of Parliament, such an argument would ignore the fact that Protestant
dissenters as well were offered toleration in the same royal edict.
One might speculate, in fact, that the equation of popery and tyranny was promoted by Anglican politicians who hoped to keep
dissenters from casting their lot with the crown against the Anglican church: if royal prerogative was identified with popery, no
self-respecting Protestant, Anglican or dissenter could support it.

The point here is that the equation between popery and tyranny was not natural. It had to be constructed, and political
pornography aided in the process of constructing it. Popery and
tyranny could be tied to one another because both were linked
to sexual debauchery. The relationship between tyranny and debauchery has already been explored above, but what were the ties
between debauchery and Catholicism?

Sexual debauchery and Catholicism were connected at a number of levels. As anti-Catholic polemicists were fond of pointing
out, the pope ran brothels in Rome. Catholicism was also thought
to be the religion which provided its believers with an excuse to
do what they wanted. In a fictitious letter purportedly written
by the king's Catholic mistress, the countess of Castlemaine, to
the whores of London, the countess presents the interests of Catholics and prostitutes as identical, promising to help out her poor,
distressed sisters by increasing the number of playhouses, which
will increase debauchery, which will increase Catholicism. She
herself, she explains, converted because "the worthy fathers and
confessors...do declare, that venereal pleasures accompanied
with looseness, debauchery and profaneness are not such heinous
crimes and crying sins, but rather...they do mortify the flesh:
and the general opinion of the holy mother church is, that venereal pleasures in the strictest sense are but venial sins, which

146

confessors of the meanest can forgive."[47] On occasion, prostitution was itself imagined as an idolatrous religion: brothels were
described as "temples to Venus," whores as "nuns" or "votaries
of Venus," sex as a sacrifice or act of worship. All of this drew
on, or fit in easily with, the long-standing tradition of referring
to the Catholic church as the "Whore of Rome," and representing
it as an overmighty, sexually profligate and obscenely rich woman.
A debauched king was, potentially, a Catholic king, and Charles's
embrace of his Catholic whores – the countess of Castlemaine,
the duchess of Portsmouth and the duchess of Mazarin – omi-
nously pointed to his embrace of the Whore of Rome, with whom
the women were conflated.[48]

Debauchery thus created a connection between popery and
tyranny, but it also complicated the meaning of tyranny. As already
noted, Charles's absolutist ambitions were represented as his rampaging penis. But, paradoxically, tyranny was just as often signi-
fied by domineering or devouring female genitalia:

> The French hag's nasty pocky bum
> So powerful is of late
> Although it is both blind and dumb
> It rules both church and state.[49]

Similarly, the common allegation that the king was spending all
the nation's treasure on his mistresses was expressed in the image
of a devouring cunt sucking up the nation's seed:

> Why art thou poor. O king? Embezzling Cunt
> That wide-mouthed, greedy monster, that has done it.[50]

The two images of cunts here are connected, since it was thought
that the king's extravagant expenditure on his whores would lead
him to tyranny.

It is tempting to assume that the images of a rampaging prick and a devouring cunt both indicate distinct political positions: one image seems to throw the blame on Charles, the other on his mistresses; one casts him as too powerful, the other as not powerful enough. In fact, they are inseparable, and often appear within the same works. In John Lacy's satire on Charles II, for example, both images are suggested, and the syntax and imagery make it difficult to tell what is devouring or engulfing what:

> Was ever Prince's soul so meanly poor
> To be enslaved to every little whore?
> The seaman's needle points always to the pole
> But thine still points to every craving hole
> Which wolflike in your breast raw flesh devours
> And must be fed all seasons and all hours.
> C—t is the mansion house where thou dost swell
> There thou art fixed as tortoise is to shell.[51]

This ambiguity as to whether pricks conquer cunts or cunts overwhelm pricks is typical of Restoration discussions of sexuality. Although it was a cliché that men "conquer" the women with whom they have sex, it was also a cliché that women were insatiable, "defeating" men because men can never satisfy them. A mock-heroic satire describes sex as a Roman spectacle, with the penis in the role of a helpless Christian set upon by beasts: "Cunt shakes her angry locks, worries the prey / Sucks out the blood and throws the skin away."[52] Similarly, "Sodom" is one long joke about men not being able to get it up or keep it up long enough. And yet women's "victory" is actually the opposite of victory – in "Sodom," they die of sexual starvation. The point about sexuality and power made in Restoration literature is that the power is elusive and unstable, and can never resolve itself in satisfaction. For men, at least, "conquering" – the moment of ejaculation – is also a loss of power and substance.

148

This enriches our understanding of what it means to equate Charles's tyranny with his debauchery. Tyranny was, for seventeenth-century political theorists, not simply an overextension of legitimate political authority, a case of there being too much royal power. Rather, tyranny was a situation in which the location and direction of power was uncertain. The ruler, pursuing nothing but private pleasure, had no power at all because he was enthralled by those who catered to his desires – people who, in turn, might be ruled by those who catered to theirs. In a political pamphlet of 1681, for example, it was asserted that an honest Parliament was essential because it is only Parliament "that hinders the subject from being given up as a prey, not only to the will of a Prince, but (which is ten times worse) to the unreasonable passions and lusts of favorites, chief ministers, and women." Without a Parliament, England might be ruled, "like the Turkish Empire under a weak Grand Signior, by the prevailing concubine of the seraglio, who is perhaps herself managed by no higher dictates than that of her chief eunuch, or she-slave."[53]

Similar ideas can be found in more formal political works, such as Paul Rycaut's *The Present State of the Ottoman Empire* (from which this pamphleteer was stealing) and Algernon Sidney's *Discourses on Government*. Both contain involved discussions of the relationship between debauchery and tyranny, and both, in different ways, emphasize that power in tyrannical regimes does not lie with the ruler. For Rycaut, the "condition of slavery" – the total resignation of everyone to the will of the sultan – that reigns at the sultan's court ultimately undermines the sultan's power, because people are too busy flattering him to tell him the truth.[54]

In Sidney's account of the workings of corrupt political systems, riches, power and vices are all means to each other as well as ends in themselves. In this sense, no one can ever achieve his goals, because every success brings with it more compelling needs.

For both monarch and courtiers, power is unstable and ephemeral. Sidney's description of the way that courtiers become addicted to corruption conveys the cyclical nature of the process:

> When riches grew to be necessary, the desire of them, which is the spring of all mischief, followed. Those who could not attain honors by the noblest actions were obliged to get wealth to purchase them from whores and villains, who exposed them to sale: and, when they were once entered into this track, they soon learnt the vices of those from whom they had received their preferment, and to delight in the ways that had brought them to it.[55]

Pleasure, once a means to acquire power, ultimately becomes the only consolation for it:

> This brought the government of the world under a most infamous traffic, and the treasures arising from it were, for the most part, dissipated by worse vices than the rapine, violence and fraud, with which they had been gotten. The authors of these crimes had nothing left but their crimes, and the necessity of committing more through the indigence into which they were plunged by the extravagance of their expenses. These things are inseparable from the life of a courtier; for as servile natures are guided by sense rather than reason, such as addict themselves to the service of courts, find no other consolation in their misery, than what they receive from sensual pleasures, or such vanities as they put a value upon; and have no other care than to get money for their supply by begging, stealing, bribing, and other infamous practices.[56]

In an atmosphere such as this, even an absolutist prince is left with only the illusion of power. Courtiers attain their office by "observing the prince's humor, flattering his vices, serving him in his pleasures, fomenting his passions, and by advancing his worst designs, to create an opinion in him that they love his person and are entirely addicted to his will."[57]

The much-feared scenario in which Charles was to sell out to Louis XIV followed the same pattern: the sell-out would make Charles "absolute" in the sense of allowing him to dispense with Parliament, but would also deprive him of sovereignty, leaving him only his pleasures. Sex was a perfect analog for tyranny – a situation in which the location of power was ambiguous and ultimately pointless.

One might also read the many references to Charles II as a priapic idol – for example, in the previously quoted "Hodges's Vision from the Monument" – as statements about royal vulnerability as well as royal power. It is true that the equation of the king with Priapus underscored Charles's pretensions to godhood, especially those pretensions encouraged by the priests of an idolatrous religion – that is, the Jesuit enthusiasts for divine right monarchy. But it was also a commonplace that idols were merely wooden things, and that the worshipper or priest was the true "deity" in the sense that he was the creator of the thing he worshipped. Satirists also delighted in pointing out that a Priapus was a giant dildo, and it is interesting to find Charles described as both a "Priapus king" and as a "Dildo-king." At first, this image seems to emphasize his power: a dildo, unlike the pathetic penises discussed above, is never satisfied, impotent or exhausted. The joke, of course, is that a dildo is also a woman's tool. The association of Charles with both a priapic god and a dildo is thus a savage jibe at the ambiguous character of tyrannical power.

The emphasis on the vulnerability and ultimate impotence of tyrants was useful to satirists because it allowed them to identify themselves as good royalists. The fact that what made Charles tyrannical – for example, the secret French alliance – could also be construed as a threat to his sovereign power was used to make attacks on his policy look like defenses of his person. Charles was presented as being in physical danger from his whores. The "Articles of High Treason" (1681) against the duchess of Portsmouth accused her of infecting the king with "foul, nauseous and contagious distempers" and of feeding him poison.[58] One poem described her as a Delilah who would shear his "tresses," adding that she "both pollutes his carcass and his power."[59] Another predicted that "she'll with her noisome breath blast even thy face / till thou thyself grow uglier than her grace."[60]

These pieces often ended with an admonition to murder the women.[61] By disposing of his whores, which can be taken either literally or as a metaphor for the political policies that the whores embodied, Charles could "make himself king again." Writers of political pornogaphy, by treating the threats emanating *from* Charles as if they were threats *to* Charles and by identifying the policies in question with the royal mistresses rather than the king, could criticize those policies while casting themselves as loyal to monarchy – a useful thing to be able to do in a political culture obsessed with the horror of regicide, and in which this sentiment was used to silence political criticism.

The contradictory and ambiguous role played by the king's body in these works is striking. The endangered body of the king can, at times, stand in for the endangered nation or bodies of his subjects. At other times, the king, as a sexual aggressor, is the danger to his subjects. Likewise, the king's penis is sometimes equated with his sovereign power, and, at other times, his penis appears to represent his point of vulnerability and his *illusion* of power. These ambiguities can be seen as a product of the unresolved relationship between the king's body and the body politic within Restoration political discourse.

This equivocation about where the king's body ended and

where his kingdom, power or the bodies of his subjects began is precisely what makes it so difficult to define the erotic intention or direction of Restoration political poems. How one relates to an erotic narrative about the king's body depends on how one sees that body in relation to one's own, and the pieces discussed in this essay offer an array of options. Some use techniques, such as ventriloquism, which invite the reader to identify with the king. A reader might, instead, identify with Charles's sexual "victims." Or the pleasure from reading the poem may lie in the opportunity to watch and mock Charles's impotence. Whatever the reader's positioning, it is clear that the fact that political discourse takes the form of sexual narratives, and the fact that these narratives have an ambiguous relationship to the category of pornography, are both related to the contested status of the king's body in Restoration political culture.

It is also clear that the line between what is and what is not considered pornography is politically constructed; that is, constructed in certain political situations to achieve certain political ends. The editions of *Poems on Affairs of State* published after the Revolution of 1688 seem to define their material as virtuous attacks on a corrupt court; hence, not pornographic. This fit in well with the Williamite regime's view of itself. The revolution had been cast by its supporters as an instance of divine providence working to rescue the nation, and, therefore, as a moment of religious and moral regeneration. The presentation of the Restoration's quasipornographic works as "virtuous" legitimized the new regime and gave it a prehistory, suggesting that there was a long-standing struggle of Protestant constitutionalist virtue against popish absolutist vice. In doing so, however, the editors of *Poems on Affairs of State* decontextualized the material they printed and made its meaning appear to be direct and simple. This essay is a first step toward restoring its complexity.

PART TWO

Philosophical and
Formal Qualities

CHAPTER FOUR

The Materialist World

of Pornography

Margaret C. Jacob

A vast philosophical transformation in European thought occurred between the seventeenth and eighteenth centuries: nature was mechanized. Its bodies were atomized, stripped of their appearances and qualities, thus rendered knowable only by virtue of their size, shape, motion and weight. They became simply, unrelentingly, matter in motion. Their telos to move in one direction or another disappeared, replaced by the mechanical interaction of bodies, their inertia if untouched, their push and pull through collision. Any standard account of the Scientific Revolution tells us about the natural philosophers who effected this transformation, and, occasionally, about the specific social context within which Boyle or Newton, Galileo or Descartes operated.[1] In most accounts, the physical bodies germane to the story are presumed to be inanimate, or, in the case of Cartesian physiology, presumed to be living animals. Transformations within European society, the relations among and between human bodies, have never been factored successfully into our understanding of the context that made possible the mechanical vision, the conceptual core of the Scientific Revolution.

Among the many genres of literature presumed to shed light on the world that permitted the mechanization of nature, one, pornography, has never been imagined as relevant. Yet pornography may have more to tell us about the world that gave rise to the new push-pull metaphysics of bodies, both animate and inanimate, than might have previously been suspected. I shall also argue here that pornography existed within, and, in some sense described, new urban social networks made up of many men and some women whose lives were privatized, atomized and individuated, rather like the eroticized bodies found in the literature. As will become evident, philosophical materialism was appropriate in the world of, as well as the texts of, pornography. Only the feared metaphysical underside of the new science could explain the ceaseless desire, the random excess, the sheer exuberance of bodies released from traditional moorings and pious inhibitions now rendered irrelevant by markets and presses, now encouraged by pens made all the more active and virile by their anonymity.

The conceptual ability to mechanize and atomize physical nature emerged roughly between the 1650s and the 1690s within a single Northern and Western European generation, the same generation that also invented a new materialist and pornographic discourse. The pornographic novel, the singular invention of the age, became the vehicle for explaining and inventing sexual bodies now eroticized and described in unprecedented narrative and discursive forms. The novels postulated for the reader a privatized space occupied only by bodies in motion. And, almost as if by design, the pornographic narratives employed philosophical materialism, which their writers extracted from the new mechanical, scientific reading of nature. By 1700, materialism became the preferred, although by no means the only, metaphysics of literary arousal and textualized desire.

Although contemporaneous with the science of Descartes and Boyle, pornography and its market were not the cause of the new scientific discourses. In fact, were there causation, it would be science that provided the needed metaphors. Yet the new erotic narratives quickly embraced mechanistic materialism. The aptness of this new metaphorical and metaphysical resource may provide a key – an imaginative resource – for postulating the lived experience of the urban world of the mid- and late seventeenth century, that social universe which permitted the articulation of both a new metaphysics of nature and a new narrative form. Atomism and materialism had many and diverse social and philosophical origins, and among their social roots would be the untamed world that produced and consumed early modern pornography.

In this social reading, metaphysical materialism, the very heresy so beloved by the new pornographic literature, may be seen as a conceptual shell that encased a new sociability, a nascent but vital civil society. This social life filled a public space that emerged after the mid-seventeenth century in the cities and larger towns of Western Europe, which were more numerous, more populated and, probably, richer. In contrast to the traditional sociability anchored in family, guild, court and church, the new social universe possessed a signal characteristic: men and some women met as individuals, not as members of the traditional corps and corporations where birth, kinship and occupation counted above all else. Freer, more anonymous, they socialized as buyers and sellers, as habitués of coffee houses, cafés, taverns and salons, of clubs, cabarets and eventually Masonic lodges. They met as merchants, shopkeepers, travelers, readers of newspapers, consumers who had some leisure and some extra money; they negotiated, discussed, and, occasionally, even conspired, or spied, or had sex with relative strangers. By the 1690s in London, they could be voters and, hence, were followers of Parliamentary news; in Paris they could be gazetteers or minor government officials; in The Hague they could be ambassadors and actresses, even clandestine agents. In all places they could be lonely visitors there on business, slavetraders, commodity factors or wholesalers. They could be prostitutes, booksellers, or what the age called sodomites, or, perhaps, speculators willing to invest in everything from cotton to pornography itself.[2]

We know about the see-and-be-seen life, the commercial and leisured to-ing and fro-ing of these towns and cities, about the social atomism and randomness and the sometimes cherished anonymity they provided – all of which the new materialism captured and rarefied – from sources as diverse as *The Spectator*, as dry as the toll collection logs of Dutch canal boats, and as juicy as Parisian police reports. From these reports we now know something about the new social universe inhabited by French pornographers and their assistants, both male and female. In the freedom it offered to buy and sell, to profit – when not caught – this new social space may be seen as the analogue of the pornographer's narration, the anonymous bedroom wherein bodies in motion, brought together by individual need and interest, collide just like the atoms of the natural philosophers. Whether in bedroom or market, participants receive pleasure or pain randomly, sometimes even furtively. Thus pornographic discourse provides a missing link between the social and the metaphysical, a link that may help us know more about the boldest men and women of the generation that invented and championed the new science. Their literature and their lives, at least as the police records report them, fit comfortably with the possessive individuals postulated by scientific materialists like Hobbes. Metaphysical materialism was seized upon by pornographers eager to describe, eroticize and, not least, to preach the ethics of the libertine driven by desire, by the relentless motion inherent in matter. Pornographic literature presented by anonymous authors spoke to the same public that read the new journals and novels, that bought and sold, that traveled far and wide and inhabited a universe now seen by us as nascently modern.

The ethical and philosophical boldness expressed by pornography was what made the new cities and the new science so potentially dangerous. In both, the authorities of church and state perceived a possible threat to morality and order, but this perception was not the fault of the major scientists. With the exception of Hobbes and Spinoza, none of the major contributors to the Scientific Revolution wished states or churches any ill will. Indeed, beginning with Galileo and continuing through Newton and Leibniz, every effort was made to Christianize the mechanical philosophy, to ward off and suppress materialism, to retain spirit or immaterial agents as the source and check on motion in the universe, however mechanical the laws were that governed it. Yet, just as pagan naturalism had lurked beneath the surface of the neoplatonic revival of the Renaissance – think of Carlo Ginzburg's lowly miller and naturalist who was eventually executed by the Inquisition for his philosophizing[3] – so too was materialism intrinsic to the philosophical transformation that ushered in the scientific version of modernity.

Materialism is the logical outcome when nature is abstractly mechanized and bodies in motion are made wholly sufficient, encapsulated by the experimental gaze of the natural philosophers. When that logic could not be readily perceived, or was vehemently resisted, a large and generally clandestine literature emerged, much of it pornographic, that drew the inevitable metaphysical conclusion. Where the pious feared the new science would go, and where the orthodox natural philosophers doggedly fought its being taken, the new natural philosophy nevertheless strayed, embraced and de-Christianized eagerly by pornographers and clandestine philosophers. They narrated new scripts imagined from experiences disdained by the traditional social and religious commentators. They enlisted science into service as an intellectual legitimator, and they gloried in both its relentless logic and its appeal to experience and experiment.

Universally censored – except for Hobbes, who slipped through the window of opportunity provided by the English Revolution and published *Leviathan* in 1651, and Spinoza, who lived in the Dutch Republic, where the presses were relatively uncensored – materialist literature was the province of clandestine coteries of publishers, booksellers and their customers. There, too, lurked pornography, the other body of literature replete with natural philosophy, which, after about 1690, became increasingly materialist. Both the materialist and the pornographer were censored, arrested and jailed and their books confiscated because their literature, although in different styles and with different purposes, offered the same threat: it challenged traditional hierarchy, and, frequently, did so intentionally.

Materialism removed the dominance of spirit and made matter and spirit essentially one, thus leaving the clergy useless as arbitrators of a separate spiritual realm. Most versions of early modern materialism – perhaps best described as pantheistic materialism – also made Nature into God, thus eliminating the traditional supernatural source of order and hierarchy in the universe. The most outrageous of the materialist tracts of the eighteenth century was *Le Traité des trois imposteurs* (1719, but in circulation at least by 1710). A portion of this work is a direct translation of Spinoza, and it simply labeled Jesus, Moses and Mohammed as the three great impostors, shifty politicians who invariably lied to their followers.[4] Not content with defaming the Almighty, materialism – like the mechanical philosophy upon which it was based – also eliminated the "forms" of scholastic philosophy. For centuries, spirit and substance had resided in them, as had the qualities and attributes that made kings kingly and the nobility noble. For Catholics, form also explained philosophically the doctrine of transubstantiation. Materialism leveled, and, not surprisingly, the first sectarian agitators for social and economic equality — the English Levellers and Diggers of the 1640s and 1650s — were led by rebel philosophers such as Gerrard Winstanley, who were also pantheists and, hence, materialists.

At the same revolutionary moment the English translation of Lucretius — one of the texts that contributed the atomism so vital to conceptualizing mechanistic nature — alerted readers in its preface to the democratic implications of Epicurean atomism: "But change and Atomes make *this All* / In Order Democratical, / Where Bodies freely run their course, / Without design, or Fate, or Force." Many decades later, when ancient atomism was old news by comparison to the scientific versions of materialism by then available, a witty poem of 1732 makes the same social point nicely: add "mind" to "Nature" and "this Mighty Mind shall be / A Democratic Deity / ...all of which we behold is God, / From Sun and Moon, to Flea and Louse / And henceforth equal — Man and Mouse."[5] Nature and society were concepts knitted together in the patterns of thought available to nascently modern Westerners.

By the late seventeenth century, readers did not have to go to Lucretius, Hobbes or Descartes, or eventually, to *Le Traité des trois imposteurs*, to learn the egalitarian implications of atomism or of nature mechanized: pornography also provided its own subversive metaphysicians and natural philosophers as guides. Invariably, they were philosophers concerned with the material and sexual order, and, by the late seventeenth century, they belonged to two overlapping schools. The first naturalist, the second materialist, they followed one another in chronological order, with materialism becoming pronounced in the 1690s. Although it would never entirely obliterate naturalism, materialism became the natural philosophy of choice among those narrators seeking to write in a voice that would now be described as fictional realism.

The older naturalists offered a heretical version of Aristotelianism, a vision of the sexual as natural, and, to use a favored metaphor for what was to be received by women, the result of the fire that propels the great virile engines. The naturalist pornographer dispensed a metaphysical potion that included Aristotle and the ancients, scholastic medical theory, perhaps even a touch of alchemy, and it relied on nature as simply being there, as a force. The naturalist's understanding of human sexuality was closer to farm and barnyard than to the demonstration tables of the new natural philosophers. Yet the naturalist pornography that surfaced in France in the 1650s, and which never entirely disappeared on either side of the English Channel for the next hundred years, did know and like simple machines. Machines, pumps and engines of indeterminate origin were favored metaphors.

By contrast, the materialists extrapolated from modern sources, such as Hobbes and Descartes, and attempted to narrate a new universe composed solely of atomized, animate bodies in motion, mechanisms driven by the laws of pleasure. The universe of the bedroom created by the materialist pornographers stands as the analogue to the physical universe of the mechanical philosophers. In both, bodies were stripped of their texture, color and smell, of their qualities, and encapsulated as entities in motion, whose very being is defined by that motion. In the universe of the materialist, however, the virile engines have lost their exclusive hold on motion and force: they have been joined by activated, energized female participants. No body, despite how much the pornographer wishes to control it, can be exempt from the newly articulated laws of nature.

Unlike the voice of the new science, some of the newly invented voices of the pornographic naturalists, as well as all of the major pornographic materialists, were women. As the natural philosophical content of pornography gradually shifts from being essentially Aristotelian to being heretically Cartesian, Newtonian or Hobbist, the woman narrator and the female body simultaneously come into their own. Through narration, these female voices move the texts along just as their bodies are compelled by their desires. Their power as narrators resides in the ability of the text to arouse; also empowered is the literary genre itself, and, perhaps in the process, all the new fictional literature of which pornography is but a part. The newly created female narrator titillates and manipulates; she services the expanded literary marketplace and, possibly, even creates new audiences within it. However much the loquacious Fanny Hill or Thérèse, the philosophe were invented to serve the needs of their invariably male, always anonymous authors, it can be argued that both escaped their bondage and gave us timeless narrations because they were speaking out of a nascent social universe that was essentially modern. They were being suggestive to an audience ripe for the invitation, one that may have even acted out in its bedrooms the prescriptions for pleasure so seductively presented by these new and naughty narrators.[6]

Although fictional, the female narrators pose in their texts as real. For our purposes, some of their spoken philosophy may be taken as truthful because it can be shown to have arisen from their creators' reading of ancient and contemporary natural philosophers. But, somewhat more controversially, it will be argued that the female narrators' statements about human nature, about their social world, may also be taken as more, rather than less, truthful when seen in relation to the universe outside the text. It is still obviously male dominated, but now must admit female participation and even female activation. The relative social truthfulness of pornography can be explored by returning to the Paris police reports, and the cells of the Parisian prisons, where we can find glimpses into the lives of the women and men who sold it. These reports permit us to witness, though fleetingly or imperfectly, the men and women whose lives could have come out of the texts, perhaps even recounted there in far too tame a fashion. Both the police reports and pornography reveal the new and atomized social and metaphysical worlds, germane to both men and women, which were being lived and in which an eroticized imagination – supposedly without limits – could exist, and could at least be imagined to flourish. First to be explored are the fictional, pornographic imaginations.

One of the earliest pieces of modern Western pornography, *L'Ecole des filles, ou la philosophie des dames* (1655), combined naturalism and storytelling in a female voice. Many elements of the soon-to-be-triumphant materialist pornography are present in this early tract, most noticeably that of the woman as teacher and describer of sex, although not as fictional narrator and actor. But, in keeping with the metaphysics of Renaissance naturalism, *L'Ecole des filles*, structured as a dialogue between two female cousins, glories in the activity of the male member – "the long engine with the most splendid pleasure in the world [Ce long engin avec le plus grand plaisir du monde]." Although the dialogue's female natural philosopher is an expert anatomist and describer of sexual intercourse who revels in the male member, she has little to say about female bodies and their motion, except as they respond to the gentlemen who come to give them pleasure – "les Messieurs [qui] viennent donner ce plaisir chez elles."[7]

In materialist pornography of the 1680s and later, however, there are numerous female narrators, who first appear in French texts, and who are also actors and philosophers. They were not exactly created by materialism. More accurately, it allowed them a new, more aggressive and dramatic role. Materialism seemed to provide a better metaphysics for the world, a world for which these narrators could now provide language. They insistently proclaim that they have experienced a supposedly uncontrolled sexual universe, which they invite the reader to enter. The female narrators are given materialism as the only philosophy available – indeed, they do not even entertain alternatives – that adequately explains the lustful universe now deemed appropriate for privatized and individualized human beings. Just as Hobbes attempted to write about the political implications of human motion – that is, the passions and the interests compelling self-willed, animate bodies, so, too, did the pornographer seek to capture their fantasies, pleasurable excesses and exploitations, the erotic desires that compel possessive individuals. On occasion, pornographers even credited Hobbes or Descartes with having inspired them.

The shift from naturalism to materialism, and, with it, the shift from description to narration, creates Tullie and Octavie in *L'Académie des dames*, which was a French translation published in Paris in 1680 and a rewrite of the 1660 Latin *Aloisiae Sigaeae Toletanae/Satyra Sotadica*... (figures 4.1 and 4.2). The generic title for the many variations of the original can be *Les Dialogues de Luisa Sigea* or, as the police reports describe it in 1718 when they arrested sellers with multiple copies, simply "D'aloisia."[8] Possibly inspired by the almost contemporaneous *L'Ecole des filles*, the Latin text (and then, in turn, the French) notes that it was authored by a woman. It preaches *libertinage* and teaches about organs and positions as it arouses. A series of dialogues introduce a bisexual mother, various boys and rather brutal men, and all are intended to shock as much by their revelations of secret liaisons and duplicities as by their descriptions of sexual prowess. The Latin dialogues between two cousins invoke by name the classical naturalists, Juvenal, Horace and Ovid, and their Renaissance successors, Boccaccio and Rabelais, Aretino and Machiavelli.

Judicium Veneris.

Jussit Hyblœis tribunal stare diva floribus:
Prœses ipsa jura dicet.   Perv. ven.

FIGURE 4.1. (left) Frontispiece to one of the Latin versions of *L'Académie des dames* (1678).

FIGURE 4.2. (above) Frontispiece to a nineteenth-century French reprint edition of *L'Académie des dames* (Grenoble, 1680). As with the title page to this work (see figure I.4), it is not obvious whether this engraving dates from the seventeenth century.

"D'aloisia's" learned and presumably male author, who chooses to "dress" in female voice could be described as a literary trans-vestite. However, the designation could work only if the obvious egalitarianism lurking in the gender play makes an appearance in our critical response to this or any other text of the new porno-graphic genre.[9]

The playfulness of Tullie and Octavie is only enhanced, and the female characters made more appealing, by the French trans-lation of 1680. It eliminates the opening philosophical oration replete with classical allusions, replacing the Latin with French dialogue and narration. The cousins meet, and, from that moment, private desire envelops them. Tullie seduces the less experienced Octavie, who will soon be married. The action that will precede their intercourse is suggested by the more aggressive Tullie: "I am ravished by seeing you; I will think entirely of you [Je suis ravie de vous voir; je pensois tout presentement à vous]." Octavie's suitor has become sexually aggressive with her: "I have always remarked on his actions, the aggressive movements of a man whom love has rendered the master... [J'ai toujours remarqué dans ses actions, les veritables mouvemens d'un homme, dont l'amours est rendu le maître: mais sur tout depuis quelque tems, il commence a estre plus hardi avec moi...]." She describes his aggressive movements, urged on by the eagerly curious Tullie: "What did he do with his hand? [Que faisoit-il avec sa main?]." Octavie wants Tullie to assist her in "the study of a science that is to me at the same time nec-essary and unknown."[10] They quickly get into bed, and Octavie responds ecstatically to Tullie's caresses: "I make you the mistress of my body."[11] Tullie senses her own power: "You make me the mistress of this path that leads to the sovereign good: ah, I see the door; but alas? I am only able to give myself this power that you give me...."[12] Octavie quickly assists, much to the joy of Tullie: "Ma chère Octavie, mon Amour, embrassé moi étroitement, & reçois, ah, ah, ah, je n'en puis plus, je décharge ah, ah, ah, je meurs de plaisirs."[13]

In the French text, the two cousins are of a similar age, and this softens the element of submission found in the Latin version of the lesbian seduction scene. It also removes most of the tedious classical allusions – the long quotations from Ovid, for example. Both texts describe lesbianism as a separate – but not equal – passion found throughout the world and they leave no doubt that although married, Tullie's preference is for women. Neither text, however, escapes a fascination with the penis, and both versions depict men as shamelessly, even violently, aggressive, dwelling at length on the pain of defloration. Intercourse between men is also mentioned, but, as in *Fanny Hill* (1748), condemned. Of course, naturalist elements remain in both versions of the story; later in the tale the penis is still an engine of force that conquers the constantly receptive Octavie.

Tullie, however, a mere twenty years after her Latin predecessor, knows precisely why and how she is ravished by desire. She is quite philosophically learned, but, in addition, she is steeped in the more contemporary texts of her time. Of course, she continues to cite the ancient philosophers – Hippocratus, Zeno and the Stoics, Empedocles, Galen and Aristotle – on the question of the seat of the soul, but she has found her own definition of the soul in contemporary materialism. In a long passage newly devised for the French text, she presents her conclusion: "I believe that the true seat of the soul is in the testicles of men and women [Je croy que son véritable siège est dans les Testicules de l'homme & de la femme]." Adopting the medical terminology of the time that gave both men and women testicles, but rejecting any of the nonsense found in some medical writing that ascribed activity to the male and passivity to the female in the physiology of reproduction,[14] Tullie believes that all ejaculations or emissions of bodily fluid by both men and women, however brief "du plaisir vénérien," stem from the material seat of both vitality and pleasure.[15] Ultimately, Tullie and Octavie's desire for one another gives way to their fixation on heterosexual pleasure – undoubtedly telling us more about their creator than about them – but not before they introduce the materialist woman narrator that occurs again in the major works of both French and English eighteenth-century pornography.

Like her eighteenth-century successors, Tullie is able to formulate her materialism in language that suggests she has been reading among the moderns. She may even be trying to tease those who would like to know what she has been reading when, just prior to placing her finger inside Octavie, she drops an assertive, italicized *ergo* in her clinching argument about the joys of sex: "I have come to tell you that if the semen is the seat of the soul... *ergo* each drop that leaves it, is a portion [Je te viens de dire, si la semence est le siège de l'ame (comme il n'en faut point douter) *ergo* chaque goût qui sort en est une portion]."[16] The Cartesian sound of the passage resonates with similar extrapolations from Descartes that justified materialism in much of Europe's clandestine literature, from the 1650s to La Mettrie and Diderot in the 1740s.[17]

Tullie and Octavie briefly introduce another theme that will recur in materialist pornography, one well known to its censors: "I certainly believe and it is true, that the civil laws are contrary to those of nature; but this is so in order to avoid the disorders that might happen in the world [Je le crois bien; & il est vrai que les loix civiles sont contraires en cela à celles de la nature; mais c'est seulement pour eviter les desordres qui pourroient arriver dans le monde]." The laws of the senses, of human nature driven by needs and interest, ultimately take precedence over the laws devised by the existing governments. Thus, pornographic or obscene literature frequently attacked the prevailing theories that justified political authority and mocked the representatives of that authority. Even the anonymous naturalist in *L'Ecole des filles* says "that if women governed the churches, as do the men who have the engines, they would turn everything upside down."[18] The men, she assures us, have introduced jealousy into the world.

In *Vénus la populaire, ou Apologie des maisons de joye* (1727), the anonymous author, who is claimed to be English (perhaps rightly given the cadence of the French), and who writes from an essentially naturalist perspective, credits Hobbes with providing the necessary analogy that permits the legal satisfaction of lust. He says that "many of those who have written about Government [have done so] by a comparison of the political body with the natural body, and it is...done by the celebrated Hobbes in *Leviathan*. In order to make use ourselves of this allegory, we can consider the spirit of debauchery as a kind of appetising [*peccante*] humor in the body politic, which envelopes the exterior parts [i.e., the penis] which it finds subject to infection."[19] The erect penis is mechanistically relieved only by giving "public permission to found houses of debauchery which [offer] a kind of legal evacuation" which, in turn, improves the health of male citizens. The rest of the tract elaborates on a traditional medical idea, describing how women capable of conceiving must have their parts lubricated so that conception will occur. In order that they are prepared "for the usage which Nature destined them, they must have a sensation subtle and delicate from the approach of the virile organs which excite in women an exquisite pleasure."[20] However happy the naturalist was in his house of joy and debauchery, he could not escape the rules of procreation. The male is the activator in procreation; the female passively awaits the engine that she craves, the engine which alone contains the seed of life. By contrast, Hobbes the materialist saw that, as animate bodies, women could be fully participant and equally desirous, could be active as initiators as well as receivers, and that only force and hereditary property rights kept them unequal.

Women in materialist pornography, often still social victims and hence social inferiors, have now become not only irrepressible participants, but also guides to the universe of the senses. Within their realm, these female materialist philosophers – now found easily on both sides of the Channel – were relentlessly philosophical about the nature of the human order. By the late eighteenth century the female philosophers of the pornographic literature had become so commonplace as to be stock characters, and were generally depicted as enlightened prostitutes. For example, there is one routinely described in *Harris's List of Covent-Garden Ladies: or, Man of Pleasure's Kalender...* (1788). This list of London prostitutes is complete with addresses that refer to real streets and places. It may have been a fictitious work and certainly its descriptions were satiric, but, for our purposes its Mrs. Gr—ff—n is real enough. She is listed as somewhat down on her luck, plying her trade near Union-Stairs, Wapping, where she can be recognized as "a comely woman, about forty.... Indeed she has acquired great experience in the course of twenty years study, in *natural philosophy*, in the University of Portsmouth, where she was long the ornament of the back of the point. She is perfectly mistress of all her actions, and can proceed regularly from the dart of her tongue...."[21] Although aged by the standards of the *Harris's List*, Mrs. Griffin is a long-schooled actor in her own right, as well as a distinctively eighteenth-century kind of prostitute, a theorist as well as a practitioner.

It seems reasonable to argue that the Mrs. Griffins are not merely narrators, but are also emblematic of the new philosophical and social universes revealed and championed in the pornographic literature that they helped sell. Before these universes came to exist, the prick (*le vit*) was the sole locus of motion, the engine in the universe of pleasure. With their advent, the female body (and the orifice, *le con* or cunt) joins in and sometimes even initiates this motion. In the pornographic moment, here focused on for its democratic implications, *le con* achieves equality with *le vit*, and both are assisted by the philosophical materialism drawn from the new science.

By the end of the eighteenth century neither organ will have to work very hard. One German pornographer of the 1790s, inspired by industrial progress, found "an English invention," *die stimulations maschiene*, which was powered electrically and swung the man and the woman in and out of each other, thus stimulating their now effortless flight to ecstasy.[22] The text assured the reader that the power of machines could compensate even for impotence (figure 4.3).

However liberating mechanistic materialism could be made to appear, it never entirely displaced the simpler, more commonplace engines found in the older naturalist literature: both pornographic discourses overlap in time and cohabitate for much of the century. In 1718, the preface to an English translation of a naturalist tract of 1629 on flogging explained how the philosophy underlying the older naturalist genre operated: "nor ought any Man to be offended at a Naturalist who searches into the Causes of a Distemper, and shews how they may proceed from the Springs of Nature herself, without having Recourse to Fancy, Fiction and Ridiculous Diabolical Inchantments."[23] More a teller of philosophical tales that often had an overtly political message than a fictional realist, the naturalist unlike the novelist, saw nature as a self-contained entity, transparent and morally neutral, without need of artifice by which to effect her conquest. Emerging early in the seventeenth century in opposition to a vast religious literature that interpreted passions as existing only to be controlled

FIGURE 4.3. The Mechanical View of Intercourse. From *Amors experimental-physikalisches Taschenbuch* (1798).

and subjugated, naturalist literature could argue that however forceful the conquest, "[t]he good effect excuses the Horror of the Application; for things are not to be esteem'd good or evil by pain or pleasure but by their usefulness and their unusefulness."[24]

For the naturalist, passions and desires are inherently good and hence useful. He could prescribe the joys of flogging, and could even proclaim that women enjoy it. These arguments did not, however, lead the naturalist to proclaim the equality of male and female desire, as a tract on hermaphrodites accompanying the essay on flogging makes clear. However often hermaphrodites find natural pleasures, the order of nature has it that "Men are more easy to be limited in the Pleasures of Venus than Women; as they are endowed with more reason." This same author describes sadism and lesbianism between female hermaphrodites, and portrays the whole disingenuously "as an innocent entertainment... without any views of inciting Masculine-Females to Amorous Tryals with their own sex."[25] Naturalists, operating within an essentially Aristotelian framework, could glory in sexual activity and create completely private worlds; they could even seek to arouse. Their artifice, though, was limited by their assumption of male activity and female passivity – which is not to imply that women wanted less sex than men – and by their assumption of male rationality which serves to bring order to the reproductive process. In this model, the naturalist simply presumed the transparently natural and unnatural in sexual matters. He presumed male desire and male reason in the activation and control of passion, however desirable and morally neutral its expression.

The naturalist claims to speak honestly and openly about things sexual, either to instruct or to arouse by just using the words – especially the naughty ones – and, in some instances, to attempt fiction while also being didactic. But by the late seventeenth century, when naturalist pornography flows into the materialist genre, the new literary form begins to look noticeably different from the naturalist. Materialism seems to be emerging as the "natural" companion of the pornographic novelist, the very teller of the sexual tale that has plot, action and characters. The metaphysics of materialism permitted randomness and the unexpected, an infinitude of desires, elaborate movements of all body parts, tensions, crescendos and carefully crafted climaxes, all of which required the artifice of fiction, like the new laws of nature, to order and explain them.

The French naturalist who created *Vénus dans le cloître ou la Religieuse en chemise* (1683, with an English translation in the same year), gives a further illustration of the subversive qualities of the older genre (figure 4.4). The author employs the dialogue form to castigate the sexual exploits of the clergy and urges that we "be guided by that pure and innocent Nature, by following intirely the Inclinations which she gives to us." He (to gender the anonymous) goes on to describe clerical promiscuity with a relish that suggests anticlericalism, and not sexual arousal, to be the tract's main purpose.[26] The distributors of the tract may have agreed with this assessment. When one of them was imprisoned in Paris in 1704 for "distributing libels, scandalous books against Religion and the State and good mores," he also had with him books aimed directly against Louis XIV and his mistress, Madame de Maintenon.[27] Naturalism may have had its philosophical limitations, but this never inhibited its ability to be subversive.

John Cleland, the most skillful eighteenth-century English pornographer, best explained the limitation naturalism imposed when it assumed a transparent understanding of "pure" nature. In his *Dictionary of Love*, he distances himself from the commonplace notion that "[n]ature gives excellent lessons; it is enough to listen to them, without other instruction." Cleland admonishes the would-be lover that such views are no longer sufficient: "this

FIGURE 4.4. Title page to *Vénus dans le cloître ou la Religieuse en chemise* (Düsseldorf, 1746).

VENUS
dans le
CLOITRE ou la RELIGIEUSE
en CHEMISE

is, however, reasoning upon the principles of antiquity, as false in love, as those of Aristotle in Natural Philosophy." Articulating the analogy to the new science, he explains that loving, like physics, "having lost its plain unsophisticate nature, and being now reduced into an art, has, like other arts, had recourse to particular words and expressions." He warns that a reliance upon Nature "may even be pernicious to those who trust to it, in a passion, of which Art has usurped the government."[28] As a novelist, Cleland knew about the wiles of artifice, and knew that, under the new dispensation provided by fictive realism, passion is so much the contrivance of artifice. When Cleland wants to express what true love might be like, he can only resort to an idealistic passage from *Clarissa*. The materialist pornographers, among whom Cleland was an unsurpassed master, sought to teach by narration all the artifices of lovemaking, all its words and expressions; they also sought to perfect and empower the newly discovered artifice of fiction.

Fanny Hill's contemporary French counterpart, *Thérèse philosophe* (1748), further elucidates the role played by materialism in the matured pornographic genre (figure 4.5). Like Fanny, Thérèse is a sexual traveler and adventurer; unlike Fanny, she is a women of some means who never takes money for sex. And unlike Fanny, who is by no means philosophically ignorant and is, of course, a materialist, Thérèse is more the philosophe. While narrating her exploits, she tells that she is not simply teaching about nature, but about living out the implications of the laws of nature: "I repeat to you that there is a need which the immutable laws of nature puts in us; it is also in the hands of nature that we hold the remedy for alleviating that need [Je vous le repeté c'est un besoin que les Loix immuables de la Nature existent en nous, c'est aussi des mains de la Nature que nous tenons le remède que je vous indique pour soulager ce besoin]."[29] She also implies that the laws of nature may be said to exist solely for their utility, because they permit the expression of human need; certainly transparent nature is no longer sufficient. The mechanization of nature holds the key to passion, just as passion verifies nature's new laws. Thérèse explains: "It is the arrangement of organs, the dispositions of the fibers, a certain movement, the liquids, which make up the genre of the passions...nature is uniform [l'arrangement des organes, les dispositions des fibres, un certain mouvement, des liqueurs, donnent le genre des passions, les dégrés de force dont elles nous agitent contraignent la raison, déterminent la volonté dans les plus petites, comme dans les plus grandes actions de notre vie...la nature est uniforme]."[30] Thus, in anal intercourse, Thérèse quickly understands that she must also move, to create "un mouvement opposé." The senses operate mechanically and, from the physical experience of good and evil, humans can derive moral definitions of good and evil: "C'est un mécanique certain, ma chère fille; nous sentons, & nous n'avons d'idées du bien & du mal physique comme du bien & du mal moral, que par la voie des sens."[31] Indeed, Thérèse's vision is so over-determined by the mechanical laws that are, nevertheless, so much controlled by her literary artifice, she eventually finds it possible to write them off altogether. But not before they had been served in her own fictive creation, as the rationale for the men and women she describes and justifies.

The late seventeenth-century shift from nature to the laws of nature, from naturalism to materialism, not only created the metaphysical underpinnings of the female narrator, it also engendered a proliferation of French and English characters that were to achieve a certain literary immortality in their genre: Tullie and Octavie in their "academy of women," Thérèse, Fanny Hill, Julie the philosophe (or the good patriot of the French Revolution), and the earlier, less well known Eulalie, whose correspondence appeared in 1785.[32] Their power derives from the descriptive force of the new narratives of arousal. These manage to arouse

because, like the scientist, the pornographic philosophical narrators rivet our attention on nature. They encapsulate bodies, capture and replicate their motions, place them in a universe of
limitless possibilities, and, in the process, abstract them from
any determining universe. The essence of the new pornographic
moment lies in the arousal induced by watching the interaction
of isolated, activated bodies, supposedly uncontrolled by any laws
save those of nature or physiology (figure 4.6). Whether they are
masturbating or observed while having sex, whether alone or in
a crowd, the atomized bodies in the new pornography are totally
privatized. In the process, they become roughly, perhaps inad-
vertently, equalized; they are as similar, as equal and metaphysi-
cally ungendered as the atoms and planets. They occupy a place
conceptually analagous to the space and time of mechanical philosophers: an abstraction divorced from the everyday space in
which are seen only the appearances or qualities of bodies clothed
and decorated, disguised by color and texture, bodies visible to
the public eye, encoded with the actual or imagined symbols of
status, power and sexuality.

Both the pornographic literature and the philosophical treatises of the new science postulate a private space where nothing
matters but the force of projectiles, the compulsive pushing and
pulling of bodies. Both promised power over the body, but, in
its ability to arouse, pornography made good on the promise. To
simplistically believe that all that needs to be said of pornography as a genre is that it was created by men for men is to miss
the subversion rationalized by materialism and symbolized by the
female narrator. That women should be the guides in so much of
pornography may be a sign of their anonymous (and probably, but
not certainly) male creators' desire – conscious or unconscious –
to postulate and advocate a commonplace, domesticated sexuality
that could be experienced by everyone, to encourage a private

space where fantasy is permitted, even if it is never quite fulfilled. They may have wanted to control this space, to justify it to the less bold, to make a profit from the sale of its literature: all these reasons provide sufficient motives for the creation of the genre. But there were real bodies, clothed and textured, who invented, distributed and purchased this literature, and it is to their subversive universe and its revelations about the invention of pornography that we must finally turn.

The Paris police records reveal that many of the major works of French pornography examined here were produced and sold by groups of men and women, sometimes with as many as two dozen people suspected of being involved. No other genre of forbidden literature found in these records can be shown so consistently to have been the work of veritable companies; sometimes seven or more people were incarcerated for their involvement with a single book. In no other genre of interest to the police, including Jansenist works, do women so regularly appear in the records. One man, a minor nobleman who already had a criminal record, was picked up in a cabaret for having put up the money for *Thérèse philosophe*. One woman stitched together the pages; men and women sold it. Another woman, Caterine Marguerite le Cocq, who went by the androgynous name she apparently volunteered, "Catin le Cocq" (*catin* being a prostitute, *le cocq* possessing the same attributes as a cock), distributed it. The work entailed the efforts of printers, engravers, distributors and booksellers, and all were assigned to Parisian prisons where on average they did two years for their trouble. The network for *Thérèse* included the publisher or, perhaps, just the distributor in Liège, and their intention, according to the police, had been to produce another edition of the very popular piece of pornography, *Histoire de Dom Bougre, portier des Chartreux*.[33] The title character translates as "Master Bugger," with *buggery*, like the old

FIGURE 4.5. Frontispiece to *Thérèse philosophe* whose text reads: "Sensual pleasure and philosophy make the sensible man happy. He embraces pleasure by taste and he loves philosophy with his reason" (The Hague, undated, 1748?).

FIGURE 4.6. Thérèse philosophe with an aristocratic lover. From *Thérèse philosophe* (The Hague, undated, 1748?).

FIGURE 4.7. Anti-clerical scene. From *Histoire de Dom B—, portier des Chartreux* (Frankfurt edition, 1748).

French *bougre*, being an arcane English word for sodomy (figure 4.7). In 1748, a few years after its publication, this work appears to have been selling well, along with "D'aloisia" and various salacious works and political satires against Louis XV and Madame de Pompadour.[34]

The original producers of *Dom Bougre* had, however, met a fate similar to that of the distributors of *Thérèse*. *Dom Bougre* recounted lesbianism, sodomy and incest while assuring its readers that the true vices were always the province of the great and the clerical. For perpetrating this distinctively anticlerical piece of work the police arrested one Charles Nourry, a "tonsured cleric, the sacristan at St. Sebastien in Triere" and put him in the Bastille in 1741. Twenty-three others involved in *Dom Bougre* were either arrested or interrogated. Nourry's sister was questioned; for her part one Mademoiselle Ollier, the young daughter of a bookseller, was exiled to Toulouse. For doing particularly salacious engravings of monks and nuns that such readers as Casanova praised for "their remarkable beauty" – a modern audience would probably find them more explicit than artful – the engraver also did time; he was accompanied by a tapestry maker and his wife. An aristocrat was suspected but not arrested, as was a Swedish baron, and one M. Stella, an Italian who was a shopkeeper. The suspected publisher, Pierre Paupie in The Hague, well known for publishing enlightened and Masonic works, was also mentioned in the reports. He, too, would have fit the police's description of an author of other infamous works of the same year: "He is a student of Voltaire."[35] The perpetrators of *Dom Bougre* may be reasonably described as a temporarily assembled international "syndicate" which, in 1741, had clearly sensed sufficient profit to make the danger worth everyone's while.

Both pornographic coteries involved with these famous works of the 1740s were hauled in by the authorities during a decade in which sedition had been exceptionally vocal. This crescendo of discontent surfaced during the War of Austrian Succession, and the police records are replete with the names of men and women arrested for selling satires against the increasingly unpopular Louis XV and his mistress, Madame de Pompadour. They were accused, quite precisely, of "making insolent discourses against the King and Madame de Pompadour." A volunteer in the cavalry and four women – one the wife of a valet, another a servant – were imprisoned for having said that "the king was an imbecile and a tyrant... who allowed himself to be governed by his whore." What was needed, they said, were people who would deliver their country from this tyranny. Two years later, in 1751, conspirators were arrested apparently attempting to do just that.[36]

In prison, these conspirators would have joined the men and women who had already spent two years there for perpetrating *Thérèse*. They would, however, have missed Diderot, long since released after his imprisonment for having written a pornographic satire, *Les Bijoux indiscrets* (1748) which, among many topics, also took aim at the king and his mistress.[37] Other cells contained yet more booksellers of libels, engravers and colporteurs involved with *L'Almanach de Priape* and various "obscene engravings," the ubiquitous sellers of Jansenist works, and others who had brought from Holland "satirical songs against respectable people." Of course there were also spies, sodomites and religious enthusiasts, and, earlier in the century, there had been many alchemists, both male and female; however, they all but disappear by the 1720s. Perhaps the most lonely of all the incarcerated was Mr. Medina, described in the records as "a Jew previously a merchant accused of the crime of sodomy in Holland... [who] had lived in Brussels where he had been imprisoned; and in prison he had composed *nouvelles politiques* which he sent to Paris, to the provinces and to other countries." When caught in Paris in 1742, Mr. Medina, undeterred, was selling the same, or similar, libelous political literature.[38]

If Mr. Medina was a Jew, a sodomite and a pamphlet trader, he was also a man with political ideas and international connections. Mr. Medina, real or fictive, may be taken as symbolic of the new urban society. By the time he arrived on the scene, the scene had existed, at least in the police records, for four or more decades. Even pornography, in its ambivalence about male homosexuality, never did justice to the world Mr. Medina may have inhabited. Neither naturalist nor materialist descriptions, however rich and, hence, reductive the sexual details, hint at what the police records suggest. As early as 1706, the Paris police had raided a cabaret and arrested a Simon Langlois, who was accused of creating "an assembly for a kind of order of young men who want to enter it and who take the names of women, making marriages together... they make these assemblies ordinarily in the Cabaret du Chaudron, rue St. Antoine... where after having drunk to excess they commit the sin of sodomy; they make certain ceremonies for the reception of proselytes and they take oaths of fidelity to the Order."[39] Langlois and his band of initiates playfully mocked the orders of the great and the clerical. Imitating the aristocratic and chivalric orders, Langlois took the title "le Grand Maître." His associate, Bertault, preferred the title "la mère des novices [the mother of novices]."[40]

Could this urban sexual underworld have been another kind of fiction, the work of the overwrought imagination of the police? It seems unlikely, because in precisely this period in London, Ned Ward recorded the existence of just such male homosexual clubs complete with rituals, female names and marriage ceremonies.[41] In 1715, the Paris police were once again in the cabarets, where they arrested Le Mar, "the principal of this troop who debauch young men."[42] In these records from both sides of the English Channel can be witnessed an internationally similar urban and homosexual culture spread by the very travelers, sellers and, possibly, sailors, who made the cities and the markets such vibrant, anonymous, intriguing and suggestive places for men and women of all proclivities.

Once it appeared, the culture of sodomy persevered despite terrifying punishments. In 1781 in Antwerp, Mr. "Stockaert" or "Mr. Stocker" – the French-speaking magistrates trying to render what was either a Flemish or an English name could not make up their minds – was imprisoned for seducing four young men aged between eighteen and twenty-one. The local authorities wrote to the Privy Council in Brussels, which represented the Austrian government in the southern Netherlands, to consult about his fate. The recommendation of the Antwerp magistrates was simple and dire: we have condemned him to death and "the judges propose that he be secretly strangled in prison...and make the four men he seduced assist in this execution." They went on to explain to the Privy Council, which had ultimate jurisdiction, that such a punishment will teach them the enormity of their crime, and a public execution would only add further shock while increasing public knowledge of the crime. Further, they said, it might also so traumatize the young men that they would never survive the terror of the experience. They, of course, will only be spared the same punishment if they swear an eternal silence. But the Privy Council had other ideas.[43] Theirs was, after all, supposed to be an enlightened regime. They ordered that Mr. Stocker be transported to the border with as much secrecy as possible and banished forever. Perhaps we can now guess why, voluntarily or not, Mr. Medina had made his way from Brussels to Paris a few decades earlier. Perhaps it is also possible to understand better why pornography was considered so shocking and wonder why it was so relatively lacking in sadism until Sade transformed the genre.

What the police and magistrates tell us, and what other less biased records from both sides of the Channel also suggest, is that the cities had become places that we would recognize. Their modernity leaps out at us from the pages of the philosophical and pornographic books, in the commercial consortia of their creators and sellers. It is found in the risk-taking of people in illicit cabarets, in pubs and clubs, even from the tame and respectable records of freemasons and their lodges. This new urban sociability, easily visible from the 1690s onward, encompassed both men and some women, heterosexual and homosexual, who could be perceived either as quite ordinary and respectable, or as dissidents, nonconformists, conspirators, or just profit-seekers or survivors in the business of subversive literature. When approaching this new urban society formally and philosophically, the movement it supported is called the Enlightenment. When seen through novels or pornography, it is the space inhabited by a newly literate public. When the police, representing both *roi et foi* dipped into the enclaves that composed it they sought the illegal and the subversive. When they saw a threat to the state, they could execute, banish or incarcerate people for years.

For his activities in the cabaret, Simon Langlois got only two months. To eighteenth-century Parisian authorities, sodomy, when not combined with other offences and not done in public, may not have always seemed as dangerous as good, philosophical pornography, such as *Thérèse philosophe*. Indeed, the political turbulence of the 1740s led to what the police called "indecent libels" against the king and his mistress, and it forms the background for a new reading of *Thérèse philosophe*. If Madame de Pompadour is the evil whore of a tyrannical king, then Thérèse is her foil, the good prostitute, the preacher of enlightenment and the religion of nature. Consciously or not, her materialism offered the only philosophy of nature capable of addressing the individualism, the passions and the interests, the freedom and nonconformity, the disrespect and subversion to be found in the cities of Western Europe from early in the eighteenth century, if not before. The War of Austrian Succession, fought incompetently by an unenlightened regime, disrupted cities from Paris to Amsterdam. Their denizens struck back with subversive *livres philosophiques* and seditious pamphlets, some of which, like *Thérèse* and *Les Bijoux indiscrets*, continued to be read and enjoyed long after the turbulent moment of their creation (figure 4.8).

Neither pornographers, scientists nor materialists could have conceptualized their bodies and space without the simultaneous existence of these privatized self-interested individuals. When endowed with erotic impulses (as distinct from illegal ones) they inhabit not prison cells but pornographically re-created bedrooms. When they enter the political arena once reserved for kings and courts, they are depicted in the political writings of the new mechanical and materialist philosophers such as Hobbes. In the pornographic literature, the Cartesian *cogito*, with all its egoism and self-reference, becomes sensate; the ego knows itself only because it sensually experiences every object that it desires. Knowing about Catin le Cocq and Mr. Medina, it can be concluded that both the philosophic and pornographic sexual literature of the age could barely keep up with the complexity and originality of a universe in which the police of the absolutist state also, though for quite different reasons, had an interest.

Sometimes, and rarely, works explored not the sexual but the social universe of Catin, Medina and Langlois, glorifying it. One such French tract of the 1720s creates a homoerotic utopia in which the narrator says, "the tribades are a visionary nation, indefinable, and incomprehensible, that enjoys pleasure to excess

FIGURE 4.8. "The Voluptuary Father Dirrag whipping Mademoiselle Eradice."
From *Thérèse philosophe* (The Hague, undated, 1748?).

[Les Bratides [tribades] sont une Nation visionnaire, indefinissable, incomprehensible, aimant le plaisir à l'exces...]." In yet another homoerotic kingdom of the Order of Manchette, the men call each other brothers. The utopian tract about the women of the tribadic nation and the men of Manchette belongs in the naturalist genre. It does not seek specifically to arouse – unless its repetitive use of certain obscene words can be considered titillating – but it does proclaim the existence of distant and free kingdoms run by buggers and tribades.[44] In 1752, a priest was exiled on "suspicion of Manchette."[45] Is this a case of life imitating art? Could there actually have been an Order of Manchette? A number of French authors of the time refer to it; so, too, do the Paris police records, which suggest the existence of "orders" with inititation rites, ceremonies and the taking of new names.[46] It is improbable that the exact nature of these orders will ever now be known. What can be known, and from a variety of sources, is that there were groups of sodomites, possibly even tribades, in the cities of Western Europe, and that a subculture appears to have existed by the mid- or late seventeenth century.

During the reign of Louis XIV (1643–1715), the pornographic and the obscene began to battle with the authorities of church and state. Early pornography found in that posture of defiance, particularly in the naturalist genre, set a theme to which the literature returned repeatedly right into the 1790s. Especially during the deeply troubled later years of Louis XIV's reign, when Protestants and religious enthusiasts populated the prisons, pornography frequently focused not on alternative kingdoms or sexualities but on the corruption of the existing authorities in church and state. In a naturalist style more obscene than pornographic, and thus, more teasing than arousing, one tract bitterly attacked the clergy and "their tyranny."[47] From this same defiant posture, other naturalist tracts attacked corruption by using animal scatology; *Le Cochon mitré* [the mitred pig] used the metaphor in 1689, precisely during the repressive period of Louis's reign, to describe the morals of the court and clergy.[48]

Naturalists had a particular ax to grind against the clergy, whose power may account for the survival of the genre throughout the century. Exemplifying this genre in the 1730s is a rare naturalist work of verse that was written in Dutch, rather than being translated into it. This work has Jesuits, who are probably in the Austrian Netherlands, flagellating the bare buttocks of those who have come to confess, enjoying anal intercourse, watching nuns urinate and, thereby, succumbing to the temptations of the devils who peer at them from sexually explicit engravings (figures 4.9 and 4.10).[49] When being subversive, naturalists could also be very naughty.

Thus, naturalism always enjoyed a place in pornographic and obscene literature well into the eighteenth century, even if, by then, purely naturalist works read very differently, and less engagingly, from narrated and materialist works. The latter embraced narration for its power to describe bodies in motion and, hence, to arouse. By contrast, naturalists made a gesture toward the new natural philosophies but, generally, continued to describe sexuality. Throughout its long history, one major purpose of the genre, which it bequeathed to the materialist, always lay elsewhere: to launch polemics against traditional authority. An example is the English tract, *A Voyage to Lethe; by Capt. Samuel Cock* (1741). Its male narrator describes the imaginary and libertine land of Lethe, which existed before the Flood: "I conceive [it] to be well worth the Consideration of the Public, and particularly of the Royal Society." Captain Cock, the narrator, is the youngest of twelve sons whose great-grandfather "had an intimacy with the mother of Oliver Cromwell and May have made Oliver." Because Lethe turns out to be a place of debauchery and obscenity inhabited by

FIGURE 4.9. A Jesuit Inspects Buttocks of a Urinating Woman. From *Historische print en Dicht Tafereelen, van Jan Baptist Girar en Juffrou Maris Catharina Cadiere* (1735).

FIGURE 4.10. Devils Watch while a Jesuit Sodomizes a Young Woman. From *Historische print en Dicht Tafereelen, van Jan Baptist Girar en Juffrou Maris Catharina Cadiere* (1735). This and figure 4.9 may have some affiliation to the literature about witchcraft and demonology.

placemen and churchmen, this work aims to be a libertine satire and it is not specifically pornographic. By making reference to the natural philosophers, Cock invokes the pornographic genre, but, like other English obscene works of the 1720s through the 1740s, this is an attack on the licentiousness and corruption of court Whiggery written from a republican perspective.[50] Its naturalism was suitable to a political message with populist overtones that was aimed against the prevailing oligarchy.

The political and philosophical never deserted the pornographic genre in both France and England up to the end of the century. As late as 1789 in England, *Harris's List* of London prostitutes takes the time to be philosophical as well as political: "no enthusiasm is so strong, so stimulous, as that of copulation; it brings its warrant from nature's closest cabinet... why should the victims of this natural propensity... be hunted like outcasts from society, be perpetually griped by the hand of petty tyrany?" The persecution of the sexual is the work of clergy and magistrates, who are the real prostitutes: "Is not the minister of state who sacrifices his country's honour to his private interest... more guilty than her?"[51] In France, just at the moment when Harris asked his rhetorical question, the guilt of the clergy and magistrates was about to be adjudicated. Only within that revolutionary process, as Lynn Hunt argues in a later essay, did pornography begin to change. In effect, the French Revolution answered Harris's question affirmatively and, in the process, reordered not only the political but also the social and sexual universe.

The anonymous French author of *Les Bordels de Paris* (1790) was responding to this reordering when he proclaimed that the old ministers of state, not the new prostitutes, were the true corrupters of virtue. Now the revolution promised to fulfill all the pornographer's fantasies. More a commentator on the possibilities for license released by the demise of clergy and magistrates than a guide, the author of the tract about Paris bordellos spoke as a good, but sensible, patriot who believed that prostitution had got somewhat out of hand. He proposed a house in every *faubourg* that would hold 400 women and be staffed by an abbess and a doctor. He also wanted "an amphitheater, a vast galerie, properly enlightened... [where] all the nymphs consecrated to public service... would be able to satisfy the curious [afin que les curieux les... amateurs puissent faire un choix capable tout à la fois de les animer et de les satisfaire]." Such a vast site for prostitution would cost money, but this industrious promoter of the art has a solution: "As it would take two million to proceed with such a useful establishment, we have found some capitalists who would furnish us with the funds, who would want, understandably, their entree assured, and who would create some matching stock, carrying interest at 5% per annum [Comme il faut deux millions pour procéder à cet etablissement utile, nous avons trouvé des capitalistes qui nous fourniront les fonds, qui auront (comme de raison) leurs grandes entrées, et qui formeront des actions partielles, portant interest à cinq pour cent par an]."[52] The author and advocate of the universe, first explored by the pornographers, is so certain of the survival of his establishment in the new revolutionary freedom that problems have become essentially managerial.

Once again affirming the relationship with their social world, the themes and interests found in pornography changed markedly in the last decades of the century. At that time, French materialist pornography turned overtly political and, in so doing, joined its concerns with the mainstream of English and French materialist writings from Toland to d'Holbach. Aided by a now commonplace self-justification based on materialism, and, thus, by a metaphysical rationale for its own usefulness, pornography also began to preach. Sexual repression is dangerous to society, and not useful among equals; according to the philosophers, the savage in the woods, master only of himself, is healthier than the religious man sequested in his cloister.[53] In a frontal assault on propriety, one French materialist writing in 1788 and posturing as a man of science could proclaim universal sexual freedom while eliminating certain practices as being the result of repression. These are generally found in the cloisters: homosexuality, masturbation and flagellation, especially if done with children. The author claimed to be an enlightened doctor, and to be writing in the service of "the state and love." And, true to the praise offered of Joseph II, there was now some despotism offered along with enlightenment.[54]

Materialism was so commonplace by the 1780s that it had itself been domesticated and become prescriptive. Some would even say it had become repressive. By then, the preachy Julie of *Julie philosophe* (1791) has had standard lessons in "experimental physics," read Rousseau and traveled through the corridor of revolution from Paris to Amsterdam.[55] Although a vehement supporter of the French Revolution and an atheist, she is hardly as naughty or philosophically astute as her mid-century predecessor, Thérèse. Julie is too busy traveling and experiencing. Julie, apparently not having read about the new houses and capitalists in *Les Bordels de Paris*, nor having taken the men of science very seriously about what could be legislated away by the supposedly enlightened, is also naively convinced that thanks "to the enlightened and to libertinism, women will be able to be all that they want."[56] Even in 1791 — perhaps the last year when that would be true — it was still possible to be naive to the complexities of the materialist world that pornography sought to narrate and describe. As an anonymous contemporary of Julie put it, the study of the great scientists should now permit new and vigorous patriots and citizens to enjoy themselves completely and to explore unimpeded "Nature the Sovereign of the entire world."[57]

Thérèse, on the other hand, is a creation of considerable sophistication, and as such, she deserves the last philosophical word. She had begun life with promiscuous parents, got caught masturbating, went to a convent where she experienced much joy, and, in the process, became a quite sophisticated natural philosopher. In her spirited book (which made her famous), Thérèse cannot decide which she enjoys more, narrating her sexual exploits or being the philosophe. She does both very well and very entertainingly. Thérèse manages one of the best explications of materialism to be found in the clandestine and anonymous literature of the century, and, in fact, goes futher than most of those explications. Thérèse has understood the usefulness, and, hence, the temporality and dispensability, of philosophical materialism itself. Borrowing an idea from Le Traité des trois imposteurs, she has figured out that the leaders of the major religions, being politicians, had lied about nature and its laws. The idea they invented, as we have seen, even got picked up by the materialists: "Dame Nature...is an imaginary being; it is a word void of sense. The first chiefs of the religions, the first politicians, embarrassed by the idea that they must give good and bad morals to the public have imagined a being between God and us, and they have rendered it the author of our passions, our miseries and our crimes." Thérèse continues: "I see clearly that both God and Nature are the same thing," and, thus, neither exists.[58]

Materialism was the perfect intellectual construction of the social world that created and circulated it. It permitted the mechanical descriptions of inanimate bodies and the atoms which composed them to be applied to newly released desires, passions and interests, now the province of the animate. First, it freed the imagination of Hobbes, then, it worked its charms on the pornographers. But only Thérèse, its practitioner as well as its theorist, understood that if early modern materialism had not existed, someone among the philosophers, or pornographers, or sodomites would have to have invented it.

CHAPTER FIVE

Truth and the Obscene Word

in Eighteenth-Century

French Pornography

Lucienne Frappier-Mazur

Diderot, in one of his *Salons,* reflects on the decency of nudity, writing that "it is not a woman in the nude that is indecent," but "a woman whose skirts are tucked up that is." And he continues: "Adorn the Medici Venus with...rose-colored garters and tightly pulled white stockings, and you will strongly feel the difference between decent and indecent."[1] He then recounts an anecdote about a rich and famous countess who, after squandering "an enormous fortune," had become quite poor and was in debt with "her butcher, her dressmaker, her chambermaids...":

> Once, [her shoemaker] came to see her in order to try and get some money out of her. "My dear, said the countess, long have I owed you, I know. But what would you have me do? I am penniless: I go naked and am so poor that one can see my arse;" and so speaking she was tucking up her skirts, and showing her behind to her shoemaker who, touched and softened, went away saying: "In faith, this is true." The shoemaker wept on one side; the countess's chambermaids laughed on the other; that was because the countess, while indecent for her women, was decent, interesting, and even pathetic for her shoemaker.[2]

This passage can serve as a starting-point to problematize the notion of the obscene. Taken at face value, and relying on Diderot's final comment, it suggests an unexpected social tolerance of crude language and gestures proffered by women of the aristocracy. A similar blurring of the demarcations between prose genres that allowed or forbade the use of obscene vocabulary could be observed well into the seventeenth century, as pointed out by Jean Marie Goulemot in his already indispensable book on eighteenth-century pornographic fiction.[3] Eighteenth-century definitions of the word *obscène* do not differ markedly from modern ones, but they are vaguer: in the *Encyclopédie*, *obscène* is defined as "all that is contrary to modesty" (*la pudeur*), a term which connotes at once women and the sexual domain, as confirmed by the examples in the *Encyclopédie*'s entry. The explicit mention of sexuality in French dictionary definitions appears only in the mid- to late twentieth century.[4] Although the perception of obscenity may vary, there is little doubt about the meaning of the word, so the previous absence of *sexual* and its cognates from the eighteenth- and nineteenth-century definitions may be ascribed to a form of self-censorship, a concern for propriety, compounded by the fact that the domain of obscenity extends to scatology. In fact, the etymology of obscene – of bad omen – refers directly to the latter connotation, through its association with the left hand.[5] In his essay, Diderot seems to avoid *obscene*, instead using a series of more common equivalents: *indecent* (four occurrences), *smutty*, *cynical*, *coarse*, *unseemly*. Nevertheless, these adjectives all point to the more precise definitions of today's Robert and Petit Larousse: "*obscène*: that which deliberately or openly hurts modesty through representations of a sexual nature."[6]

Because of an obvious contradiction between the two Diderot excerpts I have quoted, they do not merely offer elements for a definition. The countess does precisely what Diderot gives as his first example of a breach of decency: she tucks up her skirts, and the shoemaker's emotion, which displaces any thought of monetary gain, humorously conveys the seductive intent that Freud, more straightforwardly than Diderot, would later identify as the initial motivation of the obscene joke. The countess has achieved the seduction of the shoemaker by means of explicit language and an indecorous gesture.

Diderot's ambiguity is also evident in his parallel between plain nudity and plain language. He implies that nonmetaphoric, crude language is no more indecent than plain nudity: "The cynical expression is always the simplest..."[7] Significantly, the same claim is characteristic of some pornographic fiction, which justifies its own energetic language – unquestionably a factor of the pornographic effect – with similar metalinguistic comments as can be seen in this quotation from Mercier de Compiègne: "In such moments are things named by their names, without any periphrases or unwelcome veils...."[8] Truth is naked. Such justification belongs to what one critic has called the "fiction of innocence,"[9] a frequent discursive strategy in libertine and pornographic novels, destined to naturalize transgressive details. And this resemblance puts the finishing touch to Diderot's subtext, which is at once a rehearsal of and a musing on the uses of obscenity, in its visual and linguistic manifestations.

Since the linguistic representation of visual erotic scenes may be perceived as obscene without the adjunction of any obscene words, there is a great deal of overlap between pornography and the obscene. *La Messaline française* (1789), for example, is at once highly pornographic – hence, quite obscene – and most elegantly written: the word *clitoris* being its only "technical" term. Therefore, this essay will focus on the study of the interrelation of the obscene word and the pornographic effect.

Narrowly understood, the obscene word belongs to a specific

lexical category, a vulgar linguistic register associated with the naming of sexual acts and anatomical parts; that is, the obscene word functions within denotation. This definition can be extended to include technical, clinical terms, because such words were likewise – perhaps more – avoided in polite conversation. Indeed, pornography does not seem to distinguish clearly between the two categories. Thus, a metalinguistic comment in *Vénus en rut* underscores at once the directness of plain language and the "strength [of] technical terms ... which name things plainly," as opposed to figures of speech, which are polysemic and detrimental to erotic concentration.[10] And the value of sheer naming, whether with polite or vulgar vocabulary, is fully exploited by writers.

This value, however, varies considerably according to forms and degrees of contextualization. Just as nudity becomes indecent when framed by some finery, so is the pornographic effect a function of context, and the obscene word in pornography is no exception. Thus, Revolutionary pornography ranks rather low when compared to pre-Revolutionary pornography. The smuttiness of the former is not only unrelieved, it is enshrined in a prescriptive discourse that tersely extolls virile republican virtues and denounces any sexual refinement or deviation: all characteristics that run contrary to well-tried erotic recipes and detract from the erotic effect.

What kind of contextualization is it, then, that best brings out the obscene word's pornographic effect? First, there is the contrast between two registers of language, crude and polite, or, even better, crude and elegant, a contrast which actualizes the desired transgression at the linguistic level. This effect is increased when words usually associated with the lower classes are put in aristocratic mouths, especially when relayed by female narrators, a frequent occurrence which enhances their impact.[11]

The second form of contextualization is its insertion in a story, a necessity that admittedly extends to other elements in pornography, but which also affects the obscene word. When comparing erotic verse and erotic prose fiction, it becomes evident that the narrative framing is an even more significant factor than the use of prose. Thus, poems of blatant linguistic obscenity that are devoid of any narrative thread, such as Piron's *Ode à Priape* (1710), or Mercier de Compiègne's *La Foutromanie* (1780), quoted above, qualify more as comic prank or mock-heroic parody than as regular pornography. La Fontaine's *Contes*, however, which are stories in verse and not pornographic, have an erotic dimension that comes closer to the pornographic effect despite their stylistic refinement. A narrative, more than any other form, will condition and engage the reader, and even more so if it uses the past tense and the first person, a joint strategy that promotes self-voyeurism in the reader.[12] Dialogues, rather than being merely descriptive and prescriptive, also tend to incorporate some narrative, especially in the seventeenth century, when pornography began to constitute itself as a genre, with dialogue as its main form after Aretino's model. (For example, in *L'Académie des dames* and *L'Ecole des filles*.) Even the scene, the tableau or description of the sexual action, which constitutes the central, indispensable unit of pornography and around which obscene words tend to gravitate,[13] is more effective when it hangs on a story line, no matter how rudimentary. Furthermore, the tableau itself tends to turn into a narrative; the sexual performance becomes the story. Remembering that the structure of stories in general has been likened to that of the sexual act, it is not difficult to understand the insistence of the narrative form in the most successful pornography.

The last aspect of this formalist overview will bring us closer to an internal study of the working and significance of the obscene word. It concerns the respective genders of narrators and narratees, of which there are several possible combinations. Mainstream pornography, while exploiting some degree of sexual indifferentiation, is, or was, mostly heterosexual and its implicit reader was male. Freud's analysis of obscene jokes, which also had a heterosexual reference, here becomes pertinent. According to Freud, the tendentious or obscene allusion (joke) originates in the sexual arousal provoked in the speaker by a definite person, a woman. Initially, the obscenity is addressed to that particular woman and has the meaning of a seductive attempt – one that hopes to be successful but whose success is deferred, in the best cases by the presence of a third party, another man. "At higher social levels," says Freud, the woman is absent for reasons of propriety, and a group of men listening to tendentious jokes then constitutes a transformation of the original situation.[14] The man or men who were the third party now become the receiver(s) of the joke. This second situation is reproduced in pornography when a male narrator seems to be addressing a male narratee, most obviously in a first-person narrative by a male agent, but also in most third-person narratives, whose voice is male and which imply or even inscribe male narratees. Based on a limited sampling of twenty-five texts containing obscene words, all of them eighteenth-century with the exception of the two seventeenth-century examples mentioned above, this first category is the single largest by a relative majority of eleven texts and, not too surprisingly, comprises the largest number of obscene words. Freud observes that, when the person who makes the smutty joke "finds his libidinal impulse inhibited by the woman, he develops a hostile trend against [her] and calls on the originally interfering third person as his ally."[15] This typically resembles the relation between male narrator and narratee, who, in this case, talk to each other over the body of the fictitious woman. It may also be one of the factors accounting for an undercurrent of hostility toward women in pornography, obscene words, not so easily tolerated by women, being one manifestation of this hostility. As Freud puts it, "the woman is exposed," often an ambivalent procedure, and the words easily become denigrating if the "sadistic components of the sexual instinct" are summoned.[16] At worst, one gets the Sadian trend of pornography.

This initial model throws an interesting light on the numerous works that depart from it — fourteen of twenty-five, that is, more than half — by introducing a female narrator or narratee or both. With the obvious exception of Sade, they frequently obscure, alleviate or even eliminate the hostile undertones of the obscene words and complicate their significance. Thus, *Le Catéchisme libertin* (first edition, 1791) combines a male narrator and a female narratee, not the most frequent occurrence. Although this work was, erroneously or facetiously, attributed to a woman revolutionary, Théroigne de Méricourt, its format, which parodies the questions and answers of Catholic children's catechisms, implies an authoritative male speaker — a priest, doctor or lawyer -- dispensing rules of behavior to female prostitutes, and its obscenity strikes the reader as more fraternal and ostensibly well-meaning than derogatory. Something similar occurs even in Sade, in the footnotes he appends to *Histoire de Juliette*, some of which contain paternalistic sexual advice addressed to very hypothetical female narratees.

Remember that, in Diderot's anecdote, it was the woman who was engaging in the seductive attempt, which only made it more racy. Indeed, the introduction of a woman in the situation of communication between author and reader actualizes forms of complicity between the reader and the woman, or, rather, the reader's imaginary representation of woman. From a psychoanalytic standpoint, this echoes the archaic, incestuous complicity between mother and child, a connection which pornography establishes more explicitly than other genres. Drawing a parallel between the creation of the perverse scenario and artistic creation, Joyce McDougall notes that, in both cases, "the joy found in the creative act is more intense than the pleasure of contemplating the created object; the production takes precedence of the product."[17] And she points out that this feature, common to pervert and artist, finds its model in the first productions of the child during the anal phase – feces and urine – which are considered as part objects. "The child enjoys a spontaneous pleasure" in this act of creation. "He is interested in the products themselves *only in as much as his mother gives them importance; she* is the 'public' which gives them their signifying function as objects of exchange," namely, of communication.[18] According to this interpretation, a third party, be it the real or the symbolic father, appears as witness and spectator and interferes within the dual relation of mother and child.[19] In adulthood, what distinguishes the pervert from the artist are the different embodiments of the spectator's figure. Pervert and artist alike need the acceptance of a public and its enjoyment of their creation – of what, in the subject's unconscious, corresponds to the unveiling of the original part object. For the artist, this validation of his or her subjecthood, being truly public, takes place through an authentic act of exchange. For the pervert, however, it remains arrested at the level of a primal fantasy, the fantasy of "a secret, anal love between mother and child.... The artist, through his very creation, offers himself to the Other's judgment, whereas the pervert seeks to remain concealed,"[20] thus evading the intrusion of any third party. By pushing aside and repressing the symbolic father, the perverse scenario remains self-contained and, at least on the surface, enacts only the original dual relationship, in which the mother may act as both spectator and participant.

It is easy to see how different gender combinations of narrators and narratees may, at least in erotic fiction, implement different versions of this scenario. Pornography, many of the effects of which rely on "deviant" sexual situations, offers an interesting middle ground between perverse and artistic creation (a middle ground of which Sade's *oeuvre*, which goes much beyond pornography, could be considered the full realization). Itself a semi-clandestine genre, pornography injects the desired transgressive element not only into the erotic tableau, but into the choice of narrative situations. The effect of complicity is most fully achieved when the narrator is female and addresses a male narratee – the narrator frequently being a mature woman or a madam recounting her past exploits or amorous initiation to her lover or to the public at large. Such a situation of communication not only satisfies the reader's voyeurism, it introduces the mother as both agent and complicit witness in the perverse scenario, appealing to the possible survival of that "secret, anal [love] between mother and child" McDougall refers to. Needless to say the obscene utterance on the woman's part at once seals and gratifies this complicity.

The inscription of both female narrator and female narratee, although more remote from the original scenario, is the one that best caters to the real reader's voyeurism and eavesdropping, allowing for the most varied forms of identification and projection. Two women friends, or a mother and daughter, exchange confidences and advice: this is also the situation most favorable to the metalinguistic reflection on crude versus polite vocabulary, presented as a typically female concern. The most arousing pornography, however, combines more than one of these situations of communication. Thus, *Histoire de Dom Bougre, portier des Chartreux*, a constant reference in eighteenth-century pornography and considered unsurpassed as a model, modulates the genders of its narrators and narratees by means of embedded stories, reproducing at the level of narrative persona the variety of sexual combinations in the erotic scene (figures 5.1 and 5.2).

As has been mentioned above, obscene words tend to gravitate around the tableau. The description of bodies, first perceived through the narrator's chance voyeurism, becomes more focused and gives way to increasingly precise anatomical naming as the narrator becomes an active participant.[21] This crescendo either dissolves into a series of inarticulate exclamations at the point of orgasm, or culminates with the naming of the act and its effects.

Obscene words also gather around two other strategic points in the novel. Occasionally, they appear in the title, such as *Les 40 manières de foutre* (1790). More frequently they appear in its surrounding apparatus – epigraphs and fictitious places of publication, authors' names or descriptions[22] and characters' names – with those in *L'Anti-Justine* by Restif de la Bretonne being among the most notorious.[23] Goulemot considers these word games as a form of scrambling, an interference, an intellectual game in which polysemy detracts from the pornographic effect.[24] It is quite true that they do not concern the main order of business, yet they do perform an initial conditioning, which partially makes up for the alleged interference. Moreover, in some cases, they are disseminated throughout the narration and, although they dilute the strategic concentration, they contribute to the general background.

Next to be examined is the function of truth that the obscene word claims for itself, as well as its limitations. As opposed to refined language, which is the language of repression and secondary processes – that is, the conscious mental processes that are based on deferred gratification and the binding of psychic energy and which correspond to rational thinking – the plain language of obscenity relates to primary processes – that is, the unconscious processes that allow for "the free flow of psychic energy," which "tends to reinvest completely those representations attached to the gratification constitutive of desire (primitive hallucination)."[25] In other words, obscene language, more directly than ordinary language, relates to the body and to its drives, and calls up corporeal representations, which it endows with a hallucinatory quality. As such, its discourse of justification opposes the demands of the body and its pleasure to the "falsehood" of feelings. Thus, the obscene word is governed by the taboo of love, which characterizes much, though not all, pornography.[26] The obscene word assumes a function of unmasking by denouncing sentimental discourse as a kind of euphemism intended to cover up the truth of sexual desire. Indeed, the claim, which applies both to literature and social conventions, is not always without foundation. What should be pointed out, however, is that it is based on a dualistic view of sexuality, a stark dichotomy between body and soul, and that this is the very same cultural dichotomy underlying the taboo of the body in polite discourse and confining feeling to the realm of the spirit. There, perhaps, lurks an element of delusion that risks turning the claim of truth into another fiction. In Horkheimer's words, this fiction would be that of modern culture, which entertains "a love-hate relationship with the body.... The body is scorned and rejected as something inferior, and at the same time desired as something forbidden, objectified and alienated."[27] This is precisely the view of the body that underlies Sade's obscenity and which he expresses through a most violent opposition of pleasure and love:

> I do not want a woman to imagine that I owe her anything because I soil myself on top of her.... I have never believed that from the junction of two bodies could arise the junction of two hearts: I can see great reasons for scorn and disgust in this physical junction, but not a single reason for love.[28]

213

FIGURE 5.1. (above) The Lesbian Erotic Scene. From *Histoire de Dom B—, portier des Chartreux* (Frankfurt edition, 1748).

FIGURE 5.2. (right) The Voyeur. From *Histoire de Dom B—, portier des Chartreux* (Frankfurt edition, 1748).

Hence, in Sade's eroticism, there is an ambivalence toward disgust, which is both sought after and overcome by the agents, and aggressively aroused in the reader.

The truth unveiled by the obscene word lies elsewhere, in the way it works as simulacrum or fetish. This proposition, as will be seen presently, reflects the obscene word's complex relation to primary processes more accurately than the opposition, indeed alleged incompatibility, of body and soul. The association between truth and simulacrum, truth and fetish, may sound like a paradox, but only in as much as pornography is often criticized for creating a body that lacks authenticity. Thus, Nancy Armstrong speaks of "the pornographic sign as a substitute for the real body and its authentic pleasure"[29] but, although it can be readily agreed that the sign is not the real body, the distinction between authentic and inauthentic pleasure is much more problematic.[30] As previously noted, that particular pornographic sign – the obscene word – names sexual parts, but never an object (with the obvious exception of the dildo), and its recurrence reflects the prevalence of the fragmented body in pornography.

According to Marc Guillaume's definition, any perception of ourselves that we experience as "contingent" – that is, not included within the fabric of signification – is experienced as an *excess* of existence, and "this perception of an excess concentrates on the body"; in the case of the obscene, the lower body as cloaca. Various forms of socialization – dress, make-up, tattoos, dietary and funerary rituals, the conventions of civility and the many other stagings of illusion – all attempt to "avert confrontation with this excess." Nevertheless, there are always moments when the sense of contingency – "the excess of body" and of a reality outside meaning – breaks through the safety devices of the symbolic organization in the form of "irrepressible tears or laughter, anger or sexual pleasure."[31] These are also moments

216

governed by primary processes. This irrecoverable excess, when it invests the representation of the sexual and excremental, constitutes the obscene; however, it is not clear whether Guillaume extends the obscene to the other manifestations of a contingent surplus he enumerates.

Limiting ourselves to the narrower and more common acceptation, let us return to the obscene word in order to explain how, although belonging to verbal language, it brings about the experience of contingency as excess — of a reality that is unfettered by the chain of meaning. The obscene word, like the insult,[32] harks back to the time when the child does not distinguish very well between the representation of words and the representation of things and tends to treat words as things. Hence the terms *sound-body* or *organ-word* to designate the representations it triggers in the adult speaker, representations of which Pierre Fédida points out have "the power of producing in the hearer an actual regressive-hallucinatory stimulus ('Belebung') and the vivid return of mnesic images."[33] It is this proximity to the thing that exceeds ordinary language and conjures up the mental, hallucinatory representation of the body with minimal mediation. The obscene word is more than another substitute for the part object; it itself acquires the status of part object and, like the part object, may stand for the whole erotic body.

The written status of the obscene word in pornography retains these characteristics but exploits them in a particular way. Without entirely suppressing the representation of the auditory perception and its impact, the written text effects a partial shift from the auditory to the visual. Handwriting is sometimes considered a part object in psychoanalysis — the last remnant for the child of the other's body.[34] If this proposition is accepted, it can be said that the obscene word is twice a part object, both auditory and visual, once being written by hand or even set in type, and then read.

217

The obscene word exposes not only the erotic body of the woman, but also that of the man. This raises two questions: that of exhibitionism and that of gendered desire. Exhibitionism is a corollary of the wish to expose the other's body,[35] and is a frequent motivation in pornography, which may then account for many an explicit and enthusiastic description of the male organ. If the narrator is female, such descriptions take on an additional significance, that of inscribing the woman's desire. Regardless of its authenticity, which is no more questionable than that of the man's desire, this inscription through the agency of the obscene word is one of the ways in which eighteenth-century pornography presents the woman as desiring subject and the male body as desired object. Most frequently, this is achieved, as in Mirabeau's *Le Rideau levé*, by giving centrality to the woman's desired body, with a woman narrating how she observed the interaction between a man and a woman and the effects of that observation as she identified with the woman. Yet there are also cases, especially in Andréa de Nerciat, when the man is presented solely as desired object and the woman, as desiring subject, is directing the action. Sometimes the male object is a manservant or other social inferior of the woman, but, in all of his novels, Andréa de Nerciat also describes relations of total sexual – that is, social – reciprocity. As for the gendered specificity of desire, it is hardly the primary concern of pornography, and it can be proposed that this has to do as much with the necessary scrambling of sexes as with male bias. Eighteenth-century pornography leaves room for female desire, probably more than its present-day counterparts.[36]

The truth of the obscene word, then, is that it manifests the dependence of eroticism on the imaginary. While this can also be said of other narrative units, the obscene word has the most direct hold over the body and is what exhibits most forcefully the relation of desire to language. Whether or not the desire it inscribes is "authentic," it arouses an authentic desire in the reader. Functioning as part object, it reveals the fetish-word as more potent than the real object would be. In this respect, it comes close to illustrating Sebeok's extended definition of the fetish as "a supernormal sign, a 'misplaced response,' if you will, standing for – and indeed amplifying by a process of ritualization – some natural object, upon which an individual has become preferentially imprinted in lieu of the object itself."[37]

This notion of amplification attached to the obscene word as fetish or simulacrum must be examined in relation to other procedures of exaggeration that characterize pornographic fiction, in order to clarify the particular status of the obscene word. Goulemot identifies some narrative strategies, typical of the eighteenth-century novel, which eighteenth-century pornography uses with a vengeance, and he studies their bearing on questions of realism and verisimilitude. Goulemot raises several distinct but connected points that need to be confronted with one another. First and foremost, Goulemot convincingly argues that pornography's physiological effect on the reader constitutes an incursion of the book into the real world. He links this physical reaction to the agency of the imaginary and its concrete, inclusive sway when he says that, by arousing sexual desire in the reader, erotic fiction suppresses the possibility of choice and thus "bends the usual mechanism of reading, which implies play and choice.... Unable to satisfy the desire it arouses, it obliges the reader to get out of the world of imagination and forces the law of the book upon the real world."[38] Conversely, Goulemot points out in another section that, according to an eighteenth-century view, the reading of novels in general produced many physiological effects, especially in women because of their tender fibers: "a kind of quasi-pathological stimulus...(panting, insomnia, nervousness or languor)," not to mention the tears shed by female *and* male readers. In this perspective, he argues, the physiological effect of pornographic reading would become the exemplary (aggrandized) model of all fiction reading — a proposition which he does not fully endorse, however, for it is contradicted both by our contemporary reading experience and by the idea of reading as free choice.[39]

Second, Goulemot argues that pornographic novels underscore the way in which effects of reality are created in eighteenth-century fiction because they exaggerate its procedures of verisimilitude, such as its use of first-person narration and embedded stories, which either justify repetitions or favor effects of voyeurism and specularity, or both. Thus, Goulemot at times seems to suggest that there is no qualitative difference between "systems of credibility" in pornography and in other fiction, only various magnifying effects on the side of pornography. Conversely, in other places, he does point out a number of differences specific to pornography, such as the lack of characterization[40] and the impossibility of identifying with the pornographic character as a person despite the reader's identification with the character's desire,[41] and, again, the impossibility of escaping physical arousal,[42] in which cases erotic fiction cannot serve as a model (even an exaggerated one) for all novels. On balance, there *is* a qualitative difference between the reading of pornography and the reading of other novels.

The final point is an offshoot of the first and brings us back directly to the obscene word. In his conclusion, Goulemot states that the most successful pornography — that of the eighteenth century — came closest to "an effective" literary "trompe-l'oeil." Its authors, he humorously asserts, were "like those gods of whom it is said that they name in order to create,"[43] which is a way of proposing that, in pornography, the word creates the thing — another, more concise version of the view that, through its physiological effect, pornographic reading carries the law of the book —

of the imaginary – into the real world, hence the metaphor of trompe-l'oeil.

It should not be forgotten that although the pornographic effect – the reality of the reader's sexual desire – is facilitated by the presence of certain narrative techniques, it may well occur in their absence. What ultimately counts is the erotic content per se, and the fact that it is conveyed through written language in the reading situation. Verbalization itself, though, admittedly, some forms of verbalization more than others, is what triggers the workings of the imaginary, and, semiotically, it operates in two ways. For the most part, it operates at the level of literary representation (mimesis) which, as in all fiction, corresponds to the narrative and descriptive sequences that usually make up the majority of the text. Only loosely can one speak of trompe-l'oeil at that level. Erotic fiction offers a verbal minesis of sexual scenes. Representation, no matter how suggestive, is only an "imitation" in words.

What interests us is that the term *trompe-l'oeil* acquires a literal meaning in (and only in) the case of the obscene word; hence, the latter's special position within the function of literary representation. Although the totality of pornographic discourse arouses desire by appealing to the imaginary, it generally does so by using verbal language to evoke sexual acts that claim to entertain a mimetic relation with those of real human beings. Thus pornography can be viewed as a branch of "realist" fiction. However, the obscene word's relation to its referent differs from that of other words. As fetish, or simulacrum of a part object, the obscene word not only represents, but replaces, its referent. It acts as a substitute for, indeed sometimes as an improvement over, its referent. It is therefore the only unit in pornography which, strictly speaking, qualifies as trompe-l'oeil. Unlike other words, the obscene word not only represents, but is, the thing itself.

PART THREE

Eighteenth-Century
Vantage Points

Chapter Six

The Libertine Whore:

Prostitution in French Pornography

from Margot to Juliette

Kathryn Norberg

The prostitute plays a particularly important role in the history of pornography; she was present at its birth. Arguably the first pornographic text, Aretino's *Ragionamenti*, is a conversation between two whores. She was the heroine of one of the most important and enduring pornographic texts, *Memoirs of a Woman of Pleasure*. She is a participant in the ultimate pornographic world, that of the Marquis de Sade, for her debauches are the subject of one of his longest novels, *Histoire de Juliette*. From the Renaissance to the French Revolution, the courtesan fills libertine literature; her life and loves form the very stuff of many pornographic texts. The whore biography or confession is exceedingly common in the genre and, usually, the whore herself narrates the story. From *La Puttana errante* to *Fanny Hill*, from Margot to Juliette, the prostitute's chatter simply *is* much of Western pornography, and no other character, male or female, pimp or rake, can dispute her dominance in the world of the obscene.

Because she appears so frequently in libertine literature, the prostitute is an excellent instrument through which to detect changes in pornography and, in turn, changes in attitudes and beliefs. The prostitute can function as social barometer and indicate new attitudes toward old political hierarchies. Depending on the author, the prostitute can ridicule or celebrate her clients, who encompass everyone from old aristocrats to upstart bourgeois. She can be either social critic or complacent observer, and her boudoir can be a place of political agitation or simple dalliance. At the same time, the prostitute reveals a great deal about attitudes toward women, female sexuality and women's social role. The sexual politics of the time can be made evident by whether the pornographer chooses to paint her as a victim or a predator.

However, representations of prostitutes do not convey the reality of prostitution. The libertine whore is utterly fictional, an image which has more to do with male fantasy than with social reality. The bordello, like the harem, arouses all sorts of desires, and the pornographic bagnio belongs to the realm of fantasy, not to the streets of Paris or London. The whore, too, is a wholly fictional creation, but she is no less valuable for it. She can serve as a guide to an often neglected corner of European culture, pornography, and, in so doing, provide insight into changes in politics and gender.

This essay examines the representation of the prostitute in French pornographic literature from *Margot la ravaudeuse* (1750) to *Histoire de Juliette, ou Les Prospérités de la vice. Margot* appeared concurrently with several other classic French pornographic texts and, like them, defined the genre and established its conventions and clichés. Toward the end of the eighteenth century, Sade's *Juliette*, which was probably written in 1792 though published later, does not merely draw on this earlier tradition, but elaborates it and takes it to its extreme. In between these two were produced some two dozen texts that deal with prostitutes. While these are not the only eighteenth-century texts to deal with prostitutes – whores appear in many other writings, some medical, some moral, some intent upon changing the way prostitution is policed – they differ from the above in that they are pornographic;

that is, texts which are fictional, sexually explicit and contemptuous of sexual taboos.

Virtually all of the works included in this group present a particular picture of the prostitute, what I call the "libertine whore." This whore, like Margot, is independent, sensual, sensible and skilled. She is healthy and possessed of a very healthy – that is, normal – sexual appetite. She is a businesswoman and an artist who provides "varied" sex for men who can afford it. She is a courtesan who lives in luxury and abides by "philosophy," usually materialist philosophy. Intelligent, independent, proud and reasonable, she is *not* diseased or monstrous; she is not humiliated or victimized either by life or her clients.[1] She may have come from working-class roots, but she overcomes them through her education and intelligence. An *arriviste*, she can scoff at social distinctions and hoodwink the rich and powerful.

She is also the polar opposite of another kind of prostitute who appeared in eighteenth-century literature, what one specialist has called the "virtuous courtesan."[2] The virtuous courtesan was born in approximately 1760, though her antecedents could be traced back to Manon Lescaut. The new, sentimental novel clearly produced her, and Restif de la Bretonne is undoubtedly her greatest proponent. For Restif de la Bretonne and many authors thereafter, the prostitute is fundamentally good. She is a hapless victim, an impoverished working-class child who is dominated and abused, diseased in body and sometimes in spirit, doomed to endure the sadism of both men and society. Zéphire of Restif de la Bretonne's *Le Paysan perverti* is a good example of the "whore with a heart of gold." Seduced and abandoned as a teenager in Paris, Zéphire becomes a prostitute, but somehow retains "natural" goodness, even innocence, in the midst of her debauches.[3] Childlike and guileless, Zéphire is "a masterwork of nature," combining "innocence, purity, naiveté, candor, generosity, charity" in a soul "that

retains all its original beauty."[4] Authors of the time required
that Rousseauist notions of femininity prevail and that innocence
characterize all women, even those who seemed corrupt.[5] Consequently, prostitution and virtue had to be reconciled, and they
are in Restif de la Bretonne's work though not without some difficulty. In *Le Palais royal* (1790), Restif describes the streetwalkers of Paris's most notorious fleshmarket, the Palais-Royal. Here,
it would seem vice should flourish but, in fact, most of the prostitutes are virgins, victims of evil mothers and fathers who have
sold them into their disreputable trade. Despite all odds, these
hapless children have preserved their natural modesty and managed to retain their virginity. Such a conceit tries Restif de la
Bretonne's inventiveness and the reader's credulity, but it makes
its point: women are naturally modest, childlike and asexual and
even a prostitute (or, rather, a woman forced into prostitution,
since none would choose this life) will retain her virtue.

Next to this virtuous courtesan is her antithesis, the libertine whore. Fanny, Margot and Juliette have nothing in common
with Zéphire or the pseudoprostitutes of the Palais-Royal, for
they spring from a world that pre-dated or rejected Rousseauist
notions of feminine modesty. The libertine whore is a creature
of the rococo, of an age enamored of materialist philosophy and
comfortable with sensual pleasure, especially "varied" pleasure.
She owes little to the new notions of sexual difference, of which
Rousseau was the best-known spokesman. She knows nothing of
woman's supposedly inherent modesty and cares little for her
role in the family. She is a public woman of a particular sort,
who existed in a time when the division between public and private was not yet defined. She belongs to the passions, to the
sexual and to sexually explicit literature. Unlike the virtuous
courtesan, she knows no shame or guilt and never denigrates her
trade, except to suit the censors. She will, however, go out of

her way to belittle her sister type, the virtuous courtesan.

The libertine whore appears in a variety of eighteenth-century literary productions.[6] She has a long history in verse and drama, both of them genres still influenced by the bawdy spirit of eighteenth-century Parisian street culture.[7] She also lives on in a distant descendant of Aretino's *Ragionamenti*, the prostitute correspondence. This new twist on an old form allows the reader to learn tidbits about Parisian high life while keeping current with fashion, both erotic and cultural.[8] Another, more popular genre – the fictional guidebook or *guide rose* – performs much the same function. The author provides an insider's picture of the Paris sex trade, complete with addresses of prominent bordellos and prostitutes. A variant on this form, lists of prostitutes' addresses, prices and attributes, flourished after 1789. Most of these texts were extremely short – pamphlets, really – without illustrations. More elaborate and lengthy was the prostitute confession or autobiography, a genre created by John Cleland with his immensely popular *Fanny Hill*, or *Memoirs of a Woman of Pleasure*. *Fanny Hill* had many French imitators, from *Margot la ravaudeuse* through *Histoire de Marguerite, Fille de Suzon* (which also drew on the popular *Histoire de Dom Bougre, portier des Chartreux*) to *La Cauchoise* and, ultimately, to *Juliette*.

These novels provide the most complete picture of the libertine whore, and all share certain qualities. In each one, the heroine is not just a whore or a sexually promiscuous woman, but also a prostitute.[9] She accepts money or her upkeep in return for sexual favors; she spends time in a bordello or in the care of an *appareilleuse* before graduating to the status of kept woman. The course of her life and the shape of the narrative are almost always the same: the heroine briefly describes her parents and her adolescence before launching into the real substance of the novel, her training and progress as a *fille du monde*. A series of sexual

encounters follow, punctuated by momentary reversals, yet culminating in the whore's success and well-deserved retirement.
The prostitute confession is the story of a journey, not toward
self-awareness but toward professional expertise, success and,
therefore, prosperity.

It is also a story told by the whore herself: Margot, Javotte,
Pasphion, Julie and Juliette all describe their own lives. The whore
novel is the rare eighteenth-century genre in which a woman
speaks about and for herself, and French literary specialists, while
noticing this peculiarity, have not explained it.[10] I think the first-
person narrative is a device that the author would use for two reasons. First, one is able to describe a series of sexual adventures
without recourse to lengthy expositions or transitions. What is
a whore's life if not a series of clients and their perversions? Second, the reader is provided with the vicarious pleasure of an
encounter – be it only textual – with a prostitute.

The first-person narrative, however, is not a device that em-
powers the prostitute or conveys female subjectivity. Margot,
Javotte and Juliette do not have much to tell about female sexuality. The authors of these texts were men, and they probably
wrote for a predominantly, if not solely, male audience. The libertine whore is a reflection of male sexuality and a mirror of man's
lust: "she must please," Javotte tells us.[11] Complaisance (compliance) is the quality most necessary in a whore, states Margot's
first procuress, the benign Madame Florence. A whore willingly
does whatever she is asked and fulfills male fantasies, albeit for a
price. It is compliance – among other things – that distinguishes
the sensual Juliette from her stubborn sister, the virtuous Justine,
for Juliette gladly bends to her lover's whims. As Jane Gallop has
pointed out, Juliette is the perfect whore because she is an empty
vessel, a blank page, upon which her lovers can write.[12]

The libertine whore is not, however, a hapless victim who

stoically endures humiliation and pain. She knows pain, but it does not cause her to suffer. Certainly, the prostitute must satisfy her clients' whims. Margot, Javotte and Marguerite, niece of Dom Bougre, all suffer a painful loss of their "second virginity" when clients demand anal intercourse. Sometimes, the whore suffers worse. In a scene that would be repeated frequently in the prostitute literature, Margot, alone in the bordello, is forced to "service" a battalion of musketeers. "I was forced," she says, "to suffer thirty assaults in the space of two hours." She then speculates that a devout woman would have welcomed such a brutal assault but she, a minor sinner, did not. Still, she states, "Too much is too much. I was stuffed with so much pleasure that I had a kind of indigestion."[13]

Margot's reaction is at once reasonable and outrageous. She resolves to leave Madame Florence's bordello lest she suffer another such attack. But she also confesses that she enjoyed the assault, indeed too much. Marguerite La Duchapt is even more masochistic. A group of four musketeers "exploit" her, profiting from all of her orifices and her breasts, while a fifth soldier beats time on a drum. All five – including Marguerite – reach orgasm at the same time, and Marguerite tells the reader that they "drown in delirium and each other's fuck." "This new type of debauchery," she concludes, "gave me a taste for more *recherché* pleasures."[14]

This comes closer to the rapist's fantasy of the victim who "wanted it" all along. Yes, the libertine whore is *complaisante*, but only up to a point. Unlike her sisters in contemporary pornography, she will not accept and pretend to enjoy every form of abuse. Javotte rebels when a client tries to force her to engage in oral sex, and the young Cauchoise refuses to service a client with a diseased organ.[15] Such instances of rebellion are, admittedly, rare, but largely because they are rarely necessary. These texts do not, like some contemporary pornography, present scene after scene of women being abused, humiliated and dehumanized; this pornography takes little relish in recounting sadistic sexual acts. On the contrary, that honor belongs to the virtuous courtesan novels, in which the prostitute must be punished and humiliated for having betrayed her natural virtue.[16] With glee, the author of *Correspondance d'Eulalie* describes how his heroines are killed or disfigured, either by their clients or by disease.[17]

The libertine whore's clients do have "peculiarities," special tastes that the successful courtesan must satisfy, but these are more frequently bizarre or comical than deadly. Some clients like playacting, and Javotte has a client who asks that she dress like a lady of quality and virtue and yet talk like a fishwife.[18] Another lover insists that he court her, and goes through the motions of a romantic courtship. La Duchapt has a client who likes to be spanked like a child. Virtually all of the courtesans gratify clergymen, whose foremost passion is to be beaten; in fact, it is a cliché of eighteenth-century pornography that ecclesiastics can only become erect when slapped on the behind with "a handful of steel rods [*une poignée de verges*]." Old men, too, sometimes need this stimulation and a pamphlet from the revolutionary years considers the "steel rods [*verges*]" a necessary part of the average whore's equipment.[19]

The prostitute's story is made up – literally – of such encounters. Upon receiving a client, the whore is faced with a challenge: How to "animate" the "flabby," "overworked" and "lethargic" organ before her? Here is the pornographic whore's task par excellence, one that absorbs most of her story. She is, after all, a professional who, as La Cauchoise proclaims, "knows the superior art of how to make a man fuck even when his prick doesn't want to...."[20] A lively hand is the whore's most valuable asset, but she has other techniques, too, and the pornographic texts lavish narrative space on this aspect of the whore's art. Armed with an array of techniques, and even machines, the whore is in control. With her dildos, her machines, her theatrics and, of course, her hand, she makes the sexual act occur. Figuratively and literally, she seizes the phallus, and the balance of power in the sexual relationship tips in her direction.

It is evident that the libertine prostitute is — at least sometimes — in control. At her most elevated, as a *fille entretenue*, she determines when and how. "Listen my friend," Javotte tells a prospective lover, "all of this comes down to two points: you will be allowed to love me as long as you don't bore me and I will return the favor in accordance with my taste and caprice."[21] But the libertine whore is no monster, no Medusa-headed fury that strikes terror in men and elicits punishment. She does not threaten castration; on the contrary, she restores virility. And not just for the pleasure of her client. The libertine whore, unlike the virtuous courtesan, has a healthy libido. She has "a temperament"; that is, a naturally sensual character and a penchant for pleasure that she shares with all women (figure 6.1). Margot, Javotte, Marguerite and La Cauchoise all insist upon this point: "women," La Duchapt proclaims, "are all born with a taste for pleasure...."[22] "What is whorishness [*putanisme*]?" she asks. "It is a state in which one follows nature...."[23]

The prostitute may also possess a particularly fiery temperament. Margot, Marguerite, Javotte and La Cauchoise all come from lubricious stock, and they have all profited from their mothers' examples. But none has been sold into prostitution by her. The pornographic whore is neither tricked, betrayed, seduced or abandoned, nor is she an innocent country girl duped by a cunning procuress into a life of sin; unlike the virtuous courtesan, she chooses her career. Those other scenarios belong to the virtuous courtesan novels, in particular to those of Restif. The libertine whore is no fresh country girl, and she has considerable

FIGURE 6.1. The Pornographic Whore. From *Histoire de Marguerite, fille de Suzon, nièce de D — B —* (Paris: De l'Imprimerie du Louvre, 1784). The engravings to this edition had already appeared in *La Nouvelle Académie des dames* (1776).

sexual experience before she enters the bordello. She is a Parisian, a working-class girl from one of the populous *faubourgs*. Certainly, she is not rich, and money does play a part in her decision to become a prostitute. "One hundred *louis* and pleasure, who could refuse such an offer?" asks Javotte.[24] The heroines of these texts cannot, for they have fled their parents and find themselves alone and without resources. Still, the latter part of Javotte's proposition – the pleasure – is important.

Not that these whores are consumed with passion. They are not mad bacchantes, driven by an unquenchable thirst for sex. They are not a throwback to the ancient, patriarchal myth of the insatiable woman. Margot, Javotte and Marguerite are eighteenth-century girls whose sexual appetites are well moderated by a healthy dose of philosophy. Indeed, the libertine whore is well read and sophisticated. As Margot explains, prostitutes "can talk about anything for we get our education from the Public." "Is there any profession," she asks, "which we do not have occasion to hear?" The warrior, the lawyer, the financier and especially the philosopher share their wisdom with the whore.[25] A student of pleasure, the prostitute is also a student of philosophy, in particular of the Enlightenment materialism that colors so much of this libertine literature. Javotte, for example, reads "the novels of Messrs. de la Mettrie, Diderot and Crébillon." These books helped her "refine her pleasures."[26]

The libertine whore may enjoy pleasure, but she does not overindulge. As Margot says, "too much is too much." Moderation is the key and, although Margot, Javotte and their sisters can suffer physically from a surfeit of sex, otherwise they are quite healthy. Venereal disease plays only a minor role in these texts.[27] And, just as they do not overindulge in sex, neither do they allow themselves a more fashionable vice – romantic love. They are more cautious than Fanny Hill or the host of virtuous courtesans that populate Restif's and Nougaret's works. Margot warns her libertine sisters against romantic love: "Any prostitute who wishes to succeed should, like a merchant, having nothing in view but her self-interest and profit." Above all else, she continues, "[o]ne's heart should be inaccessible to love."[28] For one's pleasures, she prescribes a more rational, less entangling solution: "I have always had in my pay a young and vigorous lackey, whom I keep well-fed and clothed and who serves me in a minute and without fail unlike 'honest' men." She picks only fresh, country lads and then "educates" them herself.[29] She recommends this "method" to all, for it avoids both the inconveniences and the follies of sentimental love.

Of course, only a wealthy woman could afford to keep such a retainer and, in these texts, the prostitute becomes just that. She may begin as a laboring-class girl, the daughter of a stocking mender, a hairdresser or a tavernkeeper, but she ends up a courtesan. Her transformation is part of her story. Javotte, for example, sometimes reverts to her "fishwife" ways, and her procuress must enjoin her to "get rid of these common airs and lowly expressions; men like [good] manners."[30] Readers of eighteenth-century pornography also liked well-mannered girls and orderly, well-appointed bordellos. Madame Florence's discrete whorehouse in Montmartre is, Margot tells us, "a wonder of order and detail."[31] Madame Florence can boast that her house is "not infamous" (*malfamée*), and she has a special concern for the cleanliness of her girls. Upon Margot's arrival at Madame Florence's establishment, she is instructed in the use of the bidet, "a piece of furniture for which honest women should thank whores."[32] They also dress her as a lady would dress and teach her how to act like one. Javotte, too, goes through training, although it is interrupted by frequent orgies, until finally her lover considers her "well enough formed to take to the Opera, the theater and the balls."[33]

Finally successful, the libertine whore is now rich and adored. Margot herself wonders at her magnificence as she sits at the Opera. The luxury of her dress, the "servility of those who courted me, and my own arrogance" — all made Margot consider herself "a deity."[34] "What a life! What a position!" exclaims La Duchapt, "The pleasures of the table and those of the flesh follow one another twenty times a day." The prostitutes' life is "charming."[35]

If the whore's lot is glamorous, it is because her clients are rich, wellborn and well connected. The church, in fact, provides many of these gentlemen. Margot teams up with a Carmelite who is nothing less than "one of the finest pimps in Paris." La Cauchoise frequents a priest who escorts her to an orgy at the *maison de plaisance* of a nobleman. As in all eighteenth-century pornography, clergymen have an important role, as do financiers. Indeed, the financier is the single most frequent visitor to the bordello, where the whores make fun of his "flabby" organ, dupe him into maintaining them and then cheat on him mercilessly. Nobles are present, too, though they receive less attention. Occasionally, a musketeer may break in, but otherwise elegance prevails. Clearly, the courtesan is identified with the *haute monde*, with the worlds of the church, high finance and the court. The *maison de plaisance*, the *partie carré* in the Bois de Boulogne, the opulent homes of the Marais — this is the world of the fictional courtesan. The eighteenth-century reader apparently had no interest yet in the sordid world of the Parisian streetwalker. This is "varied" and luxurious sex for an audience that liked its pornography fine, refined and restricted to the elite.

Does the libertine whore ever hold this aristocratic world up to ridicule? Certainly, the prostitute ridicules her lovers. She, a working-class girl, makes them run around in circles and cheats on them without the slightest hesitation. She also laughs at their impotence and mocks their slavish adoration of a mere prostitute.

It is hard to tell if the eighteenth-century reader laughed with her, for the political message of the texts is ambiguous. The whore's stance toward the church, however, is clear. She rejects prejudice and removes the veils from the lust of the "hairy satyrs" – the clergymen. But her posture toward the rich and wellborn is ambiguous. She may admire the "powerful engine" – the awesome virility – of one nobleman, yet laugh at the impotence of an aging duke. Also, the eighteenth-century reader may also have harbored secret admiration for a gentleman who could purchase the services of a notorious, glamorous courtesan.

In terms of eighteenth-century sexual politics, the message of the texts is more clear, and the whore's position, unequivocal. The whore has nothing but scorn for the new cult of womanhood, with its belief in innate feminine modesty and virtue. The *pudeur* extolled by Enlightenment thinkers makes her laugh so heartily that it is possible to imagine that the novels were written primarily to refute this doctrine of sexual difference.[36] "Virtue is a vile prejudice impressed upon girls by their parents," explains a more experienced girl to the novice Javotte.[37] No whore doubts that the reward for virginity is poverty and the reward for libertinage, pleasure and riches. As for woman's "natural modesty," prostitute texts are quite clear. "[W]omen are born for pleasure," says one whore. Indeed, they are "made for it."[38] "Women are created with a taste for pleasure" and the "modesty" that is supposed to distinguish women from men is an illusion.[39]

Indeed, sexual difference, at least in terms of sensual pleasure, is a phantom. The prostitute texts preach an older, materialistic doctrine that leaves little room for biological and temperamental differences between the sexes.[40] The whores tell us that "nature exercises the same empire over women as men," and Margot, Javotte, Marguerite and the rest certainly act like men.[41] They have temperament rather than modesty, and they regard sex as its own reward and pursue it in a ruthlessly instrumental way.

To be sure, the pornographic novels do not deny the anatomical differences of men and women; in fact, they lavish attention on the female body and, through both text and illustration, the reader gets a vivid image of the female anatomy. Of course, the texts emphasize not the maternal breasts but the clitoris, that organ which most closely approximates the other emphasized organ, the penis. In fact, a few of the women with whom the whores consort, especially *tribades* (lesbians), have outsized clitorides. The seasoned whore, however, has more than just a clitoris – she has her art and her equipment, especially her dildos, which, on occasion, allow her to usurp the male role as penetrator. Likewise, many of the young men with whom the prostitutes have fleeting affairs possess the "white skin" and "beautiful buttocks" of their female lovers. Nor do the anatomical facts of sexual difference hinder the prostitute in her search for pleasure, because male and female experience the sexual act in a virtually identical manner. As orgasm approaches, both become delirious and then "discharge" repeatedly, spewing forth "waves of hot fuck." Whore and client are "drowned," "drenched" and "bathed" in a celestial liquid that is both male and female.

The whore can also usurp the traditional male role of the socially dominant partner in mercenary sex, because she can move from being kept woman and prostitute to being keeper and client. Javotte takes a soldier as a lover, and he demands that he be "reimbursed for the time and effort taken to fuck [her]."[42] Like a good whore, he provides "gaiety, value and *complaisance*." Moreover, as the pornographic whore points out, *prostitute* and *female* are not synonymous. La Cauchoise is happy to unveil a "mystery" or "scandal" that seems to contradict "eternal laws." Sodomy exists everywhere, she tells us: in Rome, St. Petersburg, Berlin, Vienna, London and Stockholm – in all the world capitals. In these cities, men penetrate each other and "what is worse depraved men who have a taste for buggery can satisfy themselves for little money. In many places, soldiers and other men will allow themselves to be sodomized (*enculé*) for only pennies!"[43] One senses some professional outrage in La Cauchoise; she does not appreciate competition, and she is equally happy to rail against the honest women who unfairly deprive her of clients. In a later text, *Vénus en rut*, the heroine is more clever and assumes the role of pimp to a male prostitute. By chance, she acquires a young "cherub" – a twelve-year-old boy – whom she initiates sexually, abuses regularly and then prostitutes to men and women, just as she does herself.[44] Her César becomes, she tells us, the "wife of all the husbands and the husband of all the wives," and, because she acts as both seller and commodity, dominator and dominated, she engages in a sensual commerce that confuses domination and subordination and, with them, sexual distinctions. At a time when sexual difference was becoming an established idea, the pornographic texts and their prostitute heroines seem curiously out-of-date.[45] The usual markers of gender either lack salience or fail to appear altogether. The libertine prostitute doesn't adhere to the new notion of womanhood. She is not modest, dependent, loving or maternal; she does not believe in romantic love and refuses to remain within the private, family sphere. Rather she is a public woman who, like Margot, is independent both financially and morally, intelligent, rational and responsible. Her reward is to end her days in a comfortable retirement, on a country estate where she can lead a peaceful and measured existence. To the "virtuous courtesan" of Restif, Rousseau and Nougaret, she leaves modesty, dependency and victimization. She stands in defiance of the new sexual politics and with the Revolution she would oppose the old power politics too.

With the Revolution came the end of censorship. Pornographic texts multiplied and so, too, did those featuring the whore, and, while most of the whore's characteristics remained the same, there were some shifts in emphasis and some changes in language. As in the past, the prostitute began in the popular *faubourgs*, and, like Margot and Javotte, she is a daughter of the *menu peuple*; however, unlike her forerunners, the Revolutionary prostitute never leaves the streets. The post-1789 whore texts dwell on the sordid side of prostitution, and like all texts of the time, are much more explicit and vulgar in their language. The prostitute not only descends from a fishwife, she talks like one, but she doesn't abandon the bishops and princes who pay for her charms. On the contrary, her connection to the aristocracy is still strong, but with politically charged consequences for the latter. For example, a handful of texts explore the old equation between prostitute and aristocracy and turn it against the aristocracy.[46]

In *Les Délices de Coblentz, ou Anecdotes des emigrés français* (1792), a description of life in Coblentz turns out to be an indictment of the nobility's corrupt ways – including their addiction to mercenary sex – which are now allowed to flourish without restraint in the emigré capital. "All one sees there," the author tells us, "is celebrations, orgies and obscene rendez-vous." While the former nobles are supposed to be preparing an assault on France, they actually divide their time between the *bonne chère* and prostitutes. All the odalisques of Europe have gathered in Coblentz to satisfy these insatiable nobles. The duc de Bourbon has brought his fishwife mistress, and Condé enjoys a sordid whore, whom he abandons occasionally so that he might sodomize a young nobleman. The count d'Artois, a habitué of the lowliest bordellos in the rue du Pélican, lives with his mistress, who, in the past, "gave lessons" to the duchesse de Polignac and "la bonne Antoinette." The noblewomen are mounted by their valets, aristocratic brothers have sex with their sisters and all engage in complicated orgies characterized by homosexuality, oral sex and sodomy. "Our princes," the author concludes, "are really bad subjects with no education and an endless source of lubricity." In a *Suite des délices*, the author reports that the nobles are exhausted, their pricks dried and flabby, their bodies weakened by unabated sexual excess. "It is in this manner," he conludes, "that all the potentates of Europe have fallen."[47]

Many of these antiaristocratic diatribes resemble older texts in which the whore narrates the proceedings. For example, *Les Derniers soupirs de la garce en pleurs adressés à la ci-devant noblesse*, probably published in 1791, contains a verse in which the whore – the *garce* of the title – addresses a long complaint to the aristocracy. She begins by complaining in very vulgar language that the nobility has "abandoned her cunt" and left her with "a venereal poison in her veins." What is she to do? The whore "who yesterday in plain view of marquises and counts, had [her] hot clitoris rubbed by prelats and her vagina sucked by barons" now has no clients. Her former lovers, Bourbon and the impotent d'Artois, have fled and begun "taking lessons in buggery." Philippe Capet responds in equally vulgar language, which prompted an unknown editor to remark that "he has forgotten none of the language he learned in the bordellos he frequented with the princesse de Lamballe." Capet returns the whore's insults, and tells her she'll have to make do without the nobility, which has found other amusements, principally buggery.[48]

In this context, the relation between courtesan and court becomes derogatory. The elegant escapades of the prostitute and her aristocratic or ecclesiastic lovers are used to discredit the nobility and equate its sexual habits to those of the lowliest subjects. Commerce between aristocrats and whores now demeans the nobles, and even the greatest princes are accused of consorting with diseased fishwives and vulgar whores. Both the nobility and the prostitute descend from the aristocratic *maison de plaisance*, and are now seen to frequent fetid bordellos and criminal taverns.

For the prostitute, the primary result of this process is swift demotion. No longer is she elegant and enviable; no longer is she prosperous. A bordello is no longer the clean, orderly establishment of the earlier whore novels, but, rather, a sordid hovel, and while the pre-Revolutionary descriptions of bordellos featured prestigious establishments like that of the dames Gourdan and Paris, they now relish in the most perverse and impoverished. During the Revolution, the common prostitute emerged from the shadows to join, if not to evince, her elegant courtesan sister. And while the courtesan has not completely disappeared, the Revolution *has* forced her to lower her standards. Virtually all the revolutionary pamphlets assumed that the prostitute's principal clients were nobility and clergy and that, without them, the whores must starve. However, the reappearance of an old form of prostitute literature – the almanac or lists of addresses – suggests the appearance of a new consumer of mercenary sex.

Between 1789 and 1792, there appear approximately forty lists or almanacs of prostitutes, complete with addresses, identifying characteristics, special services and prices. The women's physical characteristics – blonde or brunette, young or old – are cataloged, along with the services she is most likely to provide. Some prostitutes are noted for their "lively hand," others for their "fiery cunts." The women are described as "very active *citoyennes*," who "know all the Rights of Man." One whore "has a rare quality; she is a madame by day and a Monsieur by night, therefore both a passive and active citizen."[49] *Les Fastes scandaleux, Etrennes des grisettes, Almanac des demoiselles de Paris de tout genre, Protestations des filles du Palais royal et leurs veritable tarif, Tarif des filles du Palais royal, Liste complete des plus belles femmes publiques* and the *Almanac des adresses des demoiselles de Paris* are but a few of the titles.[50] Some pamphlets also include obscene verse and fiction with their lists of prostitutes' addresses. These lists appear to provide only a partially accurate guide to Parisian prostitutes: some of the women, like the famous procuress Madame Paris, were long dead by 1789; others, like the actresses Racourt, Dupré, Clairon and Arnould, were either inaccessible or had emigrated to London. It is impossible to know whether the rest actually existed. Accuracy, however, was probably not the quality sought by most men who purchased these tracts, which were quite salacious and sometimes very funny in a vulgar way. It is possible the tracts were purchased merely for entertainment.

With the publication of lists, the prostitute comes down off her pedestal; she is now available to everyone, rich or poor, common laborer or the newly created citizen, and it is the citizen that is the professed audience of some of the pamphlets. Lists prepared in 1789 target the deputies to the Estates-General; those published after 1790 are even more democratic, being intended for the "con-fédérés" visiting Paris for the first time. Because the fanciest courtesans, the former mistresses of dukes and famous actresses are included on the lists, it could be taken as a sign that pleasures once reserved for the aristocrats are now to be shared by common citizens. Stripped of her elegant trappings, the whore now becomes a *grisette*, a symbol of the laboring poor and an emblem of class, a victim in the mode of Restif and the other virtuous prostitute novelists.

The libertine whore's last stand, her final triumph and swan song, was in the early Revolution. After that, authors, both pornographic and mainstream, seemed to lose interest in prostitutes. In the years after 1791, they produced increasingly fewer texts about prostitutes, and the prostitute's confession, in particular, seems to have languished as a genre, with few additions. There are some very minor works – *L'Enfant du bordel, ou les aventures*

de chérubin (1799) or *Le Catéchisme libertin* (1792) — that include
the prostitute theme, and Restif continued to publish works very
similar to the whore biography. Restif's most sustained work on
prostitution, *Le Palais royal*, which appeared in 1790, is a series
of interviews with streetwalkers. But Andréa de Nerciat, the other
important erotic author of the period, showed less interest in
the whore, with the exception being *Julie philosophe*. The women
in Andréa de Nerciat's other novels are wealthy aristocrats who
indulge in elaborate orgies for pleasure, not for money. To use
Andréa de Nerciat's expression, the *"société d'amour"* — the gath-
ering of men and women of equal status for the purpose of rec-
reational and sometimes quite perverse sex — appears now to
be the standard. After two hundred years and a particularly bril-
liant career in the eighteenth century, the libertine whore was
almost retired.

One singular novel, Sade's *Juliette*, revived her, if only momen-
tarily, and developed her character more fully than it had ever
been before. Of course, prostitutes had appeared in Sade's work,
most notably in *Les 120 journées à Sodome*, where four seasoned
procuresses or *macquerelles* serve as ringmasters for the roué's
orgies. True to classic whore confession form, the procuresses tell
stories that later become real orgies, and the prostitutes survive
the general carnage only by skillfully "writing" themselves into
the next day's amusements. Many of the classic qualities of the
libertine whore are present in *Les 120 journées*: the prostitute narrator, with her healthy sexual appetite and indifference to "feminine" virtue or modesty. But it is in a later novel, *Juliette*, which
was probably written in 1792, at the same time as *La Philosophie
dans le boudoir*, that Sade revives and perfects the libertine whore
of the old regime (figure 6.2).

Written after the well known *Justine, ou Les Malheurs de la vertu*,
Juliette is its companion piece, and the sequel to the virtuous sis-

245

FIGURE 6.2. An engraving from the 1797 edition of Marquis de Sade's *Histoire de Juliette*.

ter's saga. It also seems to be consciously patterned on the whore confessional and borrows many of its formal conventions. For instance, Juliette tells her own story, like her predecessors Margot and Marguerite. Juliette quickly relates that she is the daughter of wealthy and relatively distinguished parents, who placed both her and her sister in a convent, where she learns the rudiments of libertinism from abbess Delbène. The mysterious death of her parents forces Juliette to leave the convent, and she goes directly to a Parisian bordello owned by the procuress, Madame Duvergier.

Like other eighteenth-century whore biographies, Juliette's story now becomes the tale of her professional progress and, in Juliette's particular case, of her personal journey toward the status of true *roué*. In the first quarter of this lengthy saga, Juliette is a Parisian prostitute. At Madame Duvergier's establishment she services a host of men, marketing her "virginity" repeatedly. Her clients are noblemen and, of course, clergymen, among whom is an archbishop with a predilection for oral intercourse. In the line of work, Juliette meets Noirceuil, the first male libertine in her life, and becomes his kept mistress. Later, she also goes to work for his friend, Saint-Fond, and graduates to the status of *appareilleuse* – that is, the procuress and arranger of pleasures. This is a typical career trajectory for an eighteenth-century whore and, even more true to the form, Juliette cheats on both Noirceuil and Saint-Fond by engaging in orgies with Belmour, a lover. She also makes extra money, thanks to Madame Duvergier, by participating in some orgies, where she meets Clairwil, the first of a series of female companions. Misfortune strikes as Juliette runs afoul of Saint-Fond, her powerful protector, and is forced to flee Paris, leaving all her savings behind. Juliette returns to her original profession and, in Angers, she opens a gambling establishment (synonymous in the eighteenth century with a bordello). She prospers and meets a gullible and virtuous gentleman, Monsieur de Lorsang, who, unaware of her past, marries her. Like any number of pornographic whores before her, Juliette is now a respectable woman.

Her saga, however, continues for another eight hundred pages, and it is at this point that Juliette's story comes uncoupled from the traditional prostitute biography, for Sade intends to make her not merely the prostitute par excellence, but a true *roué*. Bored in Angers, Juliette goes to Italy, where the rest of her story unfolds. No longer a simple *fille du monde*, Juliette prostitutes herself to heads of state, to the duke of Savoy and the king of Naples, whom she happily lectures on materialist philosophy. She shares her taste for cruelty and perverse orgies with no less a figure than the pope. Now a true *roué*, Juliette is more often a teacher than a pupil, and her grasp of philosophy is so secure that it is difficult to characterize her as a mere prostitute. (Of course, she will, at times, fall back on her original profession, and if necessary she can always open a bordello in Florence or act as an *appareilleuse* in Naples, thereby assuring renewed financial success.) But Juliette has really ceased to be a whore, even a libertine one: she has become instead the embodiment of Sade's materialist philosophy.

Though she eventually transcends her original destiny, Juliette in the early part of the novel, still shares a great deal with the libertine whore. Like Margot and Javotte, she tells her own story and feels no shame in her profession. Indeed, for one of Juliette's mentors, the lubricious abbess Delbène, the life of the prostitute is sublime:

> Yes, I would like to be declared infamous; I would like for it to be decided and declared publicly that I was a whore; I would like to break these invidious vows that prevent me from prostituting myself publicly, that prevent me from debasing myself like the lowest women! I would like to share the fate of these divine creatures who

satisfy on street corners the filthy lusts of the passerby; who squat in the mud.... Who would not want to join them?[51]

Certainly Sade would. Later, Delbène tells Juliette why the prostitute's lot is so desirable, so laudable:

> Don't let the name of whore (*putain*) frighten you.... A whore is a charming creature, young, voluptuous who sacrifices her reputation for the happiness of others, which alone would merit our praise. The prostitute is the cherished child of nature; the good girl is its execration; the prostitute merits an altar; the vestal the stake.[52]

For Sade, as for his pornographic forebears, the "prostitute is the child of nature," woman in her true form fully possessed of her sexuality. The virtuous and modest woman is the antithesis and the enemy of the whore. Delbène rails against the notion that women naturally disdain pleasure and cherish virtue. Such ideas she dismisses as "a ridiculous prejudice, absolutely belied by nature." "Chastity," she further instructs Juliette, "is only a fashion, a convention...it is not at all in nature and a girl, woman or boy who gives his body to a passerby, who prostitutes himself boldly in all senses, in all places, does nothing...contrary to nature."[53]

Like Margot and La Cauchoise, Sade's heroines have no use for Rousseauist notions of womanhood and modesty, nor for any other strictures on woman's free disposition of her own body. Marriage and motherhood they revile; prostitution, libertinage and abortion they consider natural rights. In a materialist universe, the only reward is bodily pleasure, and women are as entitled to this reward as any other human.

Sade, like his predecessors, has little interest in sexual difference and consistently confuses gender. He has Delbène explain to Juliette that "nature having created both men and women nude, it is impossible that he made either one or the other ashamed of his nudity."[54] Both male and female enjoy sex, and in much the same way. Sade's heroines are ferocious in their pursuit of pleasure, and they are not particular about the gender of those with whom they have sex. Indeed, Sade's orgies always involve the switching of roles, with men sodomizing men, women performing cunnilingus on women, one sex on top some of the time, on the bottom the rest of the time, and all positions to be changed after a massive, communal "discharge." Sade's *roués* all adore anal intercourse regardless of their gender, it being that form of copulation that comes closest to obliterating sexual difference by allowing either male or female to play the passive or the active role, since Sade's women are always armed with dildos. Moreover, there are characters in Sade whose sex is ambiguous. The witch, Durand, possesses a clitoris so long that she is able to penetrate Juliette and Clairwil. Noirceuil prefers the passive role in sodomy, and stages a fake marriage in which he, dressed as a woman, marries a man. While there is no symmetry – that is, Juliette, when dressed as a man, does not marry a woman – sexual roles are still muddled.[55]

In Sade's ideal bordello, sexual difference disappears. While for most eighteenth-century men and women, the word *prostitute* was synonymous with *woman*, the term is utterly gender-neutral for Sade. The bordello that is to provide "slaves" to the *roués* of Friends of Crime has two sections: one for female prostitutes and the other for male whores. The Florentine *bagnio* serves up both masculine and feminine flesh according to the client's wishes, not gender.

In Sade's universe, gender is *relatively* unimportant. Polymorphous perversion is the rule, as several commentators have noted, and the point could bear restatement in the light of feminist analyses of Sade's work.[56] In this regard, Sade is a throwback to the pre-Rousseauist era, a man who sees little difference – at least, most of the time – between male and female. In Sade's world, people are not divided into the categories of man and woman, but into the categories of master and slave. Here, domination is important, indeed, crucial, but it does not rely on sexual difference; women can occupy either position, and in *Juliette*, most of the *roués* are female. How one enters the master class is not spelled out, but Juliette becomes a master by an unremitting commitment to her personal happiness at the expense of that of others. Her gender is only relevant in that it makes Sade's "moral" all the more pungent. As the virtuous Justine's sister, she demonstrates more fully the irrelevance of sexual difference and the lie of virtue, and, in doing so, she joins her antecedents, the libertine whores of the mid-eighteenth century.

From Juliette and her forerunners it can be learned that pornography's assumptions are not unchanging. The obscene has not always structured domination upon gender; in the eighteenth century, a world was constructed where sex was less important than sexuality, and sexual pleasure did not necessitate the denigration of only the female participants. The pornographic world of the Enlightenment, especially as embodied in Sade's "pornotopia," was a universe built around violence and the purest, crudest domination. But women are not the only victims, the only objects.

This is not to suggest that the eighteenth-century whore constituted a "liberated" woman or that the eighteenth century was a period of gender equality. Margot and Javotte are wholly fictional characters who probably could not have survived the social realities of the eighteenth century. Nor does lack of gender difference mean gender equality; on the contrary, it is from that gender difference that women's call for equality would finally emerge in the nineteenth century. As for Margot, Javotte and the other libertine whores, they would not live to see it for they were quintessentially eighteenth-century and they spring from – and illuminate – an era before the advent of sexual difference.

The tradition of the libertine whore was clearly waning during the Revolution and did not survive the Restoration. The advent of a new doctrine of sexual difference rendered the independent philosophical prostitute obsolete. Juliette, it seems, had no nineteenth-century successors. Occasionally, the Medusa or the dominatrix – for example, Sade's Durand – resurfaced and aroused both masculine fears and domination. The prostitute, too, would have a long career in literature and art, especially mainstream literature and art. The future, however, lay not with the independent whore, but with the virtuous courtesan. The whore as victim began to replace the prostitute as philosopher, and nineteenth-century authors began to punish the public woman with disease, degradation and, ultimately, death for her unnatural sexual energy. Few nineteenth-century writers celebrated the prostitute or allowed her any independence or dignity, because notions of women's natural modesty and subordination made such characterizations unthinkable. In an age of unbreachable sexual difference, Margot, Juliette and the other libertine whores of the eighteenth century had become relics, fabulous but extinct creatures with no descendants either in the nineteenth century or today.

CHAPTER SEVEN

Erotic Fantasy and Male Libertinism

in Enlightenment England

Randolph Trumbach

In 1748 and 1749 John Cleland published the two volumes of his *Memoirs of a Woman of Pleasure*. It was to become eighteenth-century Europe's most notorious pornographic work. It contained repeated descriptions of the male sexual organs and acts of sexual intercourse. Its purpose does not seem, in any marked way, to have been political, although there were already some indications of the passion against the aristocracy that derailed Cleland's last surviving novel, *The Woman of Honour*. Instead, Cleland principally aimed at sexually arousing his reader, in a context that was neither satirical nor humorous. With that purpose and by those means, Cleland established in England the modern pornographic genre, which can be distinguished from the larger body of English erotic writing from the Restoration to the end of the eighteenth century that Roger Thompson and Peter Wagner have described. When set in the context of this larger literature and its subgenres, which ranged from the bawdy poem to the medical treatise and the trial report, Cleland's *Fanny Hill* (to give the *Memoirs* its popular name) appears unique in its singleness of purpose. But when the novel is considered with other English erotic fantasies which, in the second half of the eighteenth century, were produced for, and often, written by gentlemen, it can be seen as part of what

might be called the religion of libertinism. This religion can be
defined as believing, in contradistinction to orthodox Christianity, that sexual experience was central to human life and that sexual desire and pleasure were good and natural things. The sexual
organs and acts of sexual intercourse were, therefore, symbols of
a great life-giving force and were as worthy of human worship as
the symbols of the Christian sacraments and the grace that was
the life of the soul.[1]

Gender Roles and Sexual Behavior

This libertine religion and the new pornographic genre that Cleland's novel represented were both products of the modern system
of gender and sexual relations that was emerging in England and
the rest of northwestern Europe in the first half of the eighteenth
century. What it meant to be female or male and the connection
of gender roles to sexual behavior were both undergoing a revolution that was part of the appearance of that first modern Western culture, which historians have traditionally and usefully called
the Early Enlightenment. The behavior and status of women were
being modified by new ideals of romantic marriage, conjugal companionship and the tender care of children.[2] But the behavior and
status of men were more markedly transformed by the new meaning attached to sexual relations between males. In Europe before
1700, adult men had had sexual relations with both women and
adolescent males. Only relations with women in marriage were
legal and approved of by the church. But men engaged in other
relations with women, ranging from prostitution to adultery and
rape, all of which were illegal in England and certainly immoral
everywhere in Europe. This immoral behavior could nonetheless be honorable in men when it displayed them as powerful. Sexual relations between two males were similarly illegal, immoral
and yet honorable when conducted in ways that displayed adult

male power. In most of Europe and certainly in England, this was achieved when adult males sexually penetrated adolescent boys, who existed in a transitional state between man and woman. All men were supposed to be capable of such acts with boys. But it is as difficult to say how many actually engaged in sodomy as it is to establish the frequency of adultery. These sexual relations between men and boys did not – and this is the essential point – carry with them the stigma of effeminacy or of inappropriate male behavior, as they began to do after 1700 and have continued to ever since in modern Western societies. Adult men were deemed effeminate only when they allowed themselves to be sexually penetrated, or when an overpowering sexual desire for women caused them to surrender control into the hands of women.[3] (For recent literature on this subject see the appendix to my notes on pp. 388–90.)

After 1700, in the cities of England, France and the Netherlands – those societies most likely to produce pornographic writing – this traditional system of male homosexual behavior was replaced by a new standard of sexual relations between males. Most men were now thought to desire sexually only women and this exclusive desire was largely what gave them masculine status. This standard was one that males were expected to internalize by the onset of puberty; adolescent boys could no longer experience a period of sexual passivity with an older male. Boys in London who were approached sexually by men were, therefore, thrown into varying degrees of panic best assuaged by prosecuting, shaming and punishing the sodomite. Sodomy was now stigmatized as the behavior of an effeminate minority, regardless of whether an individual's partner was adult or adolescent, or whether an individual was active or passive in the sexual act, penetrating or penetrated. These effeminate men were imagined to desire to be women and to hate actual women. They were described as moving, speaking and dressing as women, and engaging in female occupations. There is no doubt that, in varying degrees, the new effeminate sodomite did all these things, sometimes in the open street, sometimes in the alehouse. *Molly* was the street term for these men. Its etymology precisely defines the sodomite's status. The term had first been used for female prostitutes. The molly, like the prostitute, was an individual entirely defined by his sexual behavior. Together, the prostitute and the sodomite displayed the boundaries of appropriate gender behavior for the majority of people in their societies, where true women were not whores, and real men were not sodomites.[4]

Women were not whores because by their nature they were intended for the domestic joys of motherhood. This was the new ideal. It differed from the old ideal, which held that every woman was at heart a rake, with her sexual desires more powerful and less controlled than those of men. By 1750, the families of gentlemen were affected powerfully by the new ideal. The romantic marriage began to replace the arranged. A married couple hoped to share one another's constant company after marriage rather than going out separately into the social world. Aristocratic women gave up their wet nurses, nursed their children themselves, and generally paid so close an attention to their children that the infant death rate was lowered to a level not achieved by the general population for another hundred years. These ideals and practices, of course, brought their own pains with them. The number of aristocratic divorces after 1750, though still small in absolute numbers, grew alarmingly to contemporaries, probably as a result of the higher expectations that couples came with to their marriages.[5]

It is also likely that the new level of male anxiety, displayed in the modern taboo against all homosexual acts between males, was directly tied to the new ideals of love and marriage. Males were accustomed to establishing their dominance over women and children through various forms of separation and distance; the new ideals of love, companionship and affectionate childrearing made this distance more difficult to maintain. Aristocratic boys, therefore, continued to undergo a breeching between the ages of three and five, when the formation of gender identity was completed. They discarded the sexually ambiguous coat they had worn, which resembled a woman's dress, and put on male breeches. A few years after this, boys were separated from their mothers and sisters and sent away to school to be educated in a totally male environment. These early separations from women were powerfully enforced at puberty. Adolescent boys had previously been allowed to be sexually passive with adult males. They were now socialized to avoid this. Consequently, as men they knew that no matter how close and affectionate their associations with women, there remained one unbreachable difference between men and women: men did not know what it was like to desire males sexually. Only women and sodomites knew that. Therefore, what the nineteenth century called *homosexuality* and *heterosexuality* are not distinctions to be found in universal human nature. They were, instead, products of a gender system that had appeared in the early eighteenth century and that accompanied the new forms of marital friendship and paternal affection. It is disputed whether these new forms of love affected the lives of the poor before the middle of the nineteenth century. But it is certain that the taboo on homosexual behavior was fully enacted among the London poor from whom the effeminate transvestite molly was most likely to be recruited (figure 7.1).[6]

For most of the eighteenth century it is not clear, however, that the modern homosexual taboo applied to women in the way that it did to men. In London, it was not until the last quarter of the century that there were women who were stigmatized as sapphists or tommies as men were called sodomites or mollies. Women's sexual relations with men, and whether they were faith-

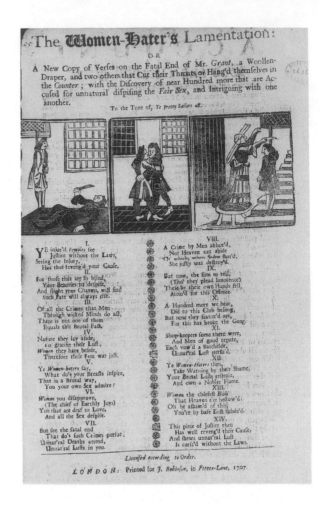

FIGURE 7.1. *The Women-Hater's Lamentation* (1707). A street ballad against effeminate sodomites who are shown kissing each other and committing suicide after they have been exposed.

ful wives and not whores, were of greater consequence for their gender standing than their avoidance of sexual relations with women. The psychology of women was not yet treated, in this respect, as equivalent to that of men. The achievement of what twentieth-century psychoanalysts have loved to call "full adult heterosexuality" was, in the later eighteenth century, still pre-served for men. Only men were, by those lights, fully human. This ideal of humanity aimed to secure the dominance of one half of society over the other, of men over women.[7]

What Is Pornography?
These developments in the history of gender and sexual desire set the boundaries within which erotic fantasy was experienced in the middle of the eighteenth century. It is even possible to argue that they forced the development of a new pornographic genre within the more general field of erotic fantasy. But before that argument is attempted, it must be made clear that, in eighteenth-century England, there was not much of what the twentieth-century viewer or reader would recognize as hard-core pornography. In fact, Cleland's *Fanny Hill* may well have been its one unam-biguous example, making it possible to think of this novel as the begetter of the twentieth-century genre.

In twentieth-century pornography, there are two kinds of sex-ual representations. First, the human sexual organs, and especially the erect penis, are depicted in photographs, prints and moving pictures. Sometimes there are also verbal descriptions of these organs, but photography has made such descriptions less vital to twentieth-century pornography than they were in the eighteenth century. Twentieth-century pornography can be found most point-edly in the repeated representation of acts of sexual intercourse in novels and stories, in photographs and, above all, in the mov-ies where acts between real persons (who are sometimes not even actors) are caught on film. The verbal or the visual techniques used in these two forms of twentieth-century pornography can vary greatly. The prose can be leaden. The film director can fail to vary camera angles, forget to show the actors' faces as opposed to their genitals, edit incompetently and accompany the images with a banal or irrelevant sound track. The actors can fail to concentrate or interact and their penises can remain flaccid. But whatever the level of technical competence displayed, the tone of all these works is very similar. It is almost never satirical or humorous. Instead, there is a level seriousness that intends to present the bodies and the sexual acts as worthy in themselves. This serious tone is probably adopted because it maximizes sexual arousal, whereas humor or satire tend to limit it. The context in which the reader's or viewer's arousal occurs can vary. An individual can use the material for solitary masturbation; or a couple or a group of individuals can achieve mutual stimulation. The written material is most likely to be used for solitary pleasure; the photographs and the movies will stimulate individuals, couples and groups.

If this is the twentieth-century practice of pornography, was there anything similar in eighteenth-century England? The answer is yes, but very little, if the standard used is the representation of repeated acts of sexual intercourse. There were as well more visual than written representations of these acts in the eighteenth century, with Cleland's *Fanny Hill* the only unambiguous instance of the written description of repeated acts of sexual intercourse. However, if the standard used is the visual representation or verbal description of the sexual organs, then there was a great deal more. Many of the verbal descriptions of genitals are to be found in medical works, and much of the visual representation, as in Rowlandson, was put in a humorous context. It was difficult to create more straightforward descriptions or representations that had the unabashed purpose of causing sexual arousal. There were, of course, no eighteenth-century pornographic films, which are probably the twentieth century's most powerful form of pornography. The nearest thing in that age was showing lewd postures, in which live women displayed their sexual parts and simulated the positions and movements of sexual intercourse.

Pornographic or erotic poetry, however, which was recited or sung to an audience, was widespread in the eighteenth century but has disappeared in the twentieth, another instance of the triumph of the novel. Most of this poetry, like a great deal of the rest of eighteenth-century sexual writing, is more usefully described as erotic rather than pornographic. It was not so much erect penises or sexual acts – and there were more penises than there were acts – that were described, as what might be called the sexual courtships that eventually led to sexual consummation. The epiphenomena of sex were far more likely to be presented in eighteenth-century English texts than was the thing itself.

The street ballad probably provided the majority of people with their most immediate experience of erotic or pornographic fantasy. Authority could be disapproving. William Crocker was arrested for singing scandalous ballads in the street. Edward Welsh sang an obscene ballad, encouraged his young son to do the same and was also arrested. But such songs, while they might get one into trouble if sung in the street, were sung by respectable tradesmen indoors. Francis Place remembered the singing of "very gross" songs in his father's parlor by men "who were much excited." Everyone who heard the songs clapped at the end and rapped the tables in delight. His friend Richard Hayward had to remind the now respectable Place of the words of "Morgan Rattler."

> First he niggled her, then he tiggled her
> Then with his two balls he began for to
> batter her

At every thrust, I thought she'd have burst
With the terrible size of his Morgan Rattler.

"Morgan Rattler" neatly combined the representation of both the erect penis and sexual intercourse. But the convivial, humorous context of such songs, especially in their group performance, could not approach the serious intentness that pornotopia seems to require to achieve the maximum level of sexual arousal.[8]

The audiences for this erotic and pornographic material in the eighteenth century were, as in the twentieth century, the individual, the couple and the group. These varying audiences can be documented most easily by considering the evidence for the use of visual materials. "Wanton pictures," wrote Henry Deacon, were among the principal causes of male erections, along with "lewd books, women's company, libidinous discourse" and hearty food and drink. "Wanton pictures," very often, were depictions of various sexual positions: they were often called "Aretino's postures" after the notorious series of illustrations. Betty Sands, a posture girl, was said to have shown "more odious postures than were invented by that most debauched nobleman of Venice named Peter Aretino": "which immodest cuts," Captain Smith piously concluded, "ought to be committed to the flames." These kinds of prints were available to all levels of society throughout the century. In 1704, Lord Dorset kept a book of them by his bedside; it was bound to look like a songbook. This presumably he used for solitary masturbation at night. A curious visiting lady on a tour of his house took a peep and found that the book contained "the most obscene lascivious pictures that ever can be imagined." Francis Place said that in his boyhood, at the end of the century, these prints were openly sold alongside schoolbooks and offered to any boy or girl. Mrs. Roach, in her shop, would ask the young if they wanted "some pretty pictures" and then encourage them to leaf through her portfolio. Once again it is probable that the pictures were first used for solitary masturbation.

Some men went directly from the inspiration of the print to their actions with a whore. Lord Grosvenor was moved by the picture of a naked woman that was hung over the fireplace in a bawdy house, to ask Elizabeth Roberts to strip herself naked. James Graham, in his sex manual, which he claimed was directed at married couples, recommended the use of lascivious prints, paintings and statues for those who were old or of languid constitutions. Graham did not mention reading lascivious texts for the same purpose.[9]

The group use of pornographic images can be documented most easily in the viewing of women who showed lewd postures. There are two literary descriptions of such women and a group of male viewers. In one, girls lay naked on a table in a bagnio, surrounded by a group of men who look closely at their sexual parts. A glass of wine is then placed on top of the mons veneris of one of the women and each man drinks from it. The women writhe and imitate various sexual postures, and finish by masturbating themselves. In the other description, a girl arrives half drunk, strips and goes down on all fours as the men gloat over her and ridicule her. Ned Ward has one whore in Bridewell describe another as "one of Posture Moll's scholars" who could show "how the watermen shoot London Bridge, or how the lawyers go to Westminster" – names, evidently, of two erotic postures. In actual commonplace bawdy houses it could be difficult to see at night. Mary Johnson said that Sarah Morrice made her strip several times in the presence of a man so that he could look "into her privities" with the help of a candle. John Northey took two girls to Elizabeth Crawford's house, where (or so she said), he "gave them money to flog him" and then "put one on the bed [and] had a candle to look at her." But in both of these cases we are back to an individual man looking at a woman's sexual parts. These actual examples confirm the realism of the many descriptions of this kind of voyeurism in Cleland's *Fanny Hill*.[10]

Any public presentation of the genitals tended to move in a pornographic direction. This can be seen in the increasing foregrounding of descriptions of the genitals in a book, which could transform it from a relatively sober medical work to an increasingly erotic and nearly pornographic one. This occurred with *Aristotle's Masterpiece*, which, in its various editions, was the best-known introduction to sex for young men. Francis Place, by the time he was thirteen, understood most of what happened in sexual intercourse because of what he had overheard in the relatively frank conversation of adults. For that which was still unclear, such as the account of the miraculous conception of Jesus in the Gospels, he sought enlightenment in *Aristotle's Masterpiece*. Most of *Aristotle's Masterpiece* in its first edition, which was probably in the late 1680s, took the form of a midwifery book, describing how children were conceived and born. The female sexual organs were not described until page ninety-nine, and the male organs even later, on pages 172–74, and in a much smaller print. The second edition, from about 1710, had a similar emphasis on childbearing, but it was reorganized to begin with a description of the female sexual organs, thereby more clearly distinguishing it from a midwifery book. It was probably intended to compete with the first translations of Venette's sex manual (1703) and John Marten's English imitation (1708) of that book, for which Marten was unsuccessfully prosecuted. The third version of *Aristotle's Masterpiece* in 1725 had, again, been rearranged. This version began with a description of the male sexual organs. This rearrangement was presumably meant to heighten further the book's appeal to a male audience. It had become less of a work on female diseases. But it still limited its libertine and pornographic intention by placing sex in the context of marriage and going back to Adam and Eve in Paradise.[11]

John Cleland's Fanny Hill

Into such a world came Cleland's *Fanny Hill* in 1748 and 1749 with its repeated and extended descriptions of penises and acts of sexual intercourse. The novel does end in marriage. Fanny happily marries Charles, with whom she falls in love after he takes her maidenhead in her first house of prostitution. But all the acts of intercourse in the novel take place outside of marriage. And when Cleland has his happy couples seek a sexual paradise, he does not conduct them into a Christian one. He takes them instead to an island in the Thames, which their imaginations transform into Cythera, the sanctuary of Venus, the pagan goddess of love. This celebration of the goodness of sexual pleasure outside of marriage sets Cleland's work apart from the other erotic fantasies about prostitutes that had appeared in England in the three generations following the Restoration. Thomas Nelson has said how difficult it was for any early eighteenth-century English writer to describe the pleasures of whoring without including its pains and disappointments. The prostitute was compassionated and feared, for, with her, came the dangers of disease and betrayal, and the decay of the aging female body. The prostitute was resented for the pretense of enjoying sexual acts that were not spontaneous for her, but a matter of business. Her financial demands, indeed, could make her seem like a second class kind of wife. Cleland's novel strikingly disregarded this approach. Its organization displayed its ideological intent. The first half showed Fanny's slow decline. Had the second half followed the usual pattern of the whore's biography, both in prose and in Hogarth's picture series, it would have continued through her arrest, imprisonment and death from disease. Instead, the book turned lyrical and arcadian. Its principal scene described the trip to Cythera organized by the young men who hoped to restore sexual pleasure to its original condition, free from pain and guilt. The couples went to Venus's island so that they might worship love with the sexual intercourse of their bodies. Sex became the sacrament of love, the outward and visible sign of inward grace.[12]

The novel used the new techniques of narrative realism, and, by these means, achieved a great deal of its sexual excitement. But it was not an especially realistic representation of the average prostitute's life, nor even of the more rarified world of prostitution for gentlemen. Fanny does not become pregnant; she avoids disease and drunkenness; and she marries her first customer for love. Most importantly, she fully shares the pleasure of her customers.

Cleland was aware of the extent of his fantasy. In his pamphlet on the sailors' riot against the prostitutes and in his imaginative writing after *Fanny Hill*, he made London prostitution a much grimmer affair. It is more difficult to say whether he recognized that his description of female sexual response in the novel was less than realistic. The clitoris, in contrast to the care taken with the penis, is not described clearly; he may even have placed it inside the vagina. (This was, perhaps, an early instance of the Freudian fantasy of the vaginal orgasm.) Cleland also supposed that the larger the penis, the greater the woman's pleasure. A woman's climaxes always equaled the man's in number and never exceeded them. Other eighteenth-century writers were much more aware of the clitoris and its role in sexual pleasure. The price of justifying pleasure in the novel's safe, domesticated environment may have been paid therefore in the coin of an increasing female passivity. In these mutual joys a new form of separation between men and women was achieved by reconstructing the female anatomy.[13]

Cleland's idealization of sexual pleasure may have broken with

a traditional Christian suspicion, but his ideology of sexual liberation was firmly contained within the new structures of romantic love and the avoidance of sodomy that were described earlier.
This is revealed by briefly comparing *Fanny Hill* with *Sodom*, the
most infamous English erotic text of the Restoration. *Sodom* in
the eighteenth century was usually attributed to Lord Rochester.
Modern scholars have tended to doubt this, but there are still
those who make a case for it. Both Rochester and *Sodom*, however,
were replaced as ideals for the libertine in the early eighteenth
century by men like Congreve or Shaftesbury and by books like
Fanny Hill. Rochester and his jokes became too crude, as Horace
Walpole and David Hume both said. *Sodom* seems to have been
printed three times, in 1684, 1689–1690, and 1707, although only
handwritten copies have survived. It was a play rather than a novel
and sexual acts were usually described in it rather than played
out. These descriptions, of course, could not compare with the
realism of the novel. But the chief objection against *Sodom* was
that it presented sex between men and adolescent youths as a
desirable alternative to sex between men and women. It presumed
that all adult males felt both kinds of desire. The play certainly
intended to present sodomy as titillating and shocking, but no
more so than the adultery, fornication, masturbation and incest
that were all part of the play's action.[14]

When *Sodom* was last printed and prosecuted in 1707, its publisher clearly meant to capitalize on the mass arrests of sodomites
in that year. These real sodomites differed considerably, however,
from the men in *Sodom*. They desired only males, and they were
likely to be passive, effeminate and even transvestite. The appearance of this new male role required that Cleland, forty years later,
treat sodomy quite differently in *Fanny Hill*. First, he never has
men and women engage in anal intercourse. There was a single
scene between two males, in which an older adolescent pene-

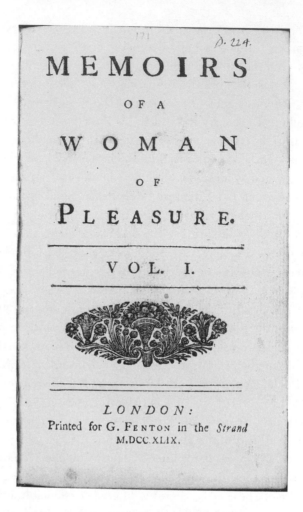

FIGURE 7.2. Title page of the first edition of *Fanny Hill* (1748–1749), which included the passage describing sodomy between two young men that was excluded from subsequent editions.

trated a younger, written with more vivid detail than in *Sodom*. But Fanny, who is so otherwise approving of all sexual pleasure, denounces the youths as members of an effeminate sect who loathe women. For this scene, in particular, the book was prosecuted, and the scene has usually been omitted from all subsequent editions of the book until the most recent, when the gay liberation movement has apparently made it possible to print it again (figure 7.2). It is not clear, however, to what extent Cleland's treatment of sodomy is accounted for by his own desire. It was claimed in 1781 that he passed "under the censure of being a sodomite" and that "in consequence thereof persons of character declined visiting him, or cultivating his acquaintance." Was this true, and if so, what does it mean? Was Cleland himself the last of the old libertines who liked both women and boys, or was he the new kind of sodomite who did not care for women? If it was the latter, it makes his novel an even greater imaginative triumph and raises interesting questions about his identification with his heroine (and, perhaps, would give another explanation as to why he placed the clitoris inside the vagina). Whatever Cleland's personal desires may have been, for his novel to appeal to a male audience in 1750, all of its men (except for the two youths) had to be presented as being (to use the twentieth-century phrase) exclusively heterosexual. This was not yet true of the women. Fanny is seduced by Phoebe Ayres, but says she "pined for more solid food, and promised tacitly to myself that I would not be put off much longer with this foolery from woman to woman." Women at mid-century still lived under the older sexual dispensation.[15]

Cleland's conscious ideological position, as opposed to the structural influences just considered, has usually been accounted for by two likely sources. There was his knowledge of other cultures as he found them in the literature of the ancient pagan Mediterranean and in the India of his own time. It is clear that India turned Cleland into a deist. It probably also confirmed his sexual libertinism. The second influence was a general, diffuse materialism that saw sex as a natural operation of the body and therefore morally good. There are, however, two other influences to consider. There was first his sodomy if the charge was true. Certainly, sodomites of the new effeminate kind who were exclusively attracted to adult men were, with libertines, among those most alienated from conventional Christian asceticism. Sodomites inverted and mocked baptism and marriage in their sexual rituals much as libertines mocked the holy communion. Cleland's sexual radicalism therefore possibly had one of its important roots in deep personal alienation. There was, finally, Lord Shaftesbury's influence on Cleland and on all of the mid-century libertines. The desire of Cleland and his contemporaries for a domesticated sexuality accompanied by love removed them from both the wild rakes of Rochester's age and the more sober Epicureans like Congreve who followed. Cleland nonetheless took Epicurus for a model, telling James Boswell that, because of *Fanny Hill,* "Epicurus was now well defended as not being a sensualist; that intellect and sense must unite in pleasure." But it was pleasure with an enthusiasm drawn from Lord Shaftesbury's doctrine of the virtuoso that discerned, behind the beauties and pleasures of the body, a deeper reality. Shaftesbury himself had been a libertine. He had written and circulated to his closest friends or "brothers," as he called them, a sexual fantasy entitled *The Adept Ladys* along with some accompanying scatological verse. Shaftesbury was concerned that the men of the fashionable world know that they might move from the physical beauty of the human body to the beauties of poetry, painting and philosophy. He had complained to Lord Somers that their fellow aristocrats were corrupted by the pursuit of women and the superstitions of Christianity. He scoffed that the beaux "go no farther than the dancing-master to seek for grace and beauty." The true virtuoso knew that "even in the arts, which are mere imitations of that outward grace and beauty, we not only confess a taste, but make it part of refined breeding to discover amidst the many false manners and ill styles the true and natural one, which represents the real beauty and Venus of the kind." From human beauty then, one proceeded to the beauty of art, but from art, one went on to virtue. This required gentlemen to surrender "brutality, insolence and riot," and turn to good breeding. They would then discover that "to philosophize, in a just signification, is but to carry good breeding a step higher." The virtuoso or "real fine gentleman" would be able to do this because he loved art and ingenuity and had seen the world. It sounds like a program for the Dilettanti Society, and it had very probably helped to form Cleland's mental world.[16]

The Libertine Dispensation

For men like the libertines who gathered in the Dilettanti Society, Cleland's *Fanny Hill* became a sacred text. The book was not in fact an accurate description of prostitution for gentlemen in 1750. But it may have served as a blueprint for a new kind of brothel that appeared in the second half of the century in which drunkenness and disease were supposedly banished and a domesticated fantasy nourished instead. Cleland may have known of Parisian brothels that were something like this. In *The Nocturnal Revels* (1777), which described these new London "seraglios," two lascivious books were mentioned as the libertines' vade mecums – *Fanny Hill* and *The Adventures of Mr F—" in Petticoats*. The relationship between the fantasy of Cleland's novel and the world of actual prostitution may, therefore, be another instance of the novel in part creating a new reality and not simply reflecting it. This would then be similar to the relationship proposed by John Bender and Nancy Armstrong between the novel and the development of both the modern total institution and the modern marriage. But the argument can work both ways. The domesticated brothel that appeared after 1750 brought into focus those conflicting aspects of the new ideals of marriage and the male gender role, which may have accounted for the appearance of the new genre of erotic writing represented by *Fanny Hill*. Romantic marriage ideally required men to be faithful to their wives. But men also needed to establish that they were real men and not sodomites by displaying a constant and exclusive sexual interest in women. These two ideals were in conflict, but the fear of sodomy was the more powerful. Men, therefore, could not give up prostitution or reconstruct the nature of male desire. Instead, there were attempts to reform the young streetwalking prostitute in houses that have been described as total institutions. The prostitute's customers, however, were left unreformed because of the fear that their exclusive desire for women might be damaged. Instead, the domesticated brothel was invented as a place for safe affectionate sex, and the realism and domesticity of the novel were taken by Cleland and applied to the repeated representations of penises and acts of sexual intercourse outside of marriage.[17]

Cleland and the gentlemen who read him were attempting to justify sexual pleasure in a world dominated by Christian asceticism. They could establish their point only by constructing a counterweight to the influence of the Christian church and its rituals. The representation of the penis and of acts of sexual intercourse between 1748, when Cleland published his novel, and 1786, when Richard Payne Knight produced his treatise on the worship of Priapus, were therefore constructed by a group of libertine gentlemen into a religion that worshipped what they would have called the generative force. These gentlemen, to some degree, enacted this religion in rituals that inverted those of the Christian church, and, more certainly, they wrote its theology in a series of erotic works in a variety of genres including the poem, the novel and the learned treatise. But this religion could hardly manage to take itself seriously. The works of its theology could seldom rise to pornographic seriousness, and very often were subverted by the humor or the satire that undermined most erotic fantasy in their society. Nonetheless, these gentlemen produced a literature that, although inchoate in form, created a valuation of sexuality that, a hundred years later, was taken up and transformed by Freud into the scientific religion of the life-giving libido. In their own day, their influence was less profound. A reformed libertine like Martin Madan used the insights of his libertine days to read the texts of the Old and New Testaments less ascetically and in opposition to the Church Fathers. Madan delighted the libertines, who did not take him seriously, and shocked his evangelical friends, who did. Madan's views then remained of marginal influence in Christianity, as they still are. But the conflicts between libertines and Christians, which were embodied in the pornographic and erotic texts about to be considered, show in another way the Enlightenment origins of the modern culture in which we still live.[18]

The gentlemen of the Dilettanti Society provide a convenient focus for a consideration of this libertine religion. The Society was founded in 1732. It aimed at promoting the knowledge of classical civilization as it could be seen in its surviving physical remains in ruins, sculpture and medals. Some of the Society's founding members, like Sir Francis Dashwood, had traveled extensively, especially in Italy, Greece and Asia Minor. When they met, the members wore robes and had various convivial rituals. The Society, however, also had an ideological program in their virtuosoship. They were libertines and often deists, opposed to conventional Christianity and interested in the justification for their sexual lives that the physical remains of ancient classical civilization seemed to provide. Some members, under the leadership of Sir Francis Dashwood, used their friendship as the basis for an additional fraternity that met during the 1750s at Medmenham Abbey, six miles from Dashwood's principal residence. It has ever since been difficult to separate fact from fiction in the history of the monks of Medmenham. Its history was written in Charles Johnstone's novel *Chrysal*, Charles Churchill's poems, Horace Walpole's *Memoirs* and John Wilkes's journalism. The most notorious English pornographic poem of the century, the *Essay on Woman*, may also have been part of Wilkes's contribution to the rituals of this brotherhood.[19]

Dashwood was largely responsible for whatever occurred at Medmenham (figure 7.3). He was widely traveled and, when at home, built extensively and with good taste. He remodeled the west portico of his house at West Wycomb on a reconstruction of a temple to Dionysus or Bacchus, which stood at what had been the principal seat of Dionysiac worship in Ionia. The temple had been investigated and engraved at the expense of the Dilettanti Society. Dashwood had a considerable interest in religious ritual. He printed, in 1773, an *Abridgement of the Book of Common Prayer*, which revised the prayers in a more deistic direction. Dashwood was also fascinated by Roman Catholic ritual and contemptuous of it. There is a sensational story that as a young man, while shouting "the devil, the devil," he had flogged with a horsewhip the surprised penitents on Good Friday as they knelt in the dark of the Sistine Chapel, baring their shoulders in the expectation of a lighter discipline. In England, he and his Dilettanti friends had their pictures painted, with Dashwood portrayed as Saint Francis with a chalice in his hand, at prayer before the statue of the Venus de Medici. But Dashwood also had his earthier side, which his most recent biographer, Betty Kemp, ignores. Walpole described him as "notorious for singing profane and lewd catches."[20]

FIGURE 7.3. William Hogarth's portrait of *Sir Francis Dashwood* (late 1750s) in a monastic habit worshipping the statue of Venus. George Knapton painted a similar portrait of Dashwood holding a communion cup in front of a statue of Venus, and Adrian Carpentier painted Dashwood as a pope standing before a bare-breasted herm.

Around 1750, Dashwood rented Medmenham Abbey. It was a converted Cistercian Abbey. Dashwood renovated it to look even more like an abbey, adding a ruined tower and a cloister and, inside the cloister, a room probably intended to serve as the chapel or the chapter room, from which "the glare of light is judiciously excluded by the pleasing gloom of ancient stained glass." Dashwood invited down a group of friends, for whom there was a costume "more like a waterman's than a monk's." The motto inscribed over the door — *Fay ce que voudras* or Do as you wish — was taken from Rabelais's Abbey of Theleme. About this much even the most skeptical historian agrees. The controversy remains over what the monks did there. Betty Kemp says that they came "to admire the gardens and to fish or sail on the river." Walpole said otherwise: each had "their cell, a proper habit, a monastic name, and a refectory in common — besides a chapel ... whatever their doctrines were, their practice was vigorously pagan: Bacchus and Venus were the deities to whom they almost publicly sacrificed." John Wilkes, who had certainly been to Medmenham, described these "English Eleusinian mysteries, where the monks assembled on all solemn occasions, the more secret rites were performed, and libations poured forth in much pomp to the BONA DEA." The gardens were filled with statues and with other mottoes, and "the younger monks" took their pleasures there. But Wilkes was careful to say that these pleasures were with women: they "seemed at least to have sinned naturally." There was no sodomy at Medmenham, whatever else might have occurred in the chapter room. In that room, Sir Francis presided over the initiates in their mysteries as Churchill wrote:

> [Dashwood] shall pour, from a Communion Cup,
> Libations to the goddess without eyes.[21]

Such a meeting would have provided an appropriate audience for the impieties of *An Essay on Woman* (figure 7.4). John Wilkes was prosecuted by the government for printing it. He has sometimes been credited with its authorship. Most modern scholars, however, ascribe it to Thomas Potter, the libertine son of an archbishop. But it is possible that, like *Sodom*, it was written by many hands. Wilkes once described the poem as being read many times to friends at the dinner table. The *Essay* was a mock learned send-up of Alexander Pope's *Essay on Man*, as it had been piously annotated by Bishop Warburton. It was full of anticlerical jeers, some of which were also antisodomitical. The poem was determinedly heterosexual. It obsessively described the female sexual parts as a country for men to traverse. It built on a series of works by Thomas Stretser and others. It constantly played on the theme that sexual intercourse was the purpose of woman's creation. It was in this way an anti-Genesis, proposing that a distant, equable fate – or Heaven – oversaw the sexual acts on earth, and recommending that each man and woman should make the most of present pleasure. The *Essay* was accompanied by three burlesques of Christian prayers, which were almost certainly written by Wilkes. In a "Veni Creator," a virgin prays to a divine penis to enter her as the Holy Spirit was invoked in the original to enter the soul. The penis and the two testes are addressed as the "thrice blessed glorious Trinity." In another of the poems, "the great first cause" was invoked as the "mother of all in every age," but the footnote created some confusion about its gender by saying that "if the *Essay on Woman* has been suspected of leaning toward naturalism, the *Universal Prayer* directly speaks of the *first Cause* as the Lord and Governor, as well as the Creator of the Universe."[22]

These poems and the descriptions of the rites of the monks at Medmenham showed a curious blend of Christian symbol and

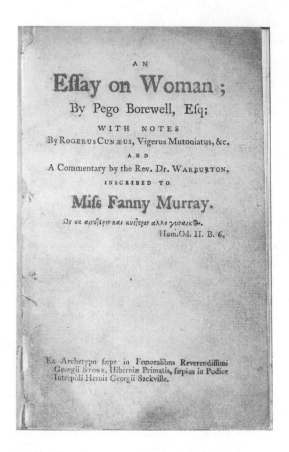

FIGURE 7.4. A version of the title page of *An Essay on Woman* (1762–1763). The Latin phrase at the bottom of the page refers to Archbishop George Stone's phallus, which was to have been engraved in the original. The phrase claims that Archbishop George Stone, the Primate of Ireland, sodomized Lord George Sackville, an instance of the anti-homosexual feelings of John Wilkes and his friends.

ancient Greek pagan rite. This very blending was probably part of the instinctive belief of Dashwood and his brothers in the Dilettanti Society that there was behind all ancient symbols – both Greek and Christian – a single religion in which the generative powers of the world were worshipped, and whose cult, appropriately, was dionysiac and priapic. What was implicit at Medmenham was eventually made explicit by the discoveries of Sir William Hamilton and the theories of the Baron d'Harcanville and Richard Payne Knight. Hamilton, while he was the British representative at Naples, discovered in the countryside what he took to be a priapic cult flourishing under the guise of a devotion to Saints Cosmos and Damian.[23] When Hamilton's letter describing this cult was printed by the Dilettanti Society, it was accompanied by Payne Knight's *Account of the Remains of the Worship of Priapus*. Payne Knight seems to have been influenced in his views by the same forces that influenced Cleland: a knowledge of ancient Mediterranean and contemporary Indian culture, a diffuse materialism, a personal sexual alienation as a sodomite and a Shaftesburian enthusiasm.[24]

Payne Knight analyzed the use in ancient religion of both the sexual organs and the act of sexual intercourse. First, in regard to the sexual organs, he wrote that Christianity had attacked the worship of Priapus more furiously than any other part of ancient polytheism. Christians had not understood that the penis was "a very natural symbol of a very natural and philosophical system of religion," and, with a sly dig at Christian sacramentalism, he pointed out that "the forms and ceremonials of a religion are not always to be understood in their direct and obvious sense; but are...symbolical representations of some hidden meaning." He continued, saying, "The female organs of generation were revered as symbols of the generative powers of nature or matter, as the male were of the generative powers of God." The male organs were sometimes represented by other forms. One of these was a cross in the form of a *T*. Sometimes, a head was added to the cross "which gives it the exact appearance of a crucifix." The crucifix was therefore an "emblem of creation and generation before the church adopted it as the sign of salvation."

Next, Payne Knight turned to the sacred use of acts of sexual intercourse. He wrote that sexual intercourse had, in fact, been a common form of ancient worship: "the male and female saints of antiquity used to be promiscuously together in the temples, and honour God by a liberal display and general communication of his bounties." There had been sacred prostitutes at Corinth and Eryx, and "the act of generation was a sort of sacrament in the island of Lesbos." The early Christian Eucharist had its holy kiss. The agape feasts and nocturnal vigils had given "too flattering opportunities to the passions and appetites of men," and had to be suppressed by the decrees of several church councils. "Their suppression may be considered as the final subversion" of the ancient phallic religion, which nonetheless survived in customs like the ex voti of Saint Cosmos and the obscene figures on gothic cathedrals. This phallic religion could also be found in ancient India, since it was a product of "the human mind in different ages, climates, and circumstances, uniformly acting upon the same principles and to the same ends." Payne Knight, however, showed his deepest intent at the beginning of his book, where he repeated the libertine doctrine that "there is naturally no impurity or licentiousness in the moderate and regular gratification of any natural appetite" and declared that "neither are organs of one species of enjoyment naturally to be considered as subjects of shame and concealment more than those of another." Both the sexual organs and the act of intercourse were worthy objects of human veneration. To establish this, he had appealed to the theology of the ancients as he understood it, and to the universal workings of the human mind, against the intolerance and austerity of the Christian religion.[25]

Payne Knight's book was privately circulated by the Dilettanti Society. Libertines like Charles Greville were liberated by it. More conventional deists like Horace Walpole were shocked by the book's open and, to their eye, socially irresponsible attack on Christianity. Once the Revolution in France had broken out, and the worship of the Supreme Being had been instituted and celebrated by supposedly orgiastic rites, Payne Knight must have seemed even more outrageous. His book became publicly known, and he was, to some degree, ostracized. The book was, therefore, both the intellectual climax of eighteenth-century English libertinism and its closure. Payne Knight also may have been obliged to mask part of his sexual libertinism from many of his friends. He seems to have liked young men. His references to sodomy as perhaps the act performed between the satyrs and hermaphrodites may have been as far as he could go in declaring himself.

While libertinism in the second half of the century may have founded itself on the Shaftesburian program of the virtuoso, it operated within the restraints of the new prohibition against sodomy between men, and it had to ignore the pederasty of the ancient world. Only the female temple prostitutes were cited, not the male. But the great appeal of the book to some libertines lay in their own orgiastic experience: they had engaged in sacred fertility worship before the theory justifying it had been composed. The libertine attempt to reconstruct the Christian attitude toward sexuality by appealing to the fertility religion of the ancient pagan world was, however, as doomed to failure as Martin Madan's appeal to the Old Testament against the Church Fathers. The rites of the monks of Medmenham had as little chance of being established as did Madan's polygamy. Madan had worked as the chaplain to the Lock Hospital for venereal disease and had been shocked by the many young girls who became infected through prostitution. He therefore had proposed to end prostitution by requiring each man to marry and care for all the girls he seduced. Such polygamy could be morally justified by appealing to the practice of the Old Testament against what he said were false ascetic readings of the New Testament. But Madan was widely mocked by the libertines for proposing that male desire should be made responsible, and by his fellow Christians for suggesting a moral standard other than monogamous ascetic restraint. It was not possible in the real world to combine an exclusive male heterosexual desire and a romantic, domesticated sexuality. Wilkes, Payne Knight and their circle could manage the one but not the other. Only in the fantasy of Cleland's great novel did they coexist.

CHAPTER EIGHT

Politics and Pornography in the Seventeenth- and Eighteenth-Century Dutch Republic

Wijnand W. Mijnhardt

In the seventeenth and early eighteenth centuries, the Dutch Republic served as one of the chief intellectual clearinghouses of early modern Europe. Many enlightened *livres philosophiques* were printed there, and, even after 1750, when the importance of the Dutch publishing industry declined in favor of cheaper and more accessible production centers such as Neuchâtel and Bouillon, an imprint of Amsterdam, Leiden or The Hague still came in useful if for no other reason than to mislead the censors. As Robert Darnton has shown, government censorship in France did not discriminate between the various genres of *mauvais livres*, labeling political criticism, philosophical treatises and pornography all as *livres philosophiques*. The Dutch book trade, which, after all, was a commercial venture, did not make such distinctions either and, consequently, produced all titles that were in demand.[1]

Although the Dutch Republic was instrumental in the distribution of much Enlightenment philosophy, pornography and politics, a distinction must be made between the international role of Dutch publishing and its native one. Recent research on the Dutch Enlightenment makes clear that Dutch culture of the eighteenth century was Janus-faced. On the one hand, the many refugees on Dutch soil, together with European authors looking for a publisher, made the Dutch Republic into one of the main publishing bases of the European Enlightenment. On the other hand, Dutch intellectuals developed a different, national version of the Enlightenment, adapted to the religious, political and intellectual values of the Republic.[2] Dutch publishers catered to both markets: the international book trade produced French books (including libertine texts) for an international clientele; the national book trade produced texts in the vernacular for an audience attached to its own brand of Enlightenment thought.

If Steven Marcus's explanation of the rise of pornography, which treats it as concomitant to a process of modernization, is accepted, then the Dutch Republic should have been a likely candidate for a strong pornographic strand in its literary production.[3] At least until the middle of the eighteenth century, the Dutch Republic was the most urbanized and most literate European society, and it fostered a greater degree of privatization than any other country in early modern Europe. Moreover, its relatively high level of religious and political toleration – if not in theory, then at least in practice – should have imposed fewer constraints on the production, distribution and consumption of pornographic literature than in most other Western European countries. Yet Dutch writers did not take a leading role in producing pornography. In order to resolve this paradox I will first delineate the origins and development of the Dutch native pornographic tradition, concentrating on pornography's relationship with philosophy and politics. Second, I will try to explain why, in the Dutch Republic, the perception and uses of pornography in the seventeenth and eighteenth centuries were so different from those in England and France.

Because the history of Dutch pornography has attracted very little scholarly attention, a definitive corpus of its native pornographic texts and prints has yet to be established.[4] The bibliographical data now compiled, though, allow for a preliminary but basically sound picture. Research on the visual tradition has hardly begun, so, of necessity, this essay will concentrate on discursive pornography. The definition of pornography I have used is quite loose: realistic representations of sexual intercourse and its variations, aimed at the arousal of sexual feelings.

The Dutch Pornographic Tradition
Although the French pornographic tradition was predominant in Europe, at least until the middle of the eighteenth century, no translations were necessary for Dutch elite consumption. After all, many French titles were printed in the Republic itself, Dutch booksellers were fully integrated in the European book exchange network and knowledge of French was widespread among the urban elites. However, there seems to have been a substantial market for translations as well. In the 1670s and 1680s, almost all the seventeenth-century pornographic classics identified by Foxon were translated into Dutch, the notable exception being Chorier's *L'Académie des dames*, originally published in Latin, which was only translated in 1770.[5] The translation of Aretino's *Ragionamenti* even included engravings made by the respectable artist Romeyn de Hooghe, the most famous Dutch engraver of the time.[6]

The increasing demand for translated pornography pushed Dutch hacks into action. As a consequence, the origins of a native Dutch pornographic tradition virtually coincided with the publication of the translations of the French and Italian classics. In the last decades of the seventeenth century, an extended series of native pornographic novels was published, some of which met with great commercial success.[7] Such titles as *Het Amsterdamsch hoerdom* [Amsterdam whores] (Amsterdam, 1681); *D'openhertige juffrouw* [The outspoken mistress] (Leiden, 1679); and *De hedendaagsche Haagsche en Amsterdamse zalet-juffers* [The salon-mistresses of contemporary Amsterdam and The Hague] (Amsterdam, 1696) must have been very popular because they were reprinted at regular intervals.[8] In Dutch literary history most of these novels are classified as picaresque, based on such genre characteristics as their autobiographical narrative technique and their emphasis on chance or fortune. However, there seems to be little doubt that the majority of these texts should be treated as at least related to the international pornographic tradition. These novels were much more advanced pornographically than their picaresque counterparts, and, in the prefaces, the authors took care to include their works in the galaxy of reputed works of pornography by advertising them as imitations of Aretino, by introducing dramatis personae that were direct references to those from, for instance, *L'Académie des dames* or by making references to *L'Ecole des filles*.[9]

However, Dutch interest in translated and homemade pornography seems to have been rather short-lived. The second international pornographic wave, which was closely related to the high tide of the Enlightenment of the 1740s and later, almost passed unnoticed. Classics like the *Histoire de Dom Bougre, portier des Chartreux*, *Thérèse philosophe*, Diderot's *Les Bijoux indiscrets*, Cleland's *Fanny Hill* or the novels of Sade were never translated during the eighteenth century. The exceptions were minor works such as *Margot la ravaudeuse* by Fougeret de Monbron, published in 1748 and translated in 1764; *Le Rideau levé, ou L'Éducation de Laure*, allegedly by Mirabeau, published in 1786 and translated in 1793; and the 1770 translation of *L'Académie des dames* already mentioned.

Moreover, the second pornographic wave, which came to include the first major English contributions, inspired hardly any native Dutch authors. Apart from occasional reprints of pre-1700 texts, the majority of which were published in the first decades of the eighteenth century, only a few new titles were put

on the market. Compared to the blatant sexuality of their seventeenth-century Dutch predecessors, these eighteenth-century novels presented rather tame stories in which the hero eventually
married safely. Neither was their popularity as great, for they were
never reprinted.[10] The only exception to this rule was *Venus en
Cupido* (1780), which, from a pornographic perspective, could
compete with seventeenth-century titles such as *D'openhertige
juffrouw*. However, whereas *Venus en Cupido* consisted of a series
of straightforward pornographic episodes, the narrative structure of *D'openhertige juffrouw* was much more convincing. Here,
a prostitute gave an account of her life, portraying herself as an
independent, resourceful and financially successful entrepeneur
who, already in 1679, mocks the bourgeois ideals of female virtue and domestic life.

The Dutch enlightened novel of the second half of the
eighteenth century was not impervious to the strong erotic
strands in its English and French counterparts, but, unlike a
century before, these foreign examples now provoked severe criticism. The Dutch novel included strong attacks on French licentious literature, which, in the eyes of novelists and moralists, had
captured the imagination of Dutch readers for far too long. The
female authors Betje Wolff and Aagje Deken, in their preface to
Sara Burgerhart (The Hague, 1782), the most influential Dutch
enlightened novel, fulminated against novels such as Crébillon's
Le Sopha, couleur de rose (1742). This indicated that, even without translations, these pornographic novels still could boast an
extensive circulation in the Dutch Republic.[11]

Thus, the native Dutch pornographic tradition may be deemed
abortive. After a promising start in the last decades of the seventeenth century, it slowly faded away to virtual nonexistence at
the end of the eighteenth. It was not only in this respect that the
Dutch pornographic genre differed from its international exam-

ples. Within the French intellectual community, philosophical materialism often had a strong sexual – even pornographic – flavor, culminating in Sade's quest for total freedom, and pornography was often used as a vehicle for expressing materialist ideas.[12] Late seventeenth-century Dutch rogue stories lacked the juxtaposition of realistic representations of sexual behavior against the hypocritical conventions of church and society. Only very rarely did Dutch authors refer to libertine ideas and, if they did, they never succeeded in presenting a convincing argument. The author of the *Leydsche straatschender* [The leyden ruffian] of 1679, for instance, limited his discussion of libertinism to short statements such as "prefering Aretino to Aristotle and Cartesius" or to allusions to his Epicurean upbringing.

Eighteenth-century Dutch rake novels contained only slightly more "philosophy." In the *Middelburgse avanturier* (1760), the male hero pleads for tolerant education and is scornful of slavery, and, in *Venus en Cupido*, allusions to the new experimental science can be found. The *Belydenis van een lichtmis* included – though superficially – the philosophical elements that formed the basis of the international pornographic tradition: a catalog of sexual variations and an attack on the ideologies and institutions that prohibited sensual pleasure such as traditional education, monogamous marriage, the celibacy of the priesthood and biblical prescriptions, all of which were denounced by a nun, aptly named Pelagia (figure 8.1). The tone, however, was much more moderate than that of its French counterparts, such as the bitterly anticlerical *Dom Bougre*. The few Dutch erotic and pornographic novels of the second half of the eighteenth century thus fell in with the moderate development of the Dutch Enlightenment, which opposed most of French high Enlightenment thought. Dutch pornographic book illustration was equally modest. Compared to the graphic and pornographically very advanced nature

FIGURE 8.1. A seduction scene. From *De Belydenis van een lichtmis* [Confessions of a rake] (1770). This engraving is a good example of the modest character of Dutch pornographic book illustrations.

of English and French pictures, Dutch illustrations may be judged tame and even chaste.

Moreover, the sexual themes discussed in Dutch pornographic novels were rather conventional. There was hardly any cataloging of sexual variations, nor any substantial discussion of masturbation, sodomy, incest or homosexuality. Dutch authors simply described women as insatiable and whores as ideal fornicating companions. The only noteworthy images of sexual excess favored by Dutch pornographic writers were flagellation scenes. However, flagellation was not treated as an attractive sexual variation; it only served to punish women who refused to give in to the justifiable wishes of the male heroes. In *Koddig en voddig leven der hedendaagsche labourlotten* (1685), which tells the story of a famous Amsterdam gang of ruffians, all members of the gang swear an oath of initiation to flagellate all females who refuse them, and especially whores. Thus, Dutch pornographic novels may be said to limit themselves to straightforward propaganda for conventional sexual license, and sexual pleasure seems to have been their unique aim.

Very little is known of the seventeenth- and early eighteenth-century readership of these pornographic novels (translated or originally Dutch), and even less about their reception. The number of copies put into circulation was probably limited, and print runs would seldom have surpassed 500 copies. There are a few surviving autobiographical documents, comparable in genre but not in quality to that of Samuel Pepys, in which individuals noted their reading experiences of pornography. The early eighteenth-century Alkmaar town architect, Simon Eikelenberg, for instance, dutifully recorded his erotic and pornographic readings – including foreign texts – together with his sexual experiences, but he was not at all interested in the libertine materialist ideology his foreign books contained. He simply used pornography to incite desire or as a replacement for sexual relations when they were unavailable to him.[13] Although this document nicely confirms my observations on the character of the Dutch pornographic tradition, it also introduces the problem of whether and why other European consumers, as is often alleged, were reading their novels so completely differently.

The absence of native Dutch pornography as a vehicle for a libertine materialist philosophy was matched by the lack of pornography for social or political purposes. In the canon of Dutch pornography discussed thus far, hardly any trace can be found of arguments intended to criticize existing social relations, or to undermine the political order and its representatives. Since the late sixteenth century, Dutch political debate was conducted by means of a continuous stream of pamphlets, which grew to enormous numbers in periods of crisis. Obviously, in the collection of the more than 30,000 seventeenth- and eighteenth-century pamphlets that have been preserved, quite a few can be found in which a variety of obscenities was used to demolish the reputation of certain regents or religious groups, but their arguments were hardly ever disguised in stories of a genuinely pornographic character.

Even in the years preceding the Patriot Revolution of 1787, a period when, in France, pornographic pamphlets were extremely effective in undermining the sacred character and prestige of the political and social institutions of the ancien régime, pornographic pamphleteering did not grow any more popular, although the French examples were known and distributed within the Republic.[14] Only in the extreme circumstances of the mid-1780s, when Dutch stadholder William V succeeded in capturing some Gelderland towns occupied by the patriot–rebels, did a few pornographic pamphlets and plays attack the person of the stadholder, the most famous being *Het gestoorde naaijpartijdje van*

Willem de Vijfden [The disturbed fornicating party of William V].[15] Compared, however, with the enormous amount of traditional pamphleteering and political journalism of this period, such scandal sheets were extremely rare.

The "Modernity" of the Dutch Republic

In various books and articles, some authors, like Robert Darnton, have demonstrated the existence in early modern France of what could be called a secular "trinity" consisting of politics, pornography and philosophy, which, in the eyes of official authority, were seldom thought of as separate categories of bad books. Only after the French Revolution did pornography slowly begin to be defined on the basis of its function as a sexual stimulant alone.[16] It seems that in the Dutch Republic, such a secular trinity never came into being. Beginning in the later seventeenth century, pornography was perceived, not only by its producers and consumers but also by official authority, as a separate category.

This fundamental difference between France and the Republic is confirmed by the various late eighteenth-century legislative proposals concerning obscene literature that were enacted after the French and Dutch Revolutions. Whereas in France the *Code Pénal* of 1791 still considered the display and distribution of immoral books as an offense against the public peace, the liberal *Crimineel Wetboek* (the Dutch equivalent of the *Code Pénal*) of 1808 only saw pornography as an offense against morality. The article in the *Crimineel Wetboek* was no novelty but was based upon a tradition that derived from an edict of the Court of Holland, enacted in 1726. This edict, which was concerned with censorship, virtually excluded pornography from the categories of books forbidden to print.[17] Obviously, this did not mean that pornography was licensed from that date on; quite the contrary, a marked increase in interdictions can be detected during the eighteenth century, especially after the 1750s. But it is only after 1726 that we find cases in which public authority acted against books for reasons of obscenity alone.

For an understanding of why this "modern" notion of pornography was adopted at such an early stage, the relative freedom of the press must be considered: in the Republic, philosophers and political writers did enjoy more freedom than in most countries of Western Europe and, as a result, did not need any vehicles such as pornography to carry their ideas. Moreover, they were addressing fundamentally different questions than their colleagues elsewhere in Europe. This tolerance should not be overestimated, however. Toleration and press freedom in the Republic have never been based on any principle, but should be considered, first of all, as political problems.[18]

Dutch authorities were forced to allow a large degree of toleration because intolerance would have been impossible to impose. For instance, reformed Protestantism was the religion of only a small majority; until the end of the eighteenth century, Catholics still made up almost 40% of the population. Also, the military power of the towns – the core of the political structure of the Republic – was weak compared to other European countries and limited only to the town militias, not always reliable bodies. Finally, the loose federal structure of the Republic precluded any firm, nationwide measures. Censoring the presses, therefore, was more a means of keeping religious and political pressures at bay than of enforcing a moral orthodoxy. It is only in such a context that the Court of Holland's argument for suppressing, in 1720, *Papekost opgedist in geuse schotelen* [Popish cooking in beggar's dishes], one of the rare obscene pamphlets against the Catholics (and of which many orthodox Calvinist regents must have approved), can be understood. The Court justified its interdiction by referring to the pamphlet's obscene language and illustrations, which the judges considered to be offensive to the Catholic citizenry of the Republic and, therefore, a potential cause of civil unrest.[19]

Ineffective press control made it possible that many titles of Darnton's recent list of pornographic best-sellers were openly distributed and sold in the Dutch Republic. We now have detailed knowledge of sales of titles of some provincial towns in the late eighteenth-century Dutch Republic. Raynal's *Histoire philosophique*, for instance, was one of the most impressive best-sellers, even in the provincial town of Zwolle.[20] Moreover, the relative press freedom allowed an enormous amount of native political criticism to be printed and distributed without any difficulties. In politically uneventful years even innocent media, such as the gossipy spectatorial press, was able to offer criticism of Dutch regents for their negligence of public affairs and, in times of crisis, there were few limits on what was said.[21] During the years preceding the Patriot Revolution, almost any political theme and everyone in authority could be discussed freely in pamphlets, political weeklies and at gatherings of political clubs. Although occasionally publications were prohibited and even journalists and printers arrested, the authorities were never able to stifle public debate.

Much more important still to an explanation of the absence of pornography in political and philosophical debate was the political, social and religious structure of the Republic. In eighteenth-century England after all, the large degree of press freedom does not seem to have hampered the eruption of native English pornography. In the Republic, however, there were no courts, no kings, no privileged nobility and no state church invested with special powers concerning dogma and morals. Although the Dutch did have a stadholder and a stadholderian court, its size was extremely small compared to other courts in Europe, and never did it function as a social and cultural center of prime importance. Moreover, in the periods from 1650–1672 and 1702–1747, there was no stadholder at all. Compared to other European states, the numbers and political influence of the Dutch nobility were limited. In the main provinces of Holland and Zeeland there were hardly any noble families left and, although some noblemen occupied high offices, politics was the explicit prerogative of the towns and their influential regent class. In the outer provinces, such as Gelderland and Overijssel, the nobility still had some influence in provincial and local affairs, but its national role was restricted. Nor did members of the nobility play any decisive role in the intellectual community. Although the Reformed Church of the Netherlands occupied a special position, it was never a state church, and although privileged to a certain extent, it never provoked the hatred against religious institutions common elsewhere.

As a result, whereas in England or France, whose courts, nobility and churches – due to their enormous political importance – were logical targets, and where the alleged or real sexual extravagances of its oligarchic dignitaries were ideal subjects for pornographic scandal sheet exploitation, the Republic had virtually no such available targets.[22] Even Catholics, who had been ideal victims of pornographical satire in England since Henry VIII, were to some degree protected in the Republic.

In my opinion, the decisive factor explaining the absence of political and religious pornography was, however, the bourgeois character of Dutch society. At a time when, in the centralized monarchies of Europe, the culture of the courts and the nobility slowly started to seep through to the middle orders, the Dutch citizenry succeeded in imposing its own bourgeois values upon society as a whole. The Dutch nobility remained attached to its own moral and sexual codes but, to Dutch citizens, the nobles functioned within a separate realm, and they were treated as an anomaly.[23] Even those regents who tried to imitate the aristocratic code of their social betters found that their pretensions to status did not seriously affect their bourgeois pattern of behavior. According to the many travelers to the Netherlands, social relations in the Republic were a peculiar phenomenon, characterized by a limited distance between social groups.[24] This limited distance was also apparent in the structure of politics, the enforcement of criminal justice and even in sexual morals. All citizens enjoyed protection under the same law, and government policies, generally speaking, were aimed at the welfare of the community as a whole. Sexual morals did not differ greatly from one social group to another. The absence of enhanced sexual, social and cultural differences made pornography useless as a political weapon.

For an explanation of the early demise of the native Dutch pornographic tradition, we have to turn to the fundamental changes in Dutch bourgeois views of sexuality during the eighteenth century. The popularity of both foreign and native pornographic novels at the end of the seventeenth century was not an isolated phenomenon, but closely related to the liberality of Dutch bourgeois sexual morals. According to contemporary commentators, like the grand pensionary and famous poet Jacob Cats, sex was a necessity and should be enjoyed by all.[25] Humanist Johan de Brune wrote that Dutch men and women alike did not need Aretino's postures, because they already enjoyed "all kinds of untimely dalliance."[26] In circles of classical scholars, the collecting of classical erotic books was a popular pastime.[27]

A similar liberal attitude can be found in the numerous sexual and erotic guidebooks that appeared in this period. The most popular of these, published in 1683, was the Dutch adaptation of Nicolas Venette's well-known manual *Venus minsieke gasthuis* [Venus's guesthouse for lovers], which openly discussed diverse variations of sexual intercourse and the methods needed to obtain maximum pleasure.[28] Dutch brothels were public institutions, and prostitution, though not approved, was generally accepted. In literature and the arts, sexuality was constantly present and hardly concealed at all. Very important in this respect are the numerous symbolic references in paintings that had direct sexual meanings.[29] In the 1660s, in the university town of Utrecht, *L'Ecole des filles* could be bought openly and was even on display in bookshop windows.[30] Most orthodox Calvinist ministers sharply protested against these sales. Other representatives of these circles, however, such as the orthodox theologian Petrus Wittewrongel, author of a well-known manual on the Christian family, allowed some sexual variations, although only within the sacred bonds of marriage.[31]

After the 1740s all this began to change. Venette's manual, like many pornographic and erotic novels, was condemned in literature as well as in the treatises of moralists and reforming societies, and was censored more often. The literary work of Cats was expurgated, erotic themes in seventeenth-century pictures were repainted, and brothels were transformed into closed private establishments.[32] In the art academies, the sexual parts of models were covered, and famous nude models were harassed on the streets.[33] In short, sexuality in all its aspects was removed from the public sphere and privatized. Obviously, pornography, and especially that of French origin, was still for sale, as can be documented from the auction catalogs of private libraries.[34] However, the sales records of late eighteenth-century bookshops show that the public sale and acquisition of pornography had become extremely difficult.

The selling of pornography, even in the liberal city of Amsterdam, seems to have been taken over by an underground circuit of shopkeepers and peddlers, who dealt not only in pornographic literature but also in condoms, dildos and other sexual aids.[35] The illicit atmosphere in which the sale of pornography now took place is demonstrated by the increasing tendency of printers to produce pornographic books in the vernacular, both translations and originals, without printer's marks. Whereas in the later seventeenth and early eighteenth century such books were produced under the printer's own name, in the second half of the eighteenth century most books were printed without reference to names, dates and places, restricting the printer's marks to anonymous announcements such as "printed for the devotees." Even reprints of titles which had been published openly before were now put on the market anonymously.[36]

For an understanding of this fundamental change in Dutch attitudes toward sexuality, two uniquely Dutch factors must be taken into account. One of the central aspects of Dutch eighteenth-century enlightened moralism was its connection to the problems of the Republic's economic and international decline.[37] Unable to explain the decline in economic or political terms, contemporary Dutch commentators perceived the cause of decline as moral. Their understanding of seventeenth-century history revealed a nation which, in a short period of time, had reached an unsurpassed level of economic prosperity, political and social stability and cultural advancement. These achievements were thought to be the product of the original Dutch character: frugal, charitable, courageous, disinterested and tolerant. In this context eighteenth-century decline was viewed as the result of a catastrophic loss of moral stamina. The catalog of vices that was created by moralists and novelists concentrated on the adoption by regents and prosperous citizens alike of a French aristocratic moral code; the reading of licentious books was just an example of this. Only if the Dutch abandoned their luxurious and sensual habits, which were, largely, of French origin, and returned to a national Dutch republican morality, could the Republic be restored to its former prosperity and prestige. As a result, sexual liberalism, eroticism and pornography were all closely associated with a nefarious French moral code and, thus, were integrated in the prevailing discourse on moral decline.

This image of Dutch moral identity, with its distaste of anything French, was, of course, primarily a fictional construct. Also evident, especially in novels and moralist tracts, was a celebration of the private and domestic spheres of life.[38] This message led to the publication of a new type of educational manual in which sexuality was separated from the rest of human life. Through benevolent societies such as the influential *Maatschappij tot Nut van 't Algemeen* [Society for Public Welfare] these booklets were distributed.[39] Thus, the idealization of marriage, love and family life had its roots in social forces.

In current Dutch historiography, the ideology of domesticity is associated with the adoption of a middle-class outlook. Its implementation is cast as part of a general civilizing process controlled by the social and cultural elites – a model derived from Norbert Elias's very influential book, *On the Civilizing Process*. It does not seem, however, that this model, which is based on aristocratic societies, applies to the Dutch case. Dutch society was characterized by a lack of distance between social groups, and this characteristic also applied to relationships between individuals. This lack of distance originated in the typical relationship patterns of the Republic, where a rapid urbanization process created a large number of chiefly small towns, and the introduction of the nuclear family helped create a complex system of social control. In the Dutch social control system, physical and psychological closeness and togetherness were crucial characteristics. Isn't it plausible that a further heightening of the psychological and physical pressures connected with a wider, more complete acceptance of that social control system developed at the expense of the external, public aspects of sexuality, resulting in an idealization of domestic and especially private life? If there is some truth in this hypothesis, then the fundamental change in attitude toward sexuality that led to the comparatively early invention of pornography as a separate category of bad books – a process begun in the mid-seventeenth century but largely manifest in the course of the eighteenth century – was also inherent within Dutch bourgeois culture itself.

CHAPTER NINE

Pornography and the
French Revolution

Lynn Hunt

Pornography and revolution might seem like uncomfortable bed-fellows. In the sixteenth, seventeenth and eighteenth centuries, pornography was written almost exclusively by men, usually, though not always for an audience of upper-class male readers, imagined to be libertine in both ideals and behavior. The aris-tocratic libertines seen in, behind and surrounding the texts discussed in preceding chapters of this book are, presumably, representative of the decadence of aristocratic morals that French revolutionaries hoped to eradicate. The common view of French revolutionaries portrays them as personally puritanical – Robes-pierre, of course, is the prime example – and it is hard to imagine such Puritans and ascetics as in any way approving of pornography.

In fact, the French Revolution and pornography had some very intimate connections, both on the personal and the social levels. At least two leading revolutionaries – Mirabeau and Saint-Just – had written pornography before the Revolution, and some of the leading pornographers, of whom Sade is the best-known exam-ple, participated directly in the Revolution itself.[1] Politically motivated pornography helped to bring about the Revolution by undermining the legitimacy of the ancien régime as a social and political system. When the Revolution began in 1789, pornography did not disappear in the flood of new publications; instead, it came to the surface of the new popular politics in the form of even more vicious attacks on leading courtiers and, in particular, on the queen, Marie Antoinette. Pornography that was not explicitly political also continued to be published in the 1790s.

The space for such publications was wider in France than it ever had been before or ever would be again until very recently, because obscenity was much lower on the revolutionary list of concerns than were counterrevolutionary publications. In the new freedom for development, political pornography also reached a wider audience than ever before. It became one of the arms of a self-consciously vulgar popular politics. After the Terror, and perhaps in reaction to it, the pornographic novel reached a kind of stylistic and ideological culmination, especially in the notorious works of the Marquis de Sade – most of which were published in the 1790s – but also in the pornographic novels of Andréa de Nerciat and Restif de la Bretonne. This essay will demonstrate these various connections between revolution and pornography.

But there is more to be revealed here than merely the relevance of pornography to the French Revolution. The French Revolution marked a turning point in the history of Western pornography, not only in France but elsewhere in the Western world. In France in the 1790s, politically motivated pornography reached its zenith – both in numbers and in viciousness – and then virtually disappeared, to be replaced by pornography that continued to test social and moral taboos without targeting political figures. Elsewhere, the specter of the French Revolution, with its threat of democratization, mass political mobilization through print and social disorder galvanized the trends toward the legal regulation of pornography as a distinct category. In Western Europe by the 1830s, at the latest, it appears that pornography had lost its previous association with subversive philosophy and politics; at the same time, it became a distinct genre on its own.

In France, we can trace the influence of the French Revolution in the history of the word *pornography*, which appears to have taken on its modern meaning during or just after the Revolution of 1789. The word *pornographe* had been used in 1769 by Restif de la Bretonne to refer to writing about prostitution. By 1806, the word was being used to mean writing that disturbed the social order and contravened good morals. In that year, a French compiler of a dictionary of forbidden works defined pornography as the category of books that were repressed for moral as opposed to religious or political reasons.[2]

The word *pornography* was not apparently in use in England until later in the nineteenth century, even though there the repression of obscene books for moral reasons was already more established than in eighteenth-century France. In 1728, the Court of King's Bench upheld a verdict of obscene libel against publisher Edmund Curll, thereby establishing a precedent in English law that remained the basis of such prosecutions until the Obscene Publications Act of 1959. Before the Curll case, however, the secular courts had refused to prosecute "for printing bawdy stuff" on the grounds that "a libel must be against some particular person or persons, or against the government."[3] The corruption of manners was not a punishable offense, according to the courts.

Action against immoral literature in England only became a crusade when the Proclamation Society was founded in 1787 for the purpose of "preventing and punishing of Vice, Profaneness, and Immorality." Like other societies for the reformation of manners that had been founded in England since the 1690s, the Proclamation Society focused its efforts on drunkenness, profanity and the breaking of the Sabbath, but, unlike its predecessors, it also included a specific reference about the need to suppress "all loose and licentious Prints, Books, and Publications, dispersing Poison to the Minds of the Young and Unwary." Yet even for England, with its earlier history of suppression of obscene libel, the French Revolution marked a watershed in attitude, for it was not until the early 1800s that "the frenzy to put pornographers behind bars," as one historian has put it, really accelerated.[4]

Central to this acceleration in England was the Society for the Suppression of Vice and the Encouragement of Religion and Virtue – known as the Vice Society – which was founded in 1801 and immediately began its campaign against the "extensive trade in obscene books, prints, drawings, toys, etc." Earlier prosecutions, such as those against Thomas Paine's *Age of Reason* in 1797 and a threatened legal action against Matthew Lewis's novel *The Monk* in the same year, paled in comparison to the sharp rise in legal actions after 1802.[5] *The Annual Register* of 1798 had explained how the French Revolution could be blamed for the spread of vice:

> The French Revolution illustrated the connection between good morals and the order and peace of society more than all the eloquence of the pulpit and the disquisitions of moral philosophers had done for many centuries. The upper ranks in society, the generality of men of rank and fortune, not always the most inquisitive on other subjects, were among the very first to take alarm at those irreligious and profligate doctrines by which the French democracy sought to shelter the profligacy of its conduct.

It was not accidental, then, that "the great age of expurgation" began in the first years of the nineteenth century. Thomas Bowdler published his expurgated *Family Shakespeare* in 1818 with a preface that explained his aim "to exclude from this publication whatever is unfit to be read aloud by a gentleman to a company of ladies."[6] The French Revolution had shown the dangers of making printed materials more widely available, and nineteenth-century moral reformers were determined to keep dangerous literature out of the hands of women and children.

The new social and moral urgency about pornography was also fostered by changes that took place in pornography as a literary genre in France during the revolutionary decade. As described in previous essays, pornography had been used for political purposes well before 1789; indeed, Peter Wagner has defined Enlightenment pornography in general as "a vehicle of protest against the authority of Church-State."[7] French pornography of the ancien régime seemed inherently subversive as a genre because it was based on materialist philosophy and often criticized priests, nuns and aristocrats. During the Revolution, political pornography proliferated, increased in stridency and extended its audience down to the popular classes. At the same time, paradoxically, pornography began to separate from politics, perhaps because of the very success of the pornographic attack on the ancien régime in France.

After the end of the Terror, French pornographers' attention shifted almost exclusively to the depiction of sexual pleasure as an end in itself. This shift marked the beginning of truly modern pornography, with its mass-produced text or images devoted to the explicit description of sexual organs or activities with the sole aim of producing sexual arousal in the reader or viewer. Paradoxically, once political pornography had become democratized, it ceased being political.

Pornography during the Revolution

Political pornography had a long lineage going back to Aretino in the sixteenth century, and it seemed to reach a crescendo in the last decades of the ancien régime in France. Robert Darnton showed how the sexual sensationalism of ancien régime pamphlets was used to attack the French court, the church, the aristocracy, the academies, the salons and the monarchy itself.[8] Recently, Sarah Maza has called attention to the gender dimension of much of this criticism. Politically motivated pornographic pamphlets in the 1770s and early 1780s often denounced the supposedly excessive influence of women at the French court.[9] Queen Marie Antoinette was the focus of much of this literature; pornographic pamphlets, couplets and ditties claimed to detail her presumed sexual misdemeanors, questioned the paternity of her children and, in the process, fatally undermined the image of royal authority.[10] If the king could not control his wife or even be sure he was the father of his children, including the heir to the throne, then what was his claim on his subjects' obedience or the future of the dynasty's claim to the throne itself?

The fear of sexual disorder went beyond the circles of the court. In his recent study of the *Mémoires secrets* and the *Correspondance secrète*, both of which were multi-volume collections of news and gossip compiled in the 1770s and 1780s, Jeffrey Merrick has discerned a widespread concern that sexual disorder was a sign of a breakdown in public order. The pages of the scandal sheets were filled with stories of increasingly brazen homosexuality, unruly and unchaste wives and marital conflicts, as well as the now well-known tales of debauchery in the highest court circles.[11] When Restif de la Bretonne commented in his *Nuits de Paris* (1786) that "delirium, debauchery, and insubordination have reached their peak," he was repeating an increasingly widespread opinion. One sociologist has concluded that such comments, together with the notorious writings of Laclos and Sade, were signs of pervasive sexual anomie in the last years of the ancien régime in France and, as such, were "leading indicators of a severe deterioration of social organization and the ultimate collapse of the legitimacy of authority."[12] Even if libertine writings are not included as one of the main causes of the French Revolution, it can still be admitted that some contemporaries saw in the spread of pornography in the 1780s the harbinger of a broader social crisis.

The number of titles in the genre of political pornography rose steadily from 1774 to 1788 and then took off after 1789, when the Revolution began. In the early years of the Revolution, politically motivated pornography accounted for about half of the obscene literature produced, and it portrayed aristocrats as impotent, riddled with venereal disease and given over to debauchery. The *Chronique Arétine* (1789), for example, offered an analysis of "the true source of all the disorders which trouble us." The "corruption of morals" was due to "the degradation of good morals by the scandalous and unpunished excesses of the courtesans of this century." Among these courtesans were leading aristocratic women.[13]

The central figure in such attacks was Queen Marie Antoinette herself. In a very pornographic pamphlet, *L'Autrichienne en goguettes*, the queen is depicted in amorous embrace with the king's brother, the count d'Artois, and with her favorite, the duchesse de Polignac. They are able to begin their orgy as soon the king passed out after drinking too much champagne. At one moment in the action, the duchess complains that she is being ignored, but she explains that she has occupied herself by masturbating while reading *Histoire de Dom Bougre, portier des Chartreux*, one of the best-known pornographic texts from the mid-eighteenth century.[14] The references to pornographic classics show that the political pornographers of the Revolution were self-consciously building on an existing tradition, even while transforming it for their own ends. In *Apparution de Thérèse philosophe à Saint-Cloud*, the famous Thérèse of the mid-eighteenth-century pornographic work appears in a dream and recounts how she instructed the queen in the uses of *volupté*.[15]

Homosexuality functioned in a manner similar to that of impo-

307

tence in this literature; it showed the decadence of the ancien régime in the person of its priests and aristocrats. The pamphlets about the queen, for instance, almost always insisted on her tribadism. *Les Enfans de Sodome à l'Assemblée Nationale* (1790) gave lists of the presumed sodomites among the clerical and aristocratic deputies of the National Assembly, and of tribades among leading aristocratic women (figure 9.1).[16] One of the main targets for such attacks was the conservative deputy abbé Maury, who was denounced as "le plus grand jean-foutre de l'univers" in a pamphlet, *Fredaines lubriques de J— F— Maury* (1790).[17] In these pamphlets, sexual degeneration went hand in hand with political corruption. Counterpoised, most often only implicitly, to the degenerate aristocrat and the sodomitic priest of the ancien régime was the healthy love of the new patriots.[18] In *Les Travaux d'Hercule* (1790), the author insists that "a male and vigorous constitution is necessary for those who wish to taste [pleasure]," and "healthy men" are contrasted to "defective and effeminate" ones.[19]

The proliferation of pornographic pamphlets after 1789 shows that political pornography cannot be viewed simply as a displacement from or substitute for "real" politics. Once participation increased dramatically, particularly with the explosion of uncensored newspapers and pamphlets, politics did not simply take the high road.[20] Alongside the flood of new political pamphlets about every issue facing the nation came a steady stream of others, like the satirical *Dom-Bougre aux Etats-Généraux, ou doléances du portier des Chartreux, par l'auteur de la foutromanie* with its fanciful publication data: "A Foutroplis, Chez Braquemart, Libraire, rue Tire-Vit, à la couille d'or. Avec permission des Supérieurs [no date given]." The pamphlet, which made satirical use of the title of the notorious eighteenth-century pornographic classic, *Histoire de Dom Bougre, portier des Chartreux* (1741), was attributed to Restif de la Bretonne, who was arrested and released, presumably for

Ce Trio Masculin, dans ses goûts ingénieux),
Vous retrace Ô! Lecteurs des vrais Bougr. les Jeux.

FIGURE 9.1. Scene of sodomy between deputies to the National Assembly.
From *Les Enfans de Sodome à l'Assemblée Nationale* (Paris, 1790). The text
reads: "This masculine trio, with its ingenious tastes, recalls for you the
readers the games of true buggers."

lack of evidence.[21] As many as 200 licentious pamphlets and books were published between 1789 and 1792 alone.[22]

Many reasons might be cited for this explosion of political pornography in the French Revolution, but surely one of the most important was the inability of legislators to agree on a policy for repressing it. The national revolutionary government exercised little control over pornography after the freeing of the presses in 1789. The deputies to the National Assembly frequently denounced scurrilous or obscene pamphlets, along with other outrages permitted to an uncontrolled press and, in January of 1790, the abbé Sieyès proposed a law against offenses committed in print. It was denounced in the left-wing press and never discussed in the Assembly. On July 7, 1791, the Assembly passed a law against "those who have made a public attempt against morals by flagrant insult against the modesty of women, by dishonest actions, and by favoring debauchery or corrupting young people of one or the other sex by means of the exposition and sale of obscene images." Interventions against the proposed law by Pétion and Robespierre showed the reluctance of many legislators in this domain. Robespierre in particular argued, unsuccessfully, that the law was too partial, that action against images would inevitably entail action against writings and that such a development would contravene liberty of the press. In fact, as all historians of the press concur, the law had virtually no effect at all.[23]

The enforcement of measures against obscenity was generally left to local authorities. The Paris municipality had tried to censor visual images from the earliest days of the Revolution. It named a censor for caricatures in July of 1789 and made efforts to seize especially obscene engravings during 1791 and 1792. The municipal government passed numerous decrees against peddlers of seditious or licentious writings in the name of public order, but the repetition of such decrees indicates their lack of success. In June of 1790, for instance, the assembly of the municipality ordered the prosecution of those connected with the publication and distribution of the anonymous *Vie privée, impartiale, politique, militaire et domestique du marquis de la Fayette*. The printer was arrested, but he was released within a month.[24]

Again and again the local police sought out and arrested peddlers of obscene literature in the Palais-Royal, the center for such activities. Their catches produced a varied lot: most were young men – jeweller's apprentices, clockmakers, secondhand dealers and hairdressers, for example – but, on occasion, they arrested women, young children or even a priest or two.[25] Sometimes they burned the offensive writings on the spot, but most of the people arrested were released within hours. During the Terror, the municipal government of Paris tried to force the expurgation of plays or to arrest actors for having appeared in obscene plays. For the most part, however, their railing against prostitution and indecency was without any real enforcement.[26]

From the fragmentary records of the Archives of the Préfecture of Police in Paris, it is possible to determine the broad outlines of the police's enforcement of these measures against licentious publications. The high points of police action were in 1790-1791, to a lesser extent in 1797, and again in the early years of the Consulate, in 1800-1802.[27] The initial swell of police activity in 1790-1791 may well have been a reaction to the flood of new publications let loose by the freeing of the presses in 1789. The renewal of activity in 1797 probably followed from the creation of a morals division by the Paris police, though activity dwindled in the next two years. Despite the claims of the Minister of Police in 1799 that "morals are the nerve of governments, especially in republics," the First Republic was not especially successful in its attempts to "make disappear anything in writings or engravings that might tend to corrupt or degrade hearts and minds."[28] The

government of the Consulate stepped up the effort to find and con-
fiscate licentious literature as part of its program to control more
closely the press and publication industry. But even its efforts
were fitful.

From 1794 – perhaps even from 1792 – until the Consulate,
repression was apparently even less effective than it had been in
the early years of the Revolution, or so it seems from the complaints of Louis-Sébastien Mercier in 1798:

> Some people display nothing but obscene books whose titles and
> engravings are equally offensive to decency and good taste. They sell
> these monstrosities everywhere, along the bridges, at the door of the-
> aters, on the boulevards. The poison is not costly; ten sous the vol-
> ume.... One could say that these purveyors of brochures are the
> privileged merchants of garbage: they seem to exclude any title that
> is not foul from their display. Young people are able to go to these
> sources of every kind of vice without any obstacle or scruple. This
> horrible manufacture of licentious books is carried on by all the
> counterfeiters, kinds of pirates who will kill the publishing indus-
> try, literature, and men of letters. It is based on that unlimited lib-
> erty of the press which has been demanded by the falsest, most
> miserable, and blindest of men.[29]

Although the leaders of the Directory regime, like Mercier,
were troubled by abuses of freedom of the press, they focused
almost exclusively on getting control over the political journals.
Their preoccupation with political dissent seems to have opened
the door to the relatively unfettered publication of nonpolitical pornography.[30]

Given the nature of pornographic publication, the constant
possibility of its repression, even in the 1790s, and the reluctance
of bibliophiles or even the police to admit to an interest in col-

lecting or recording such publications, it is very hard to trace with any certainty the actual volume of publication. Pascal Pia's catalog, *Les Livres de l'Enfer* – the list of pornographic books of the Bibliothèque Nationale – is a kind of crude index to the publication of major works,[31] "major" meaning works that were sufficiently long or notorious to make their way into the collections that were later seized by the French police and sent to a special place in the Bibliothèque Nationale. Pia's catalog seriously underestimates the pace of production for ephemeral publications, so it is impossible to interpret his lists as anything other than a crude index to proportions. According to Pia's lists, the largest number of new pornographic works was published in 1790 (counting explicitly political pornography and nonpolitical obscene works together). The numbers then declined steadily, until they reached a low point in 1795 and 1796. Production of new works increased only slightly in the last years of the revolutionary decade.

By separating political from nonpolitical pornography – not always an easy task – two separate trends become evident.[32] The high point of political pornography was also 1790, after which the numbers of new works steadily declined in 1791 and 1792 and especially from 1793 onward. Following the publication of some of the longest works against Marie Antoinette in 1793 and 1794, almost all the few pieces of political pornography published between 1795 and 1799 were anticlerical. Political pornography addressed to current issues and personalities did not pick up again until 1799–1800, when, for instance, Napoleon's wife Josephine was the subject of a new work. Nonpolitical pornography, however, had no specific high point and followed no decisive trend, beyond a slight decline in 1795–1796; it was more of a constant in revolutionary publishing.

Several tentative conclusions can be drawn from Pia's lists. Pornography flourished in the immediate aftermath of the freeing of the presses in July of 1789 but did not increase in number again when the Revolution radicalized in 1792, 1793 and 1794. The numbers began to decline in 1792–1794 for a variety of reasons. The right-wing press, which also published its own scurrilous literature, was suppressed after August 10, 1792, thereby removing one source of production. Since the aristocracy and the clergy had lost most of their influence, one set of motivations for publishing pornographic pamphlets had been superseded. Moreover, as the government of the Terror extended its hold, writers became increasingly reluctant to try their chances at any genre that might become suspect; the number of new novels published declined from a high of 112 in 1789 to forty in 1792 and then to a low of fifteen in 1794.[33]

While political pornography became virtually insignificant in the late 1790s, nonpolitical pornography revived somewhat, thereby paralleling the revival of the novel. The important new novelistic forms of pornography were published between 1795 and 1803: Sade's *Aline et Valcour*, *La Philosophie dans le boudoir* and *La Nouvelle Justine*; Restif de la Bretonne's response in *L'Anti-Justine*; the transsexual novel *Eléonore, ou L'Heureuse personne* (attributed to Andréa de Nerciat); and Andréa de Nerciat's posthumous novel, *Le Diable au corps*. It may have been the appearance of such works that so troubled observers like Mercier.

Not much is known about those who wrote, published or distributed pornographic works, except for such well-known authors as Sade and Restif de la Bretonne. Antoine de Baecque has recently uncovered fascinating information about the policing adventures of one energetic commissaire named Toublanc, who worked the Palais-Royal between November of 1790 and March of 1791. In six months, Toublanc arrested and interrogated seventy peddlers and confiscated 400 works deemed pornographic, slanderous, polemical or libelous. The peddlers sold their wares at varying prices, from five *livres* for an illustrated copy of *Arétin français* to five *sols* for the most cheaply printed, small-format pamphlets, with one *livre* equaling twenty *sols*. During an arrest for public slander of the king in July of 1790, the police came across a self-described writer, Etienne Magdelimi, who admitted to having produced three licentious works. He was a native of the eastern city of Sedan, twenty-eight years old, and had been a resident of Paris for three years. He was probably typical of the hacks who were willing to make their living in the new industry, but little is known of their motivations – besides that of commercial profit – and even less of their lives or publishing histories.[34]

It is known that pornography was not the exclusive tool of the critics of the ancien régime. Before the Revolution, anti–Marie Antoinette pamphlets, for example, were no doubt sponsored by factions at the court itself. Once the Revolution began and newspaper publishing opened up, right-wing publishers brought pornography from the underground out into the open. The royalist newspaper *Actes des Apôtres* specialized first in the lascivious "private life" essay on leading revolutionary politicians in 1789. An ultraroyalist newspaper, the *Journal de la cour et de la ville*, purveyed scurrilous gossip and scandalous anecdotes about leading revolutionary politicians and openly advertised the publication of at least one quasipornographic antirevolutionary engraving.[35] For a few months at the end of 1791 and into the beginning of 1792, the royalist presses produced as many as seven new caricatures a week, and they were designed to attract a popular audience. Few of the caricatures were frankly pornographic, but proroyalist writers were no doubt involved in the production of pornographic tracts that mocked the new revolutionary leaders.[36]

More difficult to classify are those pamphlets that attack leading democrats such as Théroigne de Méricourt, as well as the queen herself. The *Bordel National sous les auspices de la Reine, à*

315

l'usage des confédérés provinciaux; dédié et présenté à Mlle. Théroigne, présidente du district des Cordeliers, et du Club des Jacobins, for example, included a dedication to Mademoiselle Théroigne: "your insatiable flame gives you a lead on ancient and modern prostitutes." One of the engravings was described as showing the queen in an embrace with her valet, the king's brother, and deputy Le Chapelier all at once (the engraving was missing but the legend was not). Théroigne claims to have been sodomized that morning by ten deputies of the National Assembly, including the "indefatigable abbé Syeyes [Sieyès]." Lafayette, Bailly, the king's brother, Barnave and a host of other figures from each side of the political spectrum make their appearance in what is presumably an Orleanist pamphlet, since only the duke d'Orléans would benefit from the destruction of both the democrats and the family of Louis XVI. The ultrademocrats are the target of an especially focused attack. Danton asks Marat why he is there, since he had been expressly excluded as "an ignominious scribbler" and "runt." Marat replies that he has come to suck off the women and the men in order to make money, since he cannot make ends meet at his newspaper.[37]

The audience for political pornography is as difficult to specify as its authorship. Although the gossip that formed the basis of much ancien régime political pornography may have filtered through many social circuits before going into print, the audience for the actual printed political pornography seems to have been relatively limited before 1789. Works such as *Portefeuille d'un talon rouge, contenant des anecdotes galantes et secrètes de la cour de France* − a general attack on aristocratic morals − were booklength, and they seem, on the basis of their typography, length and content to have been destined for a very upper-class audience.[38]

The audience for pornography changed once the Revolution removed restrictions from the press. Although royalist publications may have led the way in bringing pornography out of the underground into the public newspaper, it was the radical critics of the ancien régime who seized upon this new tool with a vengeance. In 1789, many short pornographic pamphlets began to appear, in contrast to the usually long productions of the ancien régime: L'Autrichienne en goguettes; Bord—R— [The brothel of the queen]; Dom-Bougre aux Etats-Généraux; and another attack on the queen, Le Godmiché royal [The royal dildo], were all only sixteen pages long and, hence, accessible to a large audience. Others were as short as eight pages. The outpouring of 1790 included many longer pieces but also several in the range of twenty-four pages, thirty-two pages, forty-eight pages and sixty pages.

Although pornographic political pamphlets were more expensive than the very cheapest political pamphlets – probably because of their engravings – they were still accessible to a much wider audience than ever before, at prices as low as five sols or even less. Peddlers were arrested with scores of pamphlets or brochures in their packets, sometimes as many as a hundred. As many as thirty pamphlets at a time might be arrayed on a wooden display board by a peddler in the Palais-Royal; others were offered by wine merchants or barkeepers, or hawked outside theaters or the wax museum. Peddlers lined up early in the morning and late in the afternoon at the doors of clandestine printers and then spread out through the city to sell their wares.[39]

The new social diffusion of revolutionary pornography is evident in the engravings that accompanied the written texts. They range from the apparently highbrow, fine line engravings that accompanied novels such as Sade's La Philosophie dans le boudoir of 1795 (figure 9.2) to more vulgar and politically motivated productions directed against particular groups, such as monks, or against individual political figures (figures 9.3 and 9.4). This variety signals the beginnings of the democratization of pornography

FIGURE 9.2. (left) Typical group sex scene from Marquis de Sade's *La Philosophie dans le boudoir* (French edition, 1795).

FIGURE 9.3. (above) Pornographic lampoon of monk. The text reads: "I'm coming...I am the good Constitution" (probably Paris, 1791?).

319

les torts de M. Necker envers la france

FIGURE 9.4. Pornographic attack on Jacques Necker, Finance Minister. The text reads: "The wrongs done by M. Necker to France" (probably Paris, 1789–1790?).

as a genre during the Revolution. The libertine literature of the ancien régime, destined exclusively for upper-class men, now becomes a partly, perhaps even a predominantly, popular genre. Just as the revolutionary leadership hoped to mobilize all classes of French people, so too did political pornographers hope to tap all classes of readers and viewers.

One of the most interesting examples of the blurring of the distinction between libertinism and vulgarity can be seen in the caricatures engraved in the manner of Giuseppe Arcimboldo, a sixteenth-century Italian painter. His figures, which are composed of fruits, flowers, shells and fish, are taken as models for farcical renditions of famous political figures, with their heads made up of copulating figures and sometimes of detached penises and testicles (figures 9.5 and 9.6). Most of these *têtes composées* are obviously very hastily drawn, and the genre as a whole seems designed almost exclusively as an attack on the aristocracy and clergy. The message seems to be that both male and female aristocrats and clergymen are entirely dominated by sexual desire, that the genitals dominate the head, that the "low" lurks behind the supposedly "high" head or mind of these figures.[40] Such images are vulgar, both in terms of their audience and their message.

Direct evidence of the popularization of obscene engravings is provided in Boyer de Nîmes's *Histoire des caricatures de la révolte des Français*. Boyer was a royalist commentator who wrote a two-volume work on revolutionary engravings in 1792, just before the fall of the monarchy. He discussed obscene engravings as part of his more general analysis of both revolutionary and antirevolutionary engraving. In his view, caricatures were an *écriture parlée*, a writing that speaks: "if we should note that caricatures are the thermometer which tells the temperature of public opinion, we should also note that those who know how to master its variations know also how to master public opinion itself." Boyer claimed

FIGURE 9.5. (above) Pornographic portrait of an aristocratic woman. The text reads: "Oh! Oh! There is my portrait" (probably Paris, 1791?).

FIGURE 9.6. (right) Pornographic portrait of a clergyman. The text is a pun on *vivant* (alive) and *vit* (the slang word for penis) — *vit* like *vivant* is one of the forms of the verb *vivre* (probably Paris, 1791?).

322

L'ABBÉ M....

L'original est vivant son portrait est en VIT.

that the number of antiroyalist engravings grew alarmingly in the weeks before June 20, 1792: "a year before, some of these engravings had been shown by print merchants in the streets and along the quais of the capital, but since then, their number has so prodigiously grown and has become so considerable that one can find various of them in almost every window of the shops."[41] He went on to denounce the ways in which the Jacobins artificially inflated sales: they went around from shop to shop asking for whichever antiroyalist engravings the merchant did not have, thus requiring all of the merchants to carry a large number of such engravings.

The success of pornographic pamphlets and engravings in attracting a public is especially evident in the case of the queen. Marie Antoinette was, without question, the favorite individual target of pornographic attacks, both before and after 1789. There were not only more pamphlets about her than about any other single figure, but the pamphlets were the most sustained in their attacks; they were also, apparently, best-sellers. Heading the list of pamphlets confiscated by the Paris police in 1790–1791, for example, were *Vie privée, libertine, et scandaleuse de Marie-Antoinette*, with eighty-eight copies confiscated, and *La Messaline française*, with eighty-one copies confiscated. Next on the list was the classic *Thérèse philosophe* (1748), with twenty-seven copies taken away by the police.[42] Boyer complained that the antiqueen pamphlets were sold at the gate to the Tuileries palace, in its gardens and right under the king's window.[43] This kind of pornography had a much wider audience than ancien régime libertine literature.

The pornographic literature about the queen reflected an underlying anxiety about the role of women in the new republic and about the maintenance of clear gender boundaries. Marie Antoinette was the most visible symbol of a woman acting in the public sphere and acting through the traditional female qualities of dissimulation and seduction. In addition to commenting on women's roles in society and politics, pornography about the queen also had a democratic or leveling effect. It invariably emphasized that the queen's body served as a kind of access to sovereignty: she was married to the king and the mother of the new heir to the throne, and her body was therefore central to power. After 1789, the pornography increasingly insisted on the accessibility of the queen to everyone. Even when she was in prison, for instance, she was accused of sleeping with her valets (as well as with her son). Pornography about her behavior therefore not only degraded royalty, it elevated the common man.[44]

This democratizing effect was linked to the emphasis on specularity in the revolutionary pornographic pamphlets. The pre-1789 libertine pamphlets tended to tell the dirty stories of the court as a written version of gossip; after 1789, the public "sees" degeneracy in action rather than "hearing" court rumors. The visualization of debauchery took several forms. Obscene engravings with dialogue captions theatricalized the action, making the reader both a voyeur and moral judge. Even antiaristocratic pamphlets such as *Marie-Antoinette dans l'embarras, ou Correspondance de la Fayette avec le roi, la reine, la Tour-du-Pin et Saint-Priest*, in which only aristocrats figured as sexual partners for the queen, have this democratizing effect, for by visualizing the availability of the queen's body, the queen's body is made available to every man.[45] This effect was even more pronounced when the queen was shown in sexual liaisons with members of the lower classes. In *Le Cadran des plaisirs de la cour, ou Les Aventures du petit page Chérubin*, for instance, the queen is described in a liaison with a young page, who does not discover her identity until the Revolution breaks out.[46]

Pornography about aristocrats, priests, monks, nuns and prostitutes could have a similar leveling effect. All of these figures were imagined to be transgressors of accepted sexual behavior

325

and, therefore, subject to denunciation. However, in their weaknesses, they also resembled all other men and women. Many pamphlets also expressed outrage at the degradation of aristocratic and clerical morals. *Les Roup — tes des Calotins* denounced the clergy, exclaiming, "How many voluptuous and lubricious satyrs has the sacred college not produced?"[47] Yet, many other pamphlets spoke in a lighter tone about similar infractions. In *Dom-Bougre aux Etats-Généraux*, for example, the author is so caught up in the delights of describing a complete catalog of vices that he easily loses sight of his professed aim of teaching how to "purify morals, prevent the bastardization of the human race, destroy adultery, sodomy, bestiality and the other vices that have been degrading the French for five or six generations."[48] *Les Bijoux du petit neveu de l'Arétin, ou Etrennes libertines* is dedicated to "the women formerly of quality [noblewomen], if there are any; to chaste churchmen, whose age pushes them toward pleasure; and finally, to the sensual votaries of the pleasures of love, wherever they are found." Included among the scenes in the pamphlet is one of Père Duchesne – the stock boulevard and fair character who graced the masthead of a series of different revolutionary newspapers – having sex with a peasant girl on the back of a mule.[49] In this way, the common man participates in activities previously imagined as specially suited to the upper classes.

Pornography in the Revolution, even more so than pornography in the ancien régime, promises that sex is going to be available to everyone. The author of the pamphlet *La Confédération de la nature, ou L'Art de se reproduire, avec figures* (1790) – to take an especially telling example – used a language filled with sexual double meaning: "Vigorous patriots, amiable fellow citizens, a new FIELD which though more NARROW than that OF MARS is nonetheless agreeable, is now OPEN to you; hasten to ENTER there." In the midst of the pamphlet's various anticlerical and just generally obscene poems is one in which a prostitute promises lower prices for patriots: "Eighteen sous, instead of twenty-four; It's to that that my national cunt has been reduced [Dix-huit sous, au lieu de vingt-quatre; C'est à quoi se réduit mon con national]."[50]

The passing of public women – and perhaps all women in the pornographic imagination – from man to man is especially evident in *Julie philosophe, ou Le Bon patriote* (1791), the updated revolutionary version of *Thérèse philosophe*. Julie has affairs with the Chevalier de Morande, a prerevolutionary pornographic hack; Calonne, in his English exile; a middle-class surgeon who saves her from being lynched; Mirabeau; the Belgian revolutionary Vander-Noot; a clergyman and an aristocrat, among others (figure 9.7). She ends up rich thanks to money from her aristocrat, but she marries a peasant. Julie's body thus passes through the hands of men of every social class and every revolutionary nation; yet she is an astute observer of the political scene, passing judgment, for instance, on the leading political newspapers of the day.[51]

The political intention of *Julie philosophe* cannot be easily categorized as either prerevolutionary or antirevolutionary. The novel is clearly satirical for, as the subtitle proclaims, Julie is an example of an "active Citizeness" – a play on the political category of active citizens, which included those men with enough property to qualify for voting under the Constitution of 1791. Julie, however, is "active" in a sexual rather than a political sense. Although Julie appears to be the revolutionary version of the female narrator found in eighteenth-century pornographic works, she does not have their independence or determination. According to the subtitle, Julie is by turn agent of and victim in the recent revolutions in France, Holland and Brabant (Belgium). She has political views – prorevolutionary and democratic ones – but she is dependent on the men in her life and, finally, becomes a devoted

FIGURE 9.7. Scene from *Julie philosophe* (French edition, 1791).

peasant wife, content to "give little citizens to the state."[52] In the end, the novel ambivalently juxtaposes democratic opinions and sexual availability, political acumen and domestic desire, declamations against the aristocracy and clergy and satires of the revolutionaries.

In his work on pornographic revolutionary pamphlets, Antoine de Baecque also emphasized their democratic effect, though in somewhat different terms from those expressed above. He argues that licentious publications participated "in the apprenticeship stage of democratic life" by trying to say everything, even to the point of absurdity. In the new order, every political figure learned that his conduct was subject to attack, to democratic scrutiny, and pornographic satire was part of an insistence on transparence, publicity or openness in politics.[53]

Although there is much merit in this analysis and its attention to the modes and means of publishing, it overlooks entirely the gender dimension of the new forms of democratization. Democracy was established against monarchy through pornographic attacks on the feminization of both the aristocracy and monarchy. It was accelerated in and after 1789 by especially vicious attacks against the leading female figure of the ancien régime, the queen herself. At the same time, the fraternal bonds of democracy were established – in pornography, at least and perhaps more broadly[54] – through the circulation of images of women's bodies, especially through print media and the effect of visualization through pornographic writing. The fantasies of multiple sexual partners and of sex across class lines, like other privileged preserves of the aristocracy such as hunting, were now available to everyone, but especially to every man. Women were thus essential to the development of democracy and, in the end, excluded from it. Julie – like her real life sisters – retired from political life to raise children and tend her garden.

329

The Effects of the Revolution on the Pornographic Tradition

With its usually insistent materialist ideology, pornography had long been at the forefront of the scientific investigation of the new democratic man, which sometimes meant men and sometimes meant men and women; of the workings of his body; the similarity of his bodies to all others, aristocratic or not; and the workings of his imagination, which was portrayed as dependent on the material body. In the 1790s, materialist ideology reached its culmination and reductio ad absurdum in the writings of Sade, who demonstrated, willy-nilly, the logical and cultural pitfalls of a materialist universe. The basic similarities of all bodies was harnessed by Sade to a political and social vision dominated by masters and slaves, in which men were usually the masters and women and children the slaves.[55] In *La Philosophie dans le boudoir*, for instance, Sade used materialist ideology to undermine any notion of family feeling, religion or conventional morality, and he explicitly tied the new emphasis on equality and fraternity to the virtues of incest and the community of all women. In Sade's vision, the philosophers Thérèse and Julie would now participate like all other women in giant Temples of Venus.[56]

Sade's novels marked an important transition in the 1790s. He took the politically and socially subversive possibilities of pornography to their furthest possible extreme and, at the same time and perhaps by the same act, he paved the way for the modern, apolitical genre of pornography. His attack on every aspect of conventional morality undermined the use of pornography for political ends in the future. Pornography was now identified with a general assault on morality itself, rather than a specific criticism of the irrationalities of the ancien régime moral system. For this reason, Sade was condemned by every government, ancien régime, republican and Napoleonic. The republican and, later, the Napoleonic police devoted more energy to tracking down copies of *Justine* and *Juliette* than they did with any other works.[57]

Contemporaries immediately perceived the threat posed by Sade. The anonymous author of a book about literary life in Paris in 1799 praised Restif de la Bretonne and Laclos, even though they had written books considered scandalous by many. He called *Les Liaisons dangereuses* "one of the best-known works in Europe...it is a true story in which only the names have been changed." He reviled Sade, however, and in terms that suggested the danger he represented:

> We cite him here so that everyone will know, so that no one will forget, that he is the author of *Justine* or *les malheurs de la vertu*, an abominable work. They say that he has just died; well, so much the better, so much the better, for the existence of such a man is a true calamity, and death has done well to rid the world of him.[58]

In the preface to *L'Anti-Justine*, Restif admitted to having read *Justine*, *Aline et Valcour* and *La Philosophie dans le boudoir*, and he announced his aim of writing a book that was more titillating than all of Sade's. Yet he hoped to write a book that would have none of the violence or sadism of Sade's work; his would be a book that "wives could read to their husbands in order to be better served." "No one," he professed, "was more revolted than me by the dirty works of the infamous Dfds [Sade's initials]."[59]

Although enormously influential in the long run, Sade remained a paradoxical figure in the invention of pornography at the end of the eighteenth century. Unlike his fellow pornographers, his works always retained the political edge of earlier materialist works that was fast disappearing from other works of pornography. As the presses became freer under the revolutionary governments, apolitical as well as political pornography was published in great numbers and, after 1794, political pornography began to disappear. Pornography could make money, and it increasingly needed no other justification.

One of the central figures in the transition from a clandestine and often politically motivated pornography to the more commercial, popularized, apolitical pornography of the nineteenth and twentieth centuries was the Chevalier Andréa de Nerciat. André-Robert Andréa de Nerciat (1739–1800) was the son of a royal official in Burgundy, and, like Laclos and Sade, he began his career as a military officer. When he retired from the military in 1775, he turned his hand to writing plays, verse and light music and, when those failed, pornography. In the 1780s, he was a librarian for the Landgrave Frederick II of Hesse-Cassel, a position that may have been a cover for his work as a secret agent for the French government. He was sent to the Dutch Republic in 1787 during the Dutch revolt, which may explain why some believed him to be the author of *Julie philosophe*, with its accounts of the Dutch and Belgian revolts. Later, he went to Austria and Bohemia, where he continued to both write and serve as an agent for the French republican government. Before long, however, he was probably playing a double game, claiming to serve the French Republic but also providing information to those allied against it. The French officials knew that he wrote "dirty books" (*quelques romans orduriers*) and, in 1798, he was arrested by the French when they invaded Naples, his most recent post. He died soon after his release in 1800.[60]

The publishing career of Andréa de Nerciat spanned the ancien régime, the Revolution and the Consulate. His first known novel, *Félicia*, was published in 1775, and sixteen editions followed until 1812, seven of them appearing between 1792 and 1798.[61] It continued to have a long career thereafter, for the book was ordered destroyed in 1822, 1842 and 1865 by different French courts, and it was seized as late as 1955 in Paris.[62] His final work, published posthumously in 1803 but supposedly written before 1789, was *Le Diable au corps*, described by a noted nineteenth-century bibliographer as "the most obscene and best-known work of Nerciat," which "in my opinion... is the best erotic French novel."[63]

Andréa de Nerciat is significant not only because he was a widely read and much published author, but also because he followed and perhaps helped to create the changing pornographic conventions of this crucial time of transition. *Félicia*, like her predecessors *Thérèse philosophe* and *Margot la ravaudeuse*, was narrated in a female voice. Félicia, a foundling, tells her story to one of her favorites, a nobleman. Félicia has made her way in the world of love and writes now in order "to view and review my folies on parade, with the satisfaction of a new colonel who makes his regiment march by on a day of review, or, if you wish, like an old miser who counts and weighs the money of a repayment." She writes "to amuse myself... and to scandalize the universe!"[64]

During the Revolution, the voice of the narrator in Andréa de Nerciat's novels shifts from the female to the male and then to the omniscient position, identified neither as male nor female. In the sequel to *Félicia* called *Monrose, ou Le Libertin par fatalité* (1792), Félicia still speaks but she quickly explains that Monrose will be the principal figure in the story. Monrose then tells his story to Félicia. Félicia's voice is occasionally heard, but the male has largely supplanted the female voice in narration.[65] When Andréa de Nerciat published his next work, *Les Aphrodites, ou Fragments thali-priapiques pour servir à l'histoire du plaisir* (1793), he used the omniscient narrator to describe the fraternity of Aphrodites, which was composed of leading noblemen and women. The fraternity or order is entirely devoted to sexual pleasure and to the exploration of sexual combinations. In his last work, *Le Diable au corps*, Andréa de Nerciat used an omniscient narrator to depict a series of tableaux within the narrative structure of a novel.

The transformation of narrative voice is important because it signals a fundamental change in the representation of women. Like Thérèse, Margot and even Julie, Félicia enjoys her independence, determination and control. As the female narrator is effaced, however, so too is any ambiguity about the function of the representation of women. In the novels without a female narrator, it is clear that the female bodies in the text are there to be read about, viewed and enjoyed by men. Although a Madame Durat runs the "hospice" of the Aphrodites, the female bodies in the stories are simply counters in a male system of exchange. When an orgy is organized between seven couples of noblemen and noblewomen, for instance, it is the men who move from woman to woman in a systematic, almost machine-like series of exchanges.

The transformation in narrative voice was not always total or consistent. The marquise in *Le Diable au corps*, for example, still insists on some of the female narrator's prerogatives. In her dialogue with the younger Philippine, she teaches Philippine to use the obscene words for sexual body parts: "Learn then to speak and not to hesitate over each word like a girl in a convent." But the marquise is described as having "a tone of voice that is a little masculine," which presumably explains her ability to take the initiative. In general, gender roles are being more clearly defined, even when they occur in the same body. Each character is dissected in gender terms – a German priest, for example, has features that are a bit feminine – and one character is identified as a pederast. His desire for young boys is not denounced, but it is described as a determining characteristic. Pornography still works against sexual differentiation by emphasizing the leveling effects of bodily desires, but in the works of Andréa de Nerciat, there is an effort to reinscribe sexual differences within the pornographic mold.[66]

Politics has a curious place in Andréa de Nerciat's novels. He offers none of the philosophical and political speculation that was so striking in Sade's novels of the period, but he does, on occasion, make specific reference to the French Revolution, all of it negative or at least satirical. In *Les Aphrodites*, for example, a footnote attributes the abolition of titles of nobility to "a handful of drunkards." Madame Durat won't read pornography by Mirabeau because he supported the Revolution. And in the postface, the publishers claim that the Aphrodites dissolved themselves as an order at the end of 1791 in order to go into a "delicious exile." Several Aphrodites perished, it is claimed, in the uprising of August 10, 1792 and in the September Massacres of the same year.[67] In the slightly earlier novel, *Mon noviciat* (1792), the publisher claims in a footnote that dirty books have made him a lot of money: "The right to display them and sell them publicly... is...not one of the least advantages of this happy liberty, born in the Revolution which was made by our great courage."[68]

In general, however, politics occupies a tiny space. Many of the leading characters in *Le Diable au corps* (1803) are aristocrats or clergymen, just as they were in ancien régime pornography. But the author has no interest in denouncing their debaucheries. The marquise is beautiful and of noble bearing, the countess de Motte-en-Feu has a more tired beauty, and the abbé Boujaron is a Neapolitan priest who enjoys the vices of each nation and every station. Their pleasures are now democratic – the marquise sleeps with the man who sells her interesting new English dildos while the abbé looks on from the closet – but the focus is the depiction of their pleasures, which include bestiality with an ass, described as having "all the attractions that can make an ass interesting (figure 9.8)." The crossover of gender, racial (sexual relations with a black slave are also detailed), social and species lines is there to provoke scandal and titillation, not political reflection or com-

335

FIGURE 9.8. Bestiality scene from Andréa de Nerciat, *Le Diable au corps* (Paris, 1803).

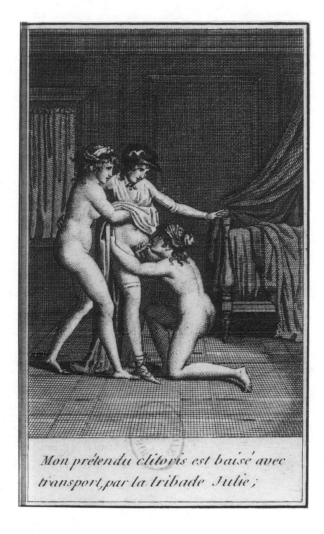

Mon prétendu clitoris est baisé avec transport, par la tribade Julie;

FIGURE 9.9. Scene from *L'Enfant du bordel* (Paris, 1800). The text reads: "My would-be clitoris is kissed with transport by the tribade [lesbian] Julie." This scene captures the gender-play potential of pornography. Here the male hero is disguised as a woman in order to seduce a lesbian.

337

mentary.[69] It does nonetheless represent a further development of eighteenth-century materialist philosophy by establishing the equality of physical attraction across every kind of boundary line.

Andréa de Nerciat proved that you did not have to be a revolutionary in order to profit from the revolutionary freeing of the presses. His work also showed that the market for pornography, which had been stimulated by criticism of the ancien régime's social and political system, could be exploited as well by those who had no interest in oppositional politics. The Héberts of the Revolution had used pornography to reach the masses of a new readership in France in order to push democratization of the political and social order. Andréa de Nerciat's books reflected the influence of a new democratic culture, but reflected no interest in any particular politics – not even a democratic politics.

Not much is known about the market for dirty books after 1799, and Andréa de Nerciat may represent a return to the old libertine market of the late seventeenth and early eighteenth centuries. But even if that was his intention, it is clear that new kinds of apolitical pornography were infiltrating and, perhaps, expanding the market for forbidden books after 1799. The anonymously written novel *L'Enfant du bordel*, for instance, took advantage of the rage for novels about orphans and foundlings that had appeared after 1795. It was written as a pornographic parody of those other "child" novels that detailed the rise of socially disadvantaged.[70] Like *Eléonore, ou L'Heureuse personne*, a novel that appeared in the same year, *L'Enfant du bordel* embroidered on the theme of transvestitism (figure 9.9). *Amélie de Saint-Far, ou la fatale erreur*, supposedly authored by a Madame de C— (according to the title page), tried to develop a space between the sentimental novel and the pornographic novel by reducing the explicit sexual descriptions to a minimum and embedding them in a narrative that was typical of the sentimental novel.

In other words, with the important exception of Sade's work, the post-1795 pornographic novel developed into a medium for the exploration of new sexual pleasures – bestiality, transvestitism and even transsexuality in *Eléonore*, but not sadism, torture or murder – but left behind its political past. Pornography did not lose all contact with social and political reality – Eléonore, for example, was the illegitimate child of a nobleman, as was the child of the brothel – but it now embarked on a career as a separate and distinct genre, clearly consigned to the underside of bourgeois, domestic life in the nineteenth and twentieth centuries. The libertine philosopher women gave way (except, of course, in their many reprintings) to the *femme fatale* and, especially, the *femmes vicieuses*, those women with lesbian tendencies who would prostitute themselves for money, ruin men with their desire for luxuries and, in the end, destroy men's virility, if they were not victimized first.[71] Pornography would continue to have political and social meanings, as it still has political and social meanings, but these would now be much less intentional and much more subtle, even as the genre became more widely accessible.

Photo Credits:

I.1. Bibliothèque Nationale, Paris.
I.2. Bibliothèque Nationale, Paris.
I.3. Bibliothèque Nationale, Paris.
I.4. Bibliothèque Nationale, Paris.
1.1. Fondazione Querini Stampalia, Venice.
1.2. The Metropolitan Museum of Art; The Elisha Whittelsey Fund, 1955.
1.3. The New York Public Library, Lenox and Tilden Foundation, Print Collection, Miriam and Ira D. Wallach Division of Art, Prints and Photographs.
1.4. Graphische Sammlung, Albertina, Vienna.
1.5. Museo del Prado, Madrid.
1.6. Bibliothèque Nationale, Paris.
1.7. Reprinted from Lynn Lawner, ed. and trans., *I modi* (Evanston, IL: Northwestern University Press, 1989). Lynn Lawner. All rights reserved. Reproduced by permission of the publisher.
1.8. Reprinted from Lynn Lawner, ed. and trans., *I modi* (Evanston, IL: Northwestern University Press, 1989). Lynn Lawner. All rights reserved. Reproduced by permission of the publisher.
1.9. Reprinted from Lynn Lawner, ed. and trans., *I modi* (Evanston, IL: Northwestern University Press, 1989). Lynn Lawner. All rights reserved. Reproduced by permission of the publisher.
1.10. Kunsthistorische Museum, Vienna.
1.11. Kunsthistorische Museum, Vienna.

1.12. Museum of Fine Arts, Boston; James Fund and by Special Contribution.
1.13. British Museum, London.
2.1. Bibliothèque Nationale, Paris.
3.1. Princeton University Libraries.
3.2. By permission of the British Library, London.
3.3. By permission of the British Library, London.
4.1. Bibliothèque Nationale, Paris.
4.2. Bibliothèque Nationale, Paris.
4.3. By permission of the British Library, London.
4.4. Bibliothèque Nationale, Paris.
4.5. Bibliothèque Nationale, Paris.
4.6. Bibliothèque Nationale, Paris.
4.7. Bibliothèque Nationale, Paris.
4.8. Bibliothèque Nationale, Paris.
4.9. By permission of the British Library, London.
4.10. By permission of the British Library, London.
5.1. Bibliothèque Nationale, Paris.
5.2. Bibliothèque Nationale, Paris.
6.1. Bibliothèque Nationale, Paris.
7.1. Guildhall Library, London.
7.2. By permission of the British Library, London.
7.3. Paul Mellon Centre, London.
7.4. Victoria and Albert Museum, London.
8.1. Royal Library, The Hague.
9.1. Bibliothèque Nationale, Paris.
9.2. Bibliothèque Nationale, Paris.
9.3. Bibliothèque Nationale, Paris.
9.4. Bibliothèque Nationale, Paris.
9.5. Bibliothèque Nationale, Paris.
9.6. Bibliothèque Nationale, Paris.
9.7. Bibliothèque Nationale, Paris.
9.8. Bibliothèque Nationale, Paris.
9.9. Bibliothèque Nationale, Paris.

Notes

Introduction

1. My understanding of pornography has been inspired in part by Michel Foucault's many works on the historical emergence of the discourses of modern life: as with medicine, madness, the prison and sexuality, pornography should be understood as the product of new forms of regulation and new desires for knowledge. Although Foucault's interest in pornography and especially the Marquis de Sade is apparent in many of his works, he did not devote any sustained attention to this subject. On Sade, see Michel Foucault, *The History of Sexuality*: vol. 1: *An Introduction*, trans. Robert Hurley (New York: Random House, 1980), pp. 148–49.

2. U.S. Department of Justice, *Attorney General's Commission on Pornography. Final Report*, 2 vols. (Washington, DC: 1986), p. 233.

3. The conclusion of the historical section of the Meese Commission report is, nonetheless, disappointingly vague: "To conclude that inhibition, in some form or another, of public discussion and representations of sexual practices is a totally modern phenomenon is to overstate the case and to misinterpret the evidence from earlier times. But to assume that public discussions and descriptions of sexuality were, prior to 1850, always as inhibited as they were in English speaking countries from 1850 to 1950 is equally mistaken" (Department of Justice, *Attorney General's Commission*, p. 236).

4. Walter Kendrick, *The Secret Museum: Pornography in Modern Culture* (New York: Penguin, 1987), p. 57.

5. Department of Justice, *Attorney General's Commission*, p. 235.

6. Kendrick, *The Secret Museum*, p. 31.

7. *Trésor de la langue française* (Paris: Centre Nationale de la Recherche Scientifique, 1988), vol. 13, pp. 786–87.

8. For a discussion of the relevant literature, see Annie Stora-Lamarre, *L'Enfer de la IIIᵉ République: Censeurs et pornographes, (1881–1914)* (Paris: Imago, 1990), pp. 14–15.

9. Etienne-Gabriel Peignot, *Dictionnaire critique, littéraire et bibliographique des principaux livres condamnés au feu, supprimés ou censurés*, 2 vols. (Paris, 1806), vol. 1, p. xij. All translations from the French are mine unless otherwise noted. Peignot used the terms *pornographique* and *sotadique* as synonyms. *Sotadique* comes from the Latin *sotadicus*, which is based on the Greek name of an obscene poet, Sotades. I am grateful to my colleague Ruth Mazo Karras for help in tracing the meaning of *sotadique*.

10. Ibid., p. vij.

11. Ibid., pp. viij–xij.

12. Full titles (Peignot gave abbreviated titles) and publication information come from *Dictionnaire des oeuvres érotiques: Domaine français* (Paris: Mercure de France, 1971).

13. Peignot, *Dictionnaire*, pp. xxiv–xxv.

14. Peter Wagner, *Eros Revived: Erotica of the Enlightenment in England and America* (London: Secker & Warburg, 1988), p. 6.

15. Robert Darnton, *Edition et sédition: L'Univers de la littérature clandestine au XVIIIᵉ siècle* (Paris: Gallimard, 1991), especially pp. v, 13–16.

16. Archives de la Préfecture de la Police [hereafter APP], Paris, Aa/132/178, Section de la Cité.

17. See, for example, the printed forms of the Bureau central of the canton of Paris from the year V (1795) in APP, Paris, Aa/153/328, Section des gardes françaises, ans III à VI.

18. APP, Paris, Aa/4/710-12. I am grateful to Margaret C. Jacob for this reference.

19. Darnton, *Edition et sédition*, pp. 220, 223.

20. Samuel Pepys, *The Diary of Samuel Pepys*, eds. Robert Latham and William Matthews, 11 vols. (Berkeley: University of California Press, 1970–1983). See entries for February 8 and 9, 1668 in vol. 9, pp. 57–59.

21. Darnton, *Edition et sédition*, p. 223.

22. I base my observations on Thomas Liebenzell, *Smut in the British Library: Register zu Kearneys Private Case* (Hamburg: C. Bell Verlag, 1986), which gives listings by country.

23. My tabulations in this paragraph are based on ibid.

24. Patrick J. Kearney, *A History of Erotic Literature* (London: Macmillan, 1982), p. 101.

25. The observations in this paragraph are based on William Hugh Hopkins, "The Development of 'Pornographic' Literature in Eighteenth- and Early Nineteenth-Century Russia," Ph.D. thesis, Indiana University, 1977.

26. Ibid., pp. 256–57.

27. The essential bibliographic work was undertaken by David Foxon, *Libertine Literature in England, 1660–1745* (New Hyde Park, NY: University Books, 1965), pp. 25–27.

28. My account is taken from Kearney, *A History*, pp. 24–29.

29. Foxon, *Libertine Literature*, p. 3.

30. Wagner, *Eros Revived*, p. 7.

31. Quoted in Foxon, *Libertine Literature*, pp. 19–20. Paula Findlen gives a slightly different translation in her essay in this volume.

32. Kearney, *A History*, pp. 29–52.

33. Foxon, *Libertine Literature*, p. ix. Foxon is an indispensable source for seventeenth-century development.

34. Lawrence Stone, *The Family, Sex, and Marriage in England, 1500–1800*, abridged ed. (New York: Harper & Row, 1977), pp. 333–34.

35. Foxon, *Libertine Literature*, pp. 48–49.

36. Kearney, *A History*, p. 53. No adequate explanation of this stagnation has been offered.

37. Susanna Åkerman, *Queen Christina of Sweden and Her Circle: The Transformation of a Seventeenth-Century Philosophical Libertine* (Leiden: E.J. Brill, 1991),

especially appendix 2, "The Libertine Pamphlets," pp. 310–15. It is unclear from Åkerman's analysis just how explicit these pamphlets were. My thanks to Paula Findlen for this reference.

38. Steven Marcus, *The Other Victorians: A Study of Sexuality and Pornography in Mid-Nineteenth-Century England* (New York: Basic Books, 1974), p. 282.

39. Robert Darnton, *The Literary Underground of the Old Regime* (Cambridge, MA: Harvard University Press, 1982).

40. Aram Vartanian, "La Mettrie, Diderot, and Sexology in the Enlightenment," in Jean Macary (ed.), *Essays on the Age of Enlightenment in Honor of Ira O. Wade* (Geneva: Librarie Droz, 1977), pp. 347–67.

41. As quoted in R.F. Brissenden, "*La Philosophie dans le boudoir*; or, A Young Lady's Entrance into the World," *Studies in Eighteenth Century Culture* 2 (1972), pp. 113–41, quote p. 124.

42. Jean Marie Goulemot, *Ces Livres qu'on ne lit que d'une main: Lecture et lecteurs de livres pornographiques au XVIIIᵉ siècle* (Aix-en-Provence: Alinéa, 1991). In fact, the gendering of pornography is still up for debate.

43. On libertinism in general, see Péter Nagy, *Libertinage et révolution*, trans. Christiane Grémillon (Paris: Gallimard, 1975), p. 29.

44. As quoted in Robert J. Ellrich, "Modes of Discourse and the Language of Sexual Reference in Eighteenth-Century French Fiction," in Robert P. Maccubin (ed.), *Unauthorized Sexual Behavior during the Enlightenment*, a special issue of *Eighteenth-Century Life* 9 (May 1985), p. 222.

45. Marcus, *The Other Victorians*, pp. 44–45, 268–71.

46. Angela Carter, *The Sadeian Woman: An Exercise in Cultural History* (New York: Pantheon, 1978), p. 16.

47. Ibid., p. 20.

48. Wagner, *Eros Revived*, p. 214.

49. Iain McCalman, *Radical Underworld: Prophets, Revolutionaries and Pornographers in London, 1795–1840* (Cambridge, UK: Cambridge University Press, 1988), especially pp. 204–321.

50. David Underdown, "*The Man in the Moon*: The Upside Down World in Popular Journalism, 1649–1650," a draft paper kindly lent to me by the author.

51. Lynn Hunt, "The Unstable Boundaries of the French Revolution," and Catherine Hall, "The Sweet Delights of Home," in Michelle Perrot (ed.), *A History of Private Life*: Vol. 4, *From the Fires of the Revolution to the Great War*, trans. Arthur Goldhammer (Cambridge, MA: Harvard University Press, 1990), pp. 13–94.

CHAPTER ONE: HUMANISM, POLITICS AND PORNOGRAPHY

1. John Addington Symonds, *Renaissance in Italy (1875-86)*, quoted in Walter Kendrick, *The Secret Museum: Pornography in Modern Culture* (New York: Penguin, 1987), p. 60.

2. The literature on Aretino is vast. The most comprehensive study of Aretino to date is Paul Larivaille, *Pietro Aretino fra Rinascimento e Manierismo* (Rome: Bulzoni, 1980), which is his Italian translation of *L'Aretin entre Renaissance et Manièrisme* (Lille: Université de Lille, Service de reproduction des thèses, 1972). There is no good biography in English, although interested readers can consult James Cleugh, *The Divine Aretino* (London: Anthony Blond, 1965); and Christopher Cairns, *Pietro Aretino and the Republic of Venice: Researches on Aretino and His Circle in Venice, 1527-1556* (Florence: Olschki, 1985). For a thorough discussion of recent bibliography on Aretino and his writings, see Giovanni Casalegno, "Rassegna aretiniana (1972–1989)," *Lettere italiane* 41 (1989), pp. 425–54.

3. John Wolfe's edition of the *Ragionamenti* billed Aretino as "M. Pietro Aretino; cognimato il Flagello de Prencipi, il Veritiero, e'l Divino." Pietro Aretino, *La Prima [-Seconda] Parte de Ragionamenti* (Bengodi, 1584). For more on Wolfe, see n. 23, below.

4. Niccolò Franco, "Rime contro Pietro Aretino con la Priapea," in Antonio Vignali, *La Cazzaria*, ed. Pasquale Stoppelli (Rome: Edizioni dell'Elefante, 1984), p. 14; and Anton Francesco Doni, *La Vita dello infame Aretino*, ed. Costantino Arlía (Città di Castello: S. Lapi, 1901), pp. 25–26, 32. Elsewhere in his *Priapea*, Franco suggested that the only thing that stopped Aretino's tongue was his unbridled sexual appetite: "You know how to eat a prick raw and cooked, . . . / Praise be to God that for now / The prick in your mouth prevents you from speaking."

In David O. Frantz, *Festum voluptatis: A Study of Renaissance Erotica* (Columbus: Ohio State University Press, 1989), p. 111.

5. Anton Francesco Doni, *La Libraria*, in Pietro Aretino, *La Cortigiana*, ed. Angelo Romano (Milan: Rizzoli, 1989), p. 28.

6. I have translated most of the materials used in this essay, including those found in Lynn Lawner's edition of *I modi* and in David Frantz's *Festum voluptatis*. Sexually explicit and obscene language is particularly difficult to convey in another language, since it is often time- and place-specific. My own approach, unlike that of Lawner, for instance, is to translate all words as directly as possible, substituting modern English equivalents where it seems appropriate. It is ironic and, of course, a reflection of our own conflicted reactions to this literature, that many people who study these materials have difficulty dealing directly with the content. As a result, anyone interested in reading further in this subject should be forewarned that most nineteenth- and twentieth-century translations should be checked against the sixteenth-century texts, because they frequently stray from the original meaning. An exception is Raymond Rosenthal's translation of Aretino's *Ragionamenti*, which compares well with the Italian critical editions: Pietro Aretino, *Sei giornate*, ed. Giovanni Aquilecchia (Bari: Laterza, 1969); and idem, *Ragionamento: Dialogo*, ed. Nino Borsellino (Milan: Garzanti, 1984).

7. Jacob Burckhardt, *The Civilization of the Renaissance in Italy* (London: George Allen & Unwin, 1960), p. 164; on this and related subjects, see pp. 100–103, 162–64, 262–79. For a more positive rendering of the same argument, see Leonard Barkan, *Transuming Passion: Ganymede and the Erotics of Humanism* (Stanford, CA: Stanford University Press, 1991).

8. Johannes Molanus, *De Picturis et imaginibus sacris* (Louvain, 1570), in David Freedberg, "Johannes Molanus on Provokative Paintings: *De Historia sanctarum imaginum et picturarum*, book 2, chapter 42," *Journal of the Warburg and Courtauld Institutes* 34 (1971), p. 245.

9. Tommaso Garzoni, *Piazza Universale* (1585), in Paul F. Grendler, *Critics of the Italian World, 1530–1560* (Madison, WI: University of Wisconsin Press, 1969), p. 192. For the basic contours of the history of early modern pornography, see David Foxon, *Libertine Literature in England, 1660–1745* (New Hyde

Park, NY: University Books, 1965); Frantz, *Festum voluptatis*; Patrick J. Kearney, *A History of Erotic Literature* (London: Macmillan, 1982); Kendrick, *The Secret Museum*, pp. 1–66; and Roger Thompson, *Unfit for Modest Ears: A Study of Pornographic, Obscene and Bawdy Works Written or Published in England in the Second Half of the Seventeenth Century* (Totowa, NJ: Rowman & Littlefield, 1979). My disagreements with the interpretations of these authors are made apparent throughout the essay. In general, however, early modern writers, readers and censors are given little agency in comparison to the motives and reactions imputed to their more modern counterparts, a tendency I hope to correct in my own forays into this subject. Much of the secondary literature tends to look at pornographic art and literature as separate entities, while I argue that it is the interplay between the different mediums that facilitated the emergence of a pornographic culture.

10. Aline Rouselle, *Porneia: On Desire and the Body in Antiquity*, trans. Felicia Pheasant (Oxford, UK: Basil Blackwell, 1988), p. 4.

11. Here I am echoing Michael Rocke's plea that we perceive homosexuality in Renaissance Italy neither as marginal nor as subculture. See his *Friendly Affections, Nefarious Vices: Homosexuality and Male Culture in Renaissance Florence* (Oxford, UK: Oxford University Press, forthcoming). In a different context, this point also is underscored by Stephanie Jed in her argument that humanist marginalia produces a powerful form of political grammar. See her *Chaste Thinking: The Rape of Lucretia and the Birth of Humanism* (Bloomington: Indiana University Press, 1989), p. 48ff. In the same spirit, pornography is not simply the product of a "subculture" of debauched literary hacks, as it often is portrayed. Aretino lived a highly public life and intersected with many of the major political, religious, artistic and intellectual figures of his age. Unless his "pornographic" writings are artificially divorced from his other literary productions, it is hard to imagine how to perceive him and his circle as being anything but center stage.

12. On the impact of printing in early modern Europe, see Roger Chartier, *The Culture of Print in Early Modern France*, trans. Lydia G. Cochrane (Princeton, NJ: Princeton University Press, 1987); Robert Darnton, *The Literary Underground*

of the Old Regime (Cambridge: Harvard University Press, 1982); and Elizabeth Eisenstein, *The Printing Press as an Agent of Change*, 2 vols. (New York: Cambridge University Press, 1979). Regarding the role of visual imagery in this transformation, see David Freedberg, *The Power of Images: Studies in the History and Theory of Response* (Chicago: University of Chicago Press, 1989), pp. 317–77; and Carlo Ginzburg, "Titian, Ovid and Sixteenth-Century Codes for Erotic Illustration," in his *Myths, Emblems, Clues*, trans. John Tedeschi and Anne C. Tedeschi (London: Hutchinson Radius, 1990), pp. 77–95.

13. I would like to thank John Paoletti for reminding me of the circumstances of display, so integral to situating the *Venus and Adonis* and *Danaë* paintings of Titian.

14. For a parallel discussion of this problem in a different arena, see William Eamon, "Arcana Disclosed: The Advent of Printing, the Books of Secrets Tradition and the Developments of Experimental Science in the Sixteenth Century," *History of Science* 22 (1984), pp. 111–50; idem, "From the Secrets of Nature to Public Knowledge: The Origins of the Concept of Openness in Science," *Minerva* 23 (1985), pp. 321–47; and Carlo Ginzburg, "High and Low: The Theme of Forbidden Knowledge in the Sixteenth and Seventeenth Centuries," *Past and Present* 73 (1976), pp. 28–41.

15. *Canons and Decrees of the Council of Trent*, trans. H.J. Schroeder (Saint Louis, MO: TAN Books, 1955), p. 275.

16. This story is recounted well by Paul Grendler, *The Roman Inquisition and the Venetian Press, 1540–1605* (Princeton, NJ: Princeton University Press, 1977).

17. In John Lievsay, *The Englishman's Italian Books, 1550–1700* (Philadelphia: University of Pennsylvania Press, 1969), pp. 17–18.

18. Piero Lorenzoni, *Erotismo e pornografia nelle letteratura italiana: Storia e antologia* (Milan: Edizioni il Formichiere, 1976), p. 40.

19. *Canons and Decrees of the Council of Trent*, in Robert Klein and Henri Zerner, *Italian Art, 1500–1600* (Evanston, IL: Northwestern University Press, 1966), p. 121.

20. Ludovico Dolce, *Aretin: A Dialogue on Painting*, trans. W. Brown (1770; New York: Scolar Press, 1970), p. 177.

21. In Roberto Zapperi, *Annibale Carracci: Ritratto di Artista da Giovane* (Turin: Einaudi, 1989), p. 89.

22. Grendler, *Critics of the Italian World*, p. 185.

23. John Wolfe published more of Aretino's works than any other individual printer, and he was the first to produce a complete edition of the *Ragionamenti* in 1584. See H.R. Hoppe, "John Wolfe, Printer and Publisher, 1579-1601," *The Library*, ser. 4, 14 (1933), pp. 241-87; A. Gerber, "All of the Five Fictitious Italian Editions of Writings of Machiavelli and Three of Those of Pietro Aretino Printed by John Wolfe of London (1584-88)," *Modern Language Notes* 22 (1907), pp. 2-6, 129-35, 201-206; and, more generally, Dennis Woodfield, *Surreptitious Printing in England, 1550-1640* (New York: Bibliographical Society of America, 1973).

24. Pietro Aretino, *Ragionamenti*, in *Aretino's Dialogues*, trans. Raymond Rosenthal (New York: Ballantine Books, 1971), p. 319.

25. Mikhail Bakhtin, *Rabelais and His World*, trans. Hélène Iswolsky (Bloomington: Indiana University Press, 1984).

26. Edgar Wind, *Pagan Mysteries in the Renaissance* (London: Faber & Faber, 1968); and Leonard Barkan, *Transuming Passion*, p. 71.

27. Freedberg, "Johannes Molanus," pp. 235 and 245.

28. Ginzburg, "Titian, Ovid and Sixteenth-Century Codes," p. 92. For a general overview of erotic engravings from this period, see Giorgio Lise, *L'Incisione erotica del Rinascimento* (Milan: Carlo Emilio Bestetti, 1975); and Henry Zerner, "L'Estampe érotique au temps de Titien," in *Convegno Internazionale di Studi, Tiziano e Venezia* (Vicenza: Neri Pozza, 1980), pp. 85-90.

29. The entirety of this sequence is reproduced in Diane DeGrazia Bohlin, *Prints and Related Drawings by the Carracci Family* (Washington, DC: National Gallery of Art, 1979), pp. 298-303.

30. Freedberg, "Johannes Molanus," p. 243; and idem, *The Power of Images*, pp. 330-31.

31. Girolamo Morlini, *Novellae* (Naples, 1520), in Freedberg, *The Power of Images*, pp. 326-27.

32. I have not yet been able to locate the source of this story, but I thank Sally Scully for bringing it to my attention.

33. October 6, 1527, in James M. Saslow, *Ganymede in the Renaissance: Homosexualiy in Art and Society* (New Haven, CT: Yale University Press, 1986), p. 71.

34. Baldesar Castiglione, *The Book of the Courtier*, trans. Charles S. Singleton (Garden City, NY: Anchor, 1959), pp. 337–38.

35. Niccolò Franco, *Sonnetti lussuriosi e satirici con la Priapea* (Alvisopoli, 1850), p. 35.

36. In saying this I am more in agreement with the interpretation offered by Carlo Ginzburg than the one put forth by Charles Hope, "Problems of Interpretation in Titian's Erotic Paintings," in *Tiziano e Venezia*, pp. 111–24, especially p. 113. Of course, I do not wish to negate the important differences between the paintings of Titian and the engravings of Raimondi and the Carracci brothers. The physical size, circumstances of production, intended audience and method of distribution have often been used to separate the "high" cultural production of Titian from the "low" cultural production of Raimondi and the Carracci. And yet, as Carlo Ginzburg observes, both drew largely upon the same stock of literary and artistic images; Titian was not necessarily better educated than the engravers, and perhaps not as well educated. While Titian saw his paintings as objects fit for princes, Raimondi and the Carracci catered to a more heterodox clientele. But they are essentially a product of the same culture, and this is the point I wish to underscore. I would like to thank Wendy Stedman Sheard for her thoughtful criticisms on this aspect of the essay.

37. "The nude of one age may seem erotically uninteresting to the eyes of another. We may even mistake an erotically intended image for an idealized one – if it lacks the shapes, proportions, and details we are accustomed to responding to in contemporary life.... Even Giulio Romano's pornographic *Sedici Modi*, showing various coital positions, so shocking to his contemporaries, have a curiously unsexy look to modern eyes because everyone is 'wearing' the Renaissance figure now associated with idealized formal nudity." In Anne Hollander, *Seeing through Clothes* (New York: Avon Books, 1975), p. 88.

38. *Raccolta di lettere sulla pittura, scultura ed architectura* (Rome, 1759),

vol. 3, pp. 259–60, and in Ginzburg, "Titian, Ovid and Sixteenth-Century Codes," pp. 81–82.

39. Pirro Ligorio, *Trattato di alcune cose appertenente alla nobiltà dell'antiche arti* (c. 1570–1580), in Claudia Lazzara, "The Visual Language of Gender in Sixteenth-Century Garden Sculpture," in Marilyn Miguel and Juliana Schiesari (eds.), *Refiguring Woman: Perspectives on Gender and the Italian Renaissance* (Ithaca, NY: Cornell University Press, 1990), p. 89; and Freedberg, "Johannes Molanus," p. 241.

40. Aretino, *I modi*, pp. 60–61, 80–81, 84–85.

41. On this subject, see Lynn Lawner, *Lives of the Courtesans: Portraits of the Italian Renaissance* (New York: Rizzoli, 1987).

42. This is taken from the conclusion of Aretino, *I modi*, pp. 90–91.

43. Giulio Ferroni, "Il teatro della Nanna," in Giulio Ferroni (ed.), *Le Voci dell'istrione: Pietro Aretino e la dissoluzione del teatro* (Naples: Liguori, 1977), pp. 136–202, and passim. This is probably the finest single essay on the *Ragionamenti*, though the introductions of Giovanni Aquileaia and Nino Borsellino to the standard Italian editions are also well worth consulting.

44. The quotes, in order, are taken from *Aretino's Dialogues*, pp. 30, 49, 21.

45. Here I follow the argument of Giulio Ferroni, "Il teatro della Nanna," p. 181ff. See n. 43, above.

46. Aretino, *Aretino's Dialogues*, pp. 50 and 224.

47. Ibid., p. 321.

48. Ibid., p. 320.

49. For more on the erotic engravings of Agostino Carracci, see DeGrazia Bohlin, *Prints and Related Drawings*, pp. 289–305.

50. Brantôme, *Vie des dames galantes*, in Harford Hyde, *A History of Pornography* (New York: Farrar, Strauss, Giroux, 1965), p. 79.

51. The work is published under the title *Il piacevol ragionamento de Aretino* in the *Capricciosi & piaceuoli ragionamenti di M. Pietro Aretino* (Cosmopoli, 1660), p. 423. This collection of Aretine and pseudo-Aretine works was published by the Elsevier press in Amsterdam.

52. Aretino, *Ragionamenti*, in *Aretino's Dialogues*, p. 39.

53. Bette Talvacchia, " 'Figure lascive per trastullo de l'ingegno,' " in *Giulio Romano* (Milan: Electa, 1989), p. 277.

54. Dolce produced the most well-known Italian translation of Ovid's *Metamorphoses* during the Renaissance, and it was first published in its entirety in 1553. Ludovico Dolce, *Le trasformationi*, ed. Stephen Orgel (New York: Garland, 1979).

55. For more on their original context, see Amy Richlin, *The Garden of Priapus: Sexuality and Aggression in Roman Humor* (New Haven, CT: Yale University Press, 1983).

56. W.H. Park, ed. and trans., *Priapea: Poems for a Phallic God* (London: Croom Helm, 1988), pp. 51–53.

57. Frantz, *Festum voluptatis*, p. 105.

58. Park, *Priapea*, pp. 53–54. On the Aldine Press, see Martin Lowry, *The World of Aldus Manutius: Business and Scholarship in Renaissance Venice* (Ithaca, NY: Cornell University Press, 1979).

59. Park, *Priapea*, p. 33.

60. Park translates this verse as "you'll be no more a girl, I say, / Than are the hairs that all around your penis lie?" (ibid., p. 137). Perhaps a better translation would be "Are you really a girl before there are hairs on your penis?" I would like to thank John Klause for offering this alternative translation. For Scaliger's commentary on the *Priapeia*, see Joseph Scaliger, *In appendicem P. Virgilii Maronis* (Leyden, 1573). For more on Scaliger, see Anthony Grafton, *Joseph Scaliger: A Study in the History of Classical Scholarship* (Oxford, UK: Oxford University Press, 1983). The description of Scaliger as a "bottomless pit of erudition" is taken from Daniel Heinsius, *Funeral Oration on the Death of Joseph Scaliger* (1609), in *Autobiography of Joseph Scaliger...and the Funeral Oration by Daniel Heinsius and Dominicus Bandius*, trans. George W. Robinson (Cambridge, MA: Harvard University Press, 1927), p. 77.

61. Park, *Priapea*, pp. 19–21.

62. Giovanni di Pagolo Morelli, *Ricordi*, ed. Vittore Branca (Florence: Le Monnier, 1956), p. 272; and Jed, *Chaste Thinking*, p. 119.

63. Pacifico Massimo, *Hecatelegium* (1489), in Lorenzoni, *Erotismo e porno-*

grafia, p. 167; Niccolò Franco, *Sonnetti lussuriosi*, pp. 26–27; idem, *Le Pistole vulgari* (Venice, 1542), p. 26. Renaissance neo-Priapism is discussed, somewhat sketchily, in Lorenzoni, ibid., pp. 18–20, 59–60; and Frantz, *Festum voluptatis*, p. 105ff. *Senza braghe* translates literally as "without underpants."

64. Ludovico Ariosto, *Satires* 6.31–33, in Barkan, *Transuming Passion*, p. 67.

65. In a letter to Beccadelli in the late 1420s, Bracciolini wrote, "Even though painters are allowed to do anything, just as poets are, still when they paint a naked woman – even though they are following nature as their guide – they cover the obscene parts of her body, or if the picture contains anything that is lewd, they keep it well out of sight." Poggio Bracciolini, *Epistolae*, in Freedberg, *The Power of Images*, pp. 360–61. For a brief analysis of the *Hermaphroditus*, see Lorenzoni, *Erotismo e pornografia*, pp. 18–19.

66. In Antonio Beccadelli, *L'Ermafrodito*, ed. and trans. Jole Tognelli (Rome: Avanzini e Torraca, 1968), pp. 24–25.

67. All quotes are taken from the English translation: Michael de Cossart, *Antonio Beccadelli and the Hermaphrodite* (Liverpool, UK: Janus, 1984), p. 25.

68. Ibid., pp. 32 and 50.

69. Ibid., p. 26.

70. Ibid., pp. 32, 43, 48, 55.

71. Ibid., pp. 58 and 63.

72. Verona, February 2, 1426, in Beccadelli, *L'Ermafrodito*, pp. 29–30.

73. See Michael Rocke, "Sodomites in Fifteenth-Century Tuscany: The Views of Bernardino of Siena," in Kent Gerard and Gert Hekma (eds.), *The Pursuit of Sodomy: Male Homosexuality in Renaissance and Enlightenment Europe* (New York: Harrington Park Press, 1989), pp. 7–31; Guido Ruggiero, *The Boundaries of Eros: Sex Crime and Sexuality in Renaissance Venice* (Oxford, UK: Oxford University Press, 1985), pp. 109–45; and James M. Saslow, *Ganymede in the Renaissance: Homosexuality in Art and Society* (New Haven, CT: Yale University Press, 1986).

74. Barkan, *Transuming Passion*, passim. In contrast, the rape of Lucretia, as Stephanie Jed recounts in her *Chaste Thinking*, was a profoundly *unerotic* tale.

75. Lorenzoni, *Erotismo e pornografia*, pp. 45–59; Frantz, *Festum voluptatis*, pp. 9–42 and passim.

76. The Accademia degli Incogniti was founded in Venice in 1630. Its prince, the patrician Giovan Francesco Loredano, wrote obscene novels that were included on the Index. Unfortunately time and space do not permit a fuller discussion of this academy, which is somewhat beyond the main chronological scope of this essay.

77. For more on Veronica Franco's peculiar role in the academy culture of sixteenth-century Venice, see Margeret Rosenthal, "Veronica Franco's Terze Rime: The Venetian Courtesan's Defense," *Renaissance Quarterly* 42 (1989), pp. 227–57. More generally, see n. 41, above, for Lawner's *Lives of the Courtesans*.

78. The title is most accurately translated as "Bunch of Pricks" though, in the playful spirit of academy culture, "The Prickery" might be truer to Vignali's intention.

79. The details of his life are given in Nino Borsellino's introduction and Pasquale Stoppelli's bio-bibliography to the recent critical edition; Vignali, *La Cazzaria*, pp. 13, 29–33.

80. Ibid., pp. 27–28.

81. Gian Paolo Lomazzo, *Il Libro dei sogni* (1548), in *Scritti sulle arti*, ed. R.P. Ciardi (Florence, 1973), vol. 1, p. 104. This passage was called to my attention in Rocke's *Friendly Affections, Nefarious Vices*, n. 11, above.

82. Antonio Rocco, *L'Alcibiade fanciullo a scola*, ed. Laura Coci (Rome: Salerno, 1988), p. 43.

83. Vignali, *La Cazzaria*, p. 29.

84. At one point, Sodo tells Arsiccio that he has read "a work...in which infinite positions of fucking repose" (ibid., p. 15) that he calls *La Cortigiana*. He probably refers to the *Sonnetti lussuriosi*.

85. This image is reproduced in *Giulio Romano*, p. 283.

86. Vignali, *La Cazzaria*, pp. 42, 48–49.

87. Ibid., pp. 59–68 and passim.

88. Ibid., p. 46.

89. Ibid., p. 41.

90. Ibid., pp. 83–84.

91. Ibid., pp. 86–87.

92. Ibid., p. 136. The political allegory can be found on pp. 94–137.

93. They are, respectively, the Pricks, Asses, Cunts and Balls of the tale.

94. Pasquale Stoppelli provides a concise summary of these events in Vignali, *La Cazzaria*, pp. 146–47, n. 173. For a more extensive discussion, see A.K. Chiancone Isaacs, "Popoli e monti a Siena del primo cinquecento," *Rivista storica italiana* 82 (1970), pp. 32–80.

95. Lucienne Bacall, *Il gioco dell'amore* (Spiel, 1991), p. 23.

96. Franco, *Priapea*, in Vignali, *La Cazzaria*, p. 153, n. 1.

97. Vignali, *La Cazzaria*, p. 23. With the exception of Borsellino's fine introduction to the 1986 critical edition of *La Cazzaria*, it has received little analysis elsewhere, though both Frantz, *Festum voluptatis*, pp. 38–42, and Lorenzoni, *Erotismo e pornografia*, pp. 60–62, discuss it briefly.

98. Aretino, *Ragionamenti*, in *Aretino's Dialogues*, pp. 107–108, 206.

99. Aretino, *I modi*, pp. 62–63, 72–75.

100. These images are explored in Barkan, *Transuming Passion*, pp. 56, 129, n. 66.

101. Rocco, *L'Alcibiade*, pp. 44 and 72. Here I am referring to Alberti's fifteenth-century *Libri della famiglia*.

102. Rocco, *L'Alcibiade*, p. 37.

103. Saslow, *Ganymede*, p. 79; Achille Olivieri, "Eroticism and Social Groups in Sixteenth-Century Venice: The Courtesan," in Philippe Ariès and André Béjin (eds.), *Western Sexuality: Practice and Precept in Past and Present*, trans. Anthony Forster (Oxford, UK: Basil Blackwell, 1985), pp. 95–102; and Ann Rosalind Jones, *The Currency of Eros: Women's Love Lyric in Europe, 1540–1620* (Bloomington: Indiana University Press, 1990), p. 192ff. Thanks to Laurie Nussdorfer for reminding me of the Enlightenment analogy of Montesquieu's *Persian Letters*.

104. Giorgio Vasari, *Lives of the Most Eminent Painters, Sculptors and Architects*, trans. Gaston DuC. De Vere (1912–1914; New York: AMS Press, 1976), vol. 6, p. 105.

105. Thomas Caldecot Chubb, *The Letters of Pietro Aretino* (n.p.: Archon Press, 1967), p. 143.

106. This story has been told many times. The most careful account, despite its brevity, is Bette Talvacchia, " 'Figure lascive,' " in *Giulio Romano*, pp. 277–80. See also the introduction to *I modi, the Sixteen Pleasures: An Erotic Album of the Italian Renaissance*, ed. and trans. Lynn Lawner (Evanston, IL: Northwestern University Press, 1988), pp. 3–17.

107. Venice, December 19, 1537, Aretino, *Lettere*, ed. Francesca Flora (Rome[?]: Mondadori, 1960), pp. 399–400. None of the published translations are as good as they could be, so I have drawn on the two most reliable ones and the Italian original to create my own rendition; Chubb, *The Letters of Pietro Aretino*, pp. 123–24; Aretino, *I modi*, p. 9.

108. In Aretino, *I modi*, p. 17; Ariosto, *I suppositi*, in Talvecchia, " 'Figure lascive,' " p. 280; Vignali, *La Cazzaria*, p. 15.

109. Franco, *Priapea*, in Carlo Simiani, *Niccolò Franco: La Vita e le opere* (Turin: L. Roux, 1894), p. 109.

110. Frantz, *Festum voluptatis*, pp. 48 and 101; *Il piacevol ragionamento de l'Aretino: Dialogo di Giulia e di Maddalena*, ed. Claudio Galderisi (Rome: Salerno, 1987), p. 43. As Frantz points out, in his English–Italian dictionary, *A Worlde of Wordes* (1598), John Florio praised Aretino, who "frames so manie new worlds" for expanding the Italian vocabulary; Frantz, ibid., p. 144.

111. Vasari, *Lives*, p. 105.

112. *Tariffa delle puttane*, in Antonio Barzaghi, *Donne o cortigiane? La prostituzione a Venezia, documenti di costume dal XVI al XVIII secolo* (Verona: Bertani, 1980), p. 175.

113. *Il Piacevol ragionamento*, pp. 96–103. The editors of this particular edition, which dates from approximately 1531, suggest that Aretino himself may have been the author, given the similarities between this work and his later *Ragionamenti*. The authorship, however, still seems to be in doubt, though it is closely tied to Aretino's works. For a brief overview of the diffusion of the postures in other works, see Foxon, *Libertine Literature*, pp. 19–37; Frantz, *Festum voluptatis*, p. 51; and Kearney, *A History of Erotic Literature*, p. 46.

114. Ferrante Pallavicino, *La Rettorica della puttana*, in *Il Gioco dell'amore: Le Cortigiane di Venezia dal Trecento al Settecento. Catalogo della mostra* (Milan: Berenice, 1990), p. 28.

115. Aretino, *Ragionamenti*, in *Aretino's Dialogues*, p. 2.

116. Ibid., p. 288. Apropos of this linguistic joke is a telling mistranslation of Castiglione's title by a contemporary English writer in a description of Urbino: "The Duke's palace is a very fair house, but not so excellent as the Conte Baldassare in his *Courtesan* doth commend it." (William Thomas, *The History of Italy (1549)*, ed. George B. Parks [Ithaca, NY: Cornell University Press, 1963], p. 127).

117. Aretino, *Ragionamenti*, in *Aretino's Dialogues*, p. 218. In another passage, Nanna advises Pippa, "good manners are the best go-between to help your rise in the world" (ibid., p. 247).

118. Ibid., p. 295.

119. Ibid., pp. 414 and 417.

120. Ibid., p. 223. In Renaissance Venice, approximately one in every ten inhabitants made their living from its prostitution industry.

121. I am indebted in this section to Laura Walvoord's unpublished paper "'A Whore's Vices are Really Virtues': Prostitution and Feminine Identity in Sixteenth-Century Venice." For the relevant passages, see Aretino, *Ragionamenti*, in *Aretino's Dialogues*, pp. 169–70.

122. Ibid., p. 142. This point is made well in Achillo Olivieri, "Eroticism," pp. 96–97.

123. Ibid., p. 257.

124. Doni, *Terremoto* (1556), in Frantz, *Festum voluptatis*, p. 114; John Wolfe, "Il Barbagrigia stampatore a gli amatori del sapere," in Aretino, *La Prima [-Seconda] Parte*, sig.A.2r.

125. Aretino, *Ragionamenti*, in *Aretino's Dialogues*, p. 169.

126. The images of a *mondo incazzito* comes from Aretino (Frantz, *Festum voluptatis*, p. 83) and that of the *monarchia puttanesca* from the *Tariffa delle puttane* (ibid., p. 103). For a broader discussion of the potentially subversive power of women, see Natalie Zemon Davis, "Women on Top," in her *Society and*

Culture in Early Modern France (Stanford, CA: Stanford University Press, 1975).

127. Rocco, *L'Alcibiade*, pp. 89 and 71. (Citations are given in the order in which they appear in the text.)

128. For a brief description of this plate and further bibliography, see Timothy Wilson, *Ceramic Art of the Italian Renaissance* (London: British Museum Publications, 1987), pp. 143–44.

129. Aretino, *I modi*, p. 60.

130. Aretino, *Letters*, pp. 8 and 36. Similar images are also discussed briefly by Arturo Graf, *Attraverso il Cinquecento* (Turin: Giovanni Chiantore, 1926), pp. 102 and 229.

131. For more on the political culture of Renaissance Venice, see Robert Finlay, *Politics in Renaissance Venice* (New Brunswick, NJ: Rutgers University Press, 1980); and Edward Muir, *Civic Ritual in Renaissance Venice* (Princeton, NJ: Princeton University Press, 1981).

132. Vignali, *La Cazzaria*, p. 117.

133. Stephanie Jed has noted the relationship between "political identity" and "textual experience" in earlier humanist writings in her *Chaste Thinking*, p. 19. As she points out, sexual experience and textual experience are never far apart, something writers like Aretino, even more than Colluccio Salutati, were quick to emphasize.

134. Barzaghi, *Donne o cortigiane*, p. 135. These are the words of a 1571 ordinance in Venice. For more on the competing images of vice, see Ruggiero, *Boundaries of Eros*; and, in a non-Italian context, Mary Elizabeth Perry, *Gender and Disorder in Early Modern Seville* (Princeton, NJ: Princeton University Press, 1985).

135. Aretino, *Ragionamenti*, in *Aretino's Dialogues*, p. 148.

136. Ibid., p. 144.

137. Dolce, *Aretin*, p. 179.

CHAPTER TWO: THE POLITICS OF PORNOGRAPHY

1. Christian Jouhaud convinced me of the centrality of Pepys's response to *L'Ecole des filles*. For more on "reading with one hand," see Jean Marie Goulemot, *Ces livres qu'on ne lit que d'une main: Lecture et lecteurs de livres pornographiques au*

XVIIIe siècle (Aix-en-Provence: Alinéa, 1991). See also Rousseau's *Confessions*.

2. Samuel Pepys, *The Diary of Samuel Pepys*, ed. H.B. Wheatley (London: George Bell, 1896), vol. 7, p. 279. The entry is for January 13, 1668.

3. Ibid., p. 311. The entry is for February 9, 1668.

4. Frédéric Lachèvre, *Le Libertinage au XVIIe siècle: Mélanges* (Paris: Honoré Champion, 1920), p. 82.

5. In a letter from August 17, 1655 recording the work's condemnation, Guy Patin described it as "*L'Escole des filles*, que l'on dit estre tiré de l'Arétin" (Lachèvre, *Le Libertinage*, pp. 83 and 90).

6. Scarron was the author of numerous parodic works, notably burlesque epics such as the *Virgile travesti* (1650) and a self-conscious novel, *Le Roman comique* (1657). At the time of *L'Ecole des filles*'s publication, his wife had no known literary activities.

7. In the interrogations that followed his arrest on charges of literary obscenity, Théophile de Viau behaved in a fashion diametrically opposed to Millot and L'Ange. He freely admitted his authorship of the contested works. He then defended himself by explaining why the works should not be considered dangerous. In the process, Théophile formulated what can be seen as a complex theory of the authorial process. His trial proceedings have been edited by Lachèvre: *Le Libertinage devant le parlement de Paris: le procès du poète Théophile de Viau*, 2 vols. (Paris: Honoré Champion, 1909). On the theory of authorship defined in the proceedings, see my "Une Autobiographe en procès: L'Affaire Théophile de Viau," *Poétique* 48 (1981), pp. 431–38.

8. Lachèvre, *Le Libertinage*, p. 101.

9. Ibid., p. 82.

10. Ibid., p. 84.

11. For information on the traffic in banned books in eighteenth-century France, see all of Robert Darnton's recent works and, in particular, *Edition et sédition: L'Univers de la littérature clandestine au XVIIIe siècle* (Paris: Gallimard, 1991).

12. Foucault develops the notion of an *episteme*, or a category in the history of knowledge delimited not by traditional temporal markers but by intel-

lectual shift, in his early works, notably *Les Mots et les choses* (Paris: Gallimard, 1966) and *L'Archéologie du savoir* (Paris: Gallimard, 1969). In place of epochs and disciplines, Foucault's archaeology of knowledge maps the strata of discursive formations. Foucault's *episteme* is the totality of relations between the sciences, analyzed at the level of their discursive practices, that can be discovered for a given period.

13. See Lachèvre, *Le Libertinage*, p. 99. See also *L'Ecole des filles*, ed. Pascal Pia (Paris: Cercle du Livre Précieux, 1959), pp. xxxvii–xxxviii.

14. On this use of *frondeur*, see Nina Rattner Gelbart, *Feminism and Opposition Journalism in Old Regime France* (Berkeley: University of California Press, 1987).

15. Lynn Hunt, p. 10.

16. It could even be argued that *La Princesse de Clèves* also demonstrates this fascination. Witness, most importantly, the novel's famous staging of female eroticism in the pavilion scene in which the princess, her clothes and hair in disarray, weaves ribbons around a cane belonging to the man she loves. In this context, Sade's predilection for *La Princesse de Clèves*, recorded in his "Idée sur les romans," should not be forgotten. I return to the example of Lafayette's masterpiece in part to suggest that the author or authors of *L'Ecole des filles* may have had intentions not so different from those of contemporary authors also experimenting with prose fiction. In its most extreme formulation, this argument could be used to suggest that *L'Ecole des filles*'s authors may have considered it simply a new type of prose fiction, a work more literarily than politically subversive. They may have been trying to produce a candidate with mainstream literary status. We can only imagine what *the* novel might have been like in the long run, had this variant not almost immediately stagnated.

17. Michel Foucault, *The History of Sexuality*: vol. 1, *An Introduction*, trans. Robert Hurley (New York: Pantheon, 1978).

18. Some of the titles given to nineteenth-century collections of Maintenon's writing on and for female education read like unintentional parodies of the 1655 dialogue – notably *Entretiens sur l'éducation des filles*. See the National Union Catalog for a complete listing of these titles.

Chapter Three: Sometimes a Scepter

1. *Poems on Affairs of State, from the time of Oliver Cromwell to the Abdication of King James the Second* (n.p., 1697), p. 171. [Hereafter POAS.] (The spellings of all the poems in this essay have been modernized.)

2. POAS, pp. 102–106.

3. POAS, preface.

4. See the *Oxford English Dictionary* for this definition of the word *pornography*.

5. Angela Carter, *The Sadeian Woman: An Exercise in Cultural History* (London: Virago Press, 1979), p. 15.

6. A list of the manuscript sources used in researching this essay includes: BL Harley 7314; BL Harley 7317; BL Harley 7319; BL Harley 6914; BL Additional 27,407; BL Additional 34,362; Bodleian Firth c. 15; Bodleian Firth c. 16; Bodleian Don. b. 8.

7. The material in POAS is fairly typical of what got published, and includes much material published in earlier collections. For an extensive list of collections of political poetry published after 1688, see George DeF. Lord (ed.), *Poems on Affairs of State: Augustan Satirical Verse, 1660–1714*, 7 vols. (New Haven, CT: Yale University Press, 1963–75), vol. 1, pp. 445–48. [Hereafter Yale POAS.]

8. See Margaret Ann Doody, *The Daring Muse* (Cambridge: Cambridge University Press, 1985) on importance and significance of these techniques in the late seventeenth century.

The "sceptre lampoon" of the earl of Rochester, beginning "In the Isle of Britain long since famous grown," might be taken as the exception that proves the rule. The poem is printed in POAS. However, according to the variant readings of the poem recorded in Yale POAS, vol. 1, pp. 479–80, a couplet in some of the manuscript editions (Bodleian Don. b. 8 and BL Harley 7317) complicates the meaning of the poem because it appears to praise Charles II. It reads "Ah generous sir! Long may you survive / For we shall never have such liberty to swive." This ironic endorsement of sexual libertinism is left out of the printed version in POAS, p. 171.

9. Bodleian Don. b. 8, pp. 513–14. See also the poem beginning, "Taking

of snuff is a mode at court" (Bodleian Don. b. 8, p. 217); and the poem beginning, "When rebels first pushed at the Crown" (BL Harley 6914, f. 21r.).

10. John O'Neill, "Oldham's 'Sardanapalus': A Restoration Mock-Encomium and Its Topical Implications," *Clio* 5 (1976), pp. 193–210.

11. The poem begins "Happy great Prince, and so much happier thou" (BL Harley 7319, ff. 128r–132v). Also in Bodleian Firth c. 15.

12. Ibid.

13. Ibid.

14. For recent discussions of how the political opposition to Charles II's policies is either caused by or expressed as disgust at royal sexuality, see Paul Hammond, "The King's Two Bodies: Representations of Charles II," in Jeremy Black and Jeremy Gregory (eds.), *Culture, Politics and Society in Britain, 1660–1800* (Manchester, UK: Manchester University Press, 1991), pp. 13–48; Steven Zwicker, "Virgins and Whores: The Politics of Sexual Misconduct in the 1660s," in Conal Condren and A.D. Cousins (eds.), *The Political Ideology of Andrew Marvell* (New York: Scolar Press, 1990), pp. 85–110; and Richard Elias, "Political Satire in 'Sodom,' " *Studies in English Literature* 18 (1978), pp. 423–48.

15. For a recent argument for the need to revise our view of the political and cultural divisions in the Restoration, see Tim Harris, "Introduction: Revising the Restoration," in Tim Harris, Paul Seaward and Mark Goldie (eds.), *The Politics of Religion in Restoration England* (Oxford, UK: Blackwell, 1990). On Buckingham, see ibid., p. 7, and Gary S. De Krey, "London Radicals and Revolutionary Politics," in ibid., pp. 142–43.

16. See the essay by Joan DeJean in this volume. See also Robert Darnton, *Edition et sédition: L'Univers de la littérature clandestine au XVIIIe siècle* (Paris: Gallimard, 1991). Note that their explanations vary. For DeJean, pornography becomes "oppositional" because the monarchy tries to censor it. For Darnton, it is politically subversive because it attacks established moral values associated with the monarch.

It may be possible to detect the same link between sexual libertinism and radical politics in eighteenth-century England. See the essay by Margaret Jacob in this volume. For evidence that this link existed in the early nineteenth century, see Iain McCalman, "Unrespectable Radicalism: Infidels and Pornography in Early Nineteenth-Century London," *Past and Present* 104 (1984), pp. 74–110.

17. *Eikon Basilike Deutera* (n.p., 1694).

18. Ibid., p. 3.

19. Ibid., p. 133.

20. Ibid., p. 134.

21. It is tempting to speculate that if the poem was written after the publication of "Absalom and Achitophel" in 1681, the speaker is meant to be a parody of the real poet laureate, John Dryden, who began his own royalist satirical poem with what appeared to be a celebration of libertine sexuality: "In pious times ere priestcraft did begin / before polygamy was made a sin...."

22. Zwicker, "Virgins and Whores."

23. See, for example, the poem beginning, "Awake Britannia, rouse thyself and say" (Bodleian Firth b. 20, attached at f. 140); and Rachel Jevon, *Exultationis Carmen* (London, 1660).

24. Poem beginning, "If any do the authors name inquire" (BL Additional 34,362, ff. 4r–15v).

25. The classic study of this is Ernst Kantorowicz, *The King's Two Bodies: A Study in Medieval Political Theology* (Princeton, NJ: Princeton University Press, 1957). For a recent exploration of this theme in the context of court culture, see David Starkey et al., *The English Court* (New York: Longman, 1987).

26. Starkey, *The English Court*, introduction, pp. 1–24.

27. Samuel Pepys, *The Shorter Pepys*, ed. Robert Latham (Berkeley: University of California Press, 1985), p. 760. See entry for April 26, 1667.

28. See the poem beginning, "Hard by Pall Mall lives a wench called Nell" (Yale POAS, vol. 1, p. 420); poem beginning, "Long days of absence dear I could endure" (Bodleian Don. b. 8, p. 504); and poem beginning "When to the king I bid good morrow" (Bodleian Firth c. 15, p. 25).

29. See, for example, "The Substance of the Conference between the late King Charles II...[and] the then duchess of Orleans" (Bodleian Carte 198, ff. 28r–30r); and poem beginning "O heavens we have signs below," in which

the Duke of York acts as pander: "and then to your [Charles'] incestuous eyes / will show again her highness' thighs / Strip her of greatness for the cause / And show her scut to change the laws" (BL Additional 34,362, ff. 48r–49v). See also the episode in *Eikon Basilike Deutera*, discussed in n. 19, above.

30. *The Secret History of the Dutchess of Portsmouth* (Richard Baldwin, 1690), pp. 128–32; and *The Secret History of the Reigns of K. Charles II and K. James II* (n.p., 1690), p. 87. See also poem beginning, "As in the days of yore was odds" (Yale POAS, vol. 1, pp. 263–65).

31. Bodleian Don. b. 8.

32. On this, see Larry Carver, "The Restoration Poets and their Father King," *Huntington Library Quarterly* 40 (1977), pp. 333–51.

33. See "Sardanapalus" and *The Amours of the Sultana of Barbary* (London: Richard Baldwin, 1689).

34. Algernon Sidney, *Discourses on Government*, 3 vols. (1698; New York: Richard Lee, 1805), vol. 2, p. 128.

35. In *The Secret History of the Reigns of K. Charles II and K. James II*, pp. 25 and 26. See also *Eikon Basilike Deutera* for the same idea.

36. In Act I of "Sodom" (Princeton University Library, AM 14401, pp. 37–108).

37. Poem beginning, "The Spaniards gravely teach in politick schools" (BL Harley 7317, ff. 67r–68v).

38. Poem beginning, "Close wrapt in Portsmouth's smock his senses are" (BL Additional 34, 362, f. 47r).

39. Poem beginning, "In the isle of Britain, long since famous grown" (POAS, p. 171).

40. Ibid.

41. Poem beginning, "Ah Raleigh, when thy breath thou didst resign" (Yale POAS, vol. 1, p. 232).

42. Poem beginning, "After two sittings now our Lady state" (ibid., p. 136). See also Zwicker, "Virgins and Whores," for a discussion.

43. See, for example, Pepys, *The Shorter Pepys*, p. 275 (entry for May 15, 1663), p. 727 (entry for February 17, 1667), p. 760 (entry for April 26, 1667),

and pp. 797–98 (entry for June 24, 1667).

44. See n. 37, above.

45. Pepys, *The Shorter Pepys*, pp. 701–702 (entry for December 12-13, 1666), pp. 812-13 (entry for July 27, 1667), pp. 814-15 (entry for July 29, 1667), and p. 1013-14 (entry for April 28, 1669).

46. For a discussion of the unstable and contradictory meanings attached to popery and the significance of this instability, see Peter Lake, "Anti-Popery: The Structure of a Prejudice," in Richard Cust and Ann Hughes (eds.), *Conflict in Early Stuart England* (New York: Longman, 1989), pp. 72-105.

47. "The Most gracious answer of Dame Barbara Countess of C. to ye peti-con of undone, poore, and distressed company of Whores" (Bodleian Don. b. 8, pp. 190-93).

48. On this mode of representing the Catholic Church, see Lyndal Roper, "Discipline and Respectability: Prostitution and the Reformation in Augsburg," *History Workshop Journal* 19 (1985), pp. 3-28.

49. "His Holiness has three grand friends" (Yale POAS, vol. 2, p. 291).

50. Poem beginning, "Of all the plagues with which this world abounds" (BL Harley 7319, ff. 68r-70v).

51. Poem beginning, "Preserved by wonder in the oak, O Charles" (Yale POAS, vol. 1, pp. 425-28).

52. Poem beginning, "Deep in an unctious vale, twixt swelling hills" (BL Harley 7319, ff. 11v-15v).

53. *An Address to the Honorable City of London... Concerning their Choice of a New Parliament* (n.p., 1681).

54. Paul Rycaut, *The Present State of the Ottoman Empire* (New York: Arno Press, 1971), p. 9.

55. Sidney, *Discourses*, vol. 2, pp. 292-93.

56. Ibid., p. 293.

57. Ibid., pp. 293-94.

58. "Articles of High-Treason, and other High-Crimes and Misdeameanours, against the Duchess of Portsmouth," in *The Harleian Miscellany*, 10 vols. (London: John White and John Murray, 1808-13), vol. 3, pp. 507-510.

THE INVENTION OF PORNOGRAPHY

59. See n. 37, above.

60. See n. 50, above.

61. See poem beginning, "We have raised up a legion of lusty young wenches" (BL Harley 7317, f. 57v).

CHAPTER FOUR: THE MATERIALIST WORLD OF PORNOGRAPHY

1. Such studies are still few and far between. See Steven Shapin and Simon Schaffer, *Leviathan and the Air-Pump* (Princeton, NJ: Princeton University Press, 1985); Pietro Redondi, *Galileo Heretic* (Princeton, NJ: Princeton University Press, 1987); Margaret C. Jacob, *The Cultural Meaning of the Scientific Revolution* (New York: McGraw-Hill, 1988). The conceptualization of this essay has been aided by C.B. Macpherson, *The Political Theory of Possessive Individualism: Hobbes to Locke* (Oxford, UK: Oxford University Press, 1962).

2. For a general discussion of this conceptual framework see Margaret C. Jacob, *Living the Enlightenment: Freemasonry and Politics in Eighteenth Century Europe* (Oxford, UK: Oxford University Press, 1991), introduction.

3. Carlo Ginzburg, *The Cheese and the Worms: The Cosmos of a Sixteenth-Century Miller*, trans. John Tedeschi and Anne C. Tedeschi (Baltimore, MD: The Johns Hopkins University Press, 1980).

4. For the most recent scholarship on the text see Sylvia Berti, "The First Edition of the *Traité des trois imposteurs*, and its Debt to Spinoza's Ethics," in Michael Hunter and David Wootton (eds.), *Atheism from the Reformation to the Enlightenment* (Oxford, UK: Clarendon Press, 1992), pp. 183–220.

5. *War with Priestcraft Or, the Freethinkers' Iliad: A Burlesque Poem* (London, 1732), pp. 36–37. The 1656 poem by Edmund Waller comes with a disclaimer printed in the margin by John Evelyn, the translator of *Essay on the First Book of T. Lucretius Carus, De Rerum Natura* (London, 1656), quoted in Robert H. Kargon, *Atomism in England from Hariot to Newton* (Oxford, UK: Oxford University Press, 1966), p. 92.

6. This is a suggestion made in an essay that reached me after the present one had been written. See Lawrence Stone, "Libertine Sexuality in Post-Restoration England: Group Sex and Flagellation among the Middling Sort in Norwich

in 1706-07," *Journal of the History of Sexuality* 2 (1992), pp. 511-26. One of the men in this circle was a bookseller.

7. Page fifteen reads "il est grossi et allongé de la moitié, il est dur & long comme un baston, & a force de se bander comme je dis..." *L'Escole des filles, ou La Philosophe des Dames, divisée en deux dialogues* (Paris, 1667), pp. 12-15. Found in the Bibliothèque Nationale, Paris; call number: Enfer 112 (Hereafter B.N., Enfer and the number). All copies of the 1655 edition appear to have disappeared; certainly, when the police went after its publishers they sought to destroy the books. A good summary of those events can be found in Patrick J. Kearney, *A History of Erotic Literature* (London: Macmillan, 1982), pp. 29-33.

8. Archives de la Préfecture de la Police [hereafter APP], Paris, Aa/4/710-12. By this date, the bookseller almost certainly was selling the French text, which is often mistakenly assumed to be a straightforward translation. For a good English translation of *Aloisiae: The Dialogues of Luisa Sigea* (Paris, 1890), see B.N., Enfer 108. For a guide to Enfer see Pascal Pia (ed.), *Les Livres de l'Enfer du XVIe siècle à nos jours*, 2 vols. (Paris: C. Coulet & A. Faure, 1978). I am using B.N., Enfer 258. Enfer 257 is a different edition of *Aloisiae sigeae* (with this variant spelling on the title page and no place or date), and it has a shorter introduction, but the dialogues are the same as those in 258. For the Latin, I rely on the 1678 Amsterdam edition.

9. Madeleine Kahn, *Narrative Transvestism: Rhetoric and Gender in the Eighteenth-Century English Novel* (Ithaca, NY: Cornell University Press, 1991), in which, however useful the analysis, this implication fails to appear. Note that atoms, the building blocks of materialist matter theory, are ungendered.

10. *L'Académie des Dames* (Paris, 1680), p. 6.

11. Ibid., p. 19.

12. The text reads: "Tu me fais donc la maitresse de ce chemin qui conduit au souverain bien: ah! j'en vois la porte; mais hélas? je ne puis me servir du pouvoir que tu me donnes..." (ibid.).

13. Ibid., p. 20.

14. Thomas Laqueur, *Making Sex: Body and Gender from the Greeks to Freud*

(Cambridge, MA: Harvard University Press, 1990), pp. 126–48. Pornography does not, however, support the discussion found in chapter 5.

15. *L'Académie des dames, ou Les Sept entretiens galants / d'Aloisia* (Cologne, Ignace le Bas, 1691), p. 61. This is Enfer 271, in Pia, *Les Livres*, pp. 322–27, and it is being compared to the Latin text, Enfer 258, also in Pia. See n. 8, above.

16. Ibid., compared to Enfer 258/259 in Pia.

17. Aram Vartanian, "La Mettrie, Diderot, and Sexology in the Enlightenment," in Jean Macary (ed.), *Essays on the Age of Enlightenment in Honor of Ira O. Wade* (Geneva: Librarie Droz, 1977), pp. 347–67.

18. *L'Ecole des filles* (Paris, 1667), p. 30. This is Enfer 112 in Pia.

19. *Vénus la populaire, ou Apologie des maisons de joye* (London: A. Moore, 1727), p. 87. This is Bodleian copy O f. 37. Bernard de Mandeville has been mentioned as a possible author of this text, though I have no insight to offer on the suggestion.

20. Ibid., pp. 61–62.

21. *Harris's List…* (London: H. Ranger…nr Drury Lane, Play-House, 1788), p. 141. All the other prostitutes are portrayed as being between nineteen and twenty-four.

22. For a description of the machine, see *Amors experimental–physikalisches Taschenbuch: Erstes Bändchen mit Kupfern* (1798; British Library, Private Case 31.i.12), sect. 8, pp. 211–12 and 260.

23. [John Henry Meibomius], *A Treatise of the Use of Flogging In Venereal Affairs: Also Of the Office of the Loins and Reins. To which is Added, A Treatise of Hermaphrodites* (London: E. Curll, 1718), preface, p. 13.

24. Ibid., p. 13.

25. Ibid., and I also quote from [Giles Jacob], *Treatise of Hermaphrodites*, see the preface, and pp. ii, 14 and 55 for sadism. The flogging treatise first came out in Latin in 1629. The publisher Curll was widely accused in his day of being a sodomite. These tracts are very similar, and the second was apparently by Jacob, a hack writer and denizen of Grub Street. The second may bear resemblance to Beccadelli's *Hermaphroditus* as mentioned in David F. Greenberg, *The Construction of Homosexuality* (Chicago: University of Chicago Press, 1988), p. 308. Other

earlier English naturalist tracts – actually, more marriage manuals than pornography – that could be included are: *The XV Comforts of Rash and Inconsiderate Marriage, or Select Animadversions upon the Miscarriage of the Wedded State. Done out of French* (London: Walter David, 1682), which is bound with *The Womens Advocate: Or, Fifteen Real Comforts of Matrimony, being In requital of the late Fifteen Sham-Comforts with Satyrical Reflections on Whoring... Written by a Person of Quality of the Female Sex* (2nd ed.; London, 1683). This is Bodleian Wood 750.

26. I am using *Venus in the Cloister: Or, The Nun in her Smock. By a Person of Honour* (London, 1725), p. 3. A copy may be found in the Private Case of the British Library, 25 A.63.

27. This was the arrest, in 1704, of Antoine Galoche for distributing *La Religieuse en chemise, ou Vénus dans le Cloître* and *Les Amours du Roy et de Madame de Maintenon.* See APP, Paris, Aa/5/215.

28. *A Dictionary of Love* (London: J. Bell & C. Etherington, 1776), pp. iv–v. I am using Bodleian Vet.45.g.9. Cleland is identified as the book's author in John Cleland, *Memoirs of a Woman of Pleasure,* ed. Peter Sabor (Oxford, UK: Oxford University Press, 1985), p. xxxi; based on Radier's *Dictionnaire d'Amour.*

29. *Thérèse philosophe, ou Mémoires pour servir à l'Historie de D. Dirriq....* This is Bodleian Vet.B5.e.129, p. 80.

30. *Thérèse philosophe, ou Mémoires pour servir à l'Histoire de D. Dirrag, & de Mademoiselle Eradice* (The Hague, 1748), p. 23. The copy here being cited is in the British Library, and its pagination may differ from the copy at the Bibliothèque Nationale.

31. Ibid., p. 31.

32. As mentioned: Tullie and Octavie are the principal actors in *Les Dialogues de Luisa Sigea,* the generic title for *Aloisiae Sigaeae Toletanae,* which becomes *L'Académie des dames* (1678). See Enfer 623 in Pia, *Les Livres de Enfer.* Julie appears in *Julie philosophe, ou Le Bon patriote* (Paris, 1791), vols. 1 and 2; and *Thérèse philosophe.* For Fanny Hill I use *Memoirs of a Woman of Pleasure,* ed. Peter Sabor (1748–1749; Oxford, UK: Oxford University Press, 1985). See also *Correspondance d'Eulalie, ou Tableau du libertinage de Paris. Avec la vie de plusieurs filles celebres de ce siècle* (London: Nourse, 1785), Enfer 623.

33. This piece, dated 1748, is entitled "Affaire de Thérèse Philosophe et du Portier des Chartreux," in which François Xavier d'Arles de Montigny is described as "Escuyer interrné dans les fermer du Roy entre à la Bastille le 1er fevrier 1749 sorti le 25 aout 1750, a ete arreté des l'annee 1744..." APP, Paris, Aa/7/592-97. This affair is briefly described from the records in the Bibliothèque Arsenal in the preface by Philippe Roger to *Oeuvres anonymes du XVIIIe siècle: L'Enfer de la Bibliothèque Nationale* (Paris: Fayard, 1985), vol. 3, pp. 18-19. The large number of people rounded up who were involved in Jansenism do indeed include women.

34. These handwritten arrest records for the 1740s are interesting and important, see APP, Paris, Aa/7/461-752. They can also be supplemented with those that describe pornography and satires against the king mixed together and sold by people arrested for the activity, see APP, Paris, Aa/5/443-650. Others show books about Jansenism and "debauchery" being sold together, an unusual coupling, see APP, Paris, Aa/7/339. There is another arrest record for sodomites in 1742, see APP, Paris, Aa/7/409. By far the bulk of the people being incarcerated in the 1740s for selling books are trafficking in pornography and political diatribe. There is one big Jansenist round-up, see APP, Paris, Aa/7/482-91. F. 517 has three men and one woman (not a wife) selling pornography, "Les nouvelles ecclesiastiques," (transcribed as written and clearly Jansenist) in 1746. In 1746-1747, there were many spies arrested. In 1747, Claude Crespy was incarcerated for political, pornographic and masonic literature, see APP, Paris, Aa/7/541. Others arrested include, f. 545, husband and wife with a thousand copies of "Amusements philosophiques sur le langage des Betes," "Lettre a Mad. de Pompadour," with fifty-four copies of *L'Art de faire des garçons*, le *Colporteur et le Secret de la Maçonnerie*, f. 565, 1748; and in f. 624, a bookseller with works by philosophes and Jansenists; and in ff. 640-46 from 1749, "discours insolents contre le Roy et Mad. de Pompadour."

35. APP, Paris, Aa/7/363-66; for Bacculard d'Arnaud ("c'etoit un Eleve de Voltaire") see APP, Paris, Aa/7/361. The manuscript interrogation reports are discussed in Roger, pp. 22-28; for Casanova, see his *Memoires, 1744-56*, ed. René Demoris (Paris: Garnier-Flammarion, 1977), p. 440.

36. They were said to be plotting against the king, see APP, Paris, Aa/5/650.

37. Kearney, *A History*, p. 62.

38. In APP, Paris, Aa/7/424. It is also said that he has had contact with one Roussel, possibly the same Roussel named in the *Dom Bougre* affair; and, in the same piece, Roussel is described as the author of "un libelle" and other critical works, see APP, Paris, Aa/5/591.

39. "Une assemblée pour un espece d'ordre des jeunes garçons qui vouloient entrer et prenoient des noms de femmes [,] faisoient des mariages ensemble, les endroits où ils faisoient ces assemblees etoient ordinairement au Cabaret du Chaudron rue St. Antoine...où apres avoir bu par exces ils commettoient le péché de Sodomie, ils faisoient certaines Cérémonies pour la Reception des Prozelites et leur faisoient prêter serment de fidelles a l'Ordre." This is quoted from APP, Paris, Aa/4/205. See also Michel Rey, "Police and Sodomy in Eighteenth-Century Paris: From Sin to Disorder," in Kent Gerard and Gert Hekma (eds.), *The Pursuit of Sodomy: Male Homosexuality in Renaissance and Enlightenment Europe* (New York: Harrington Park Press, 1989), pp. 129–46. Rey works from a different set of archival records, which also contain further evidence on sodomy in the period.

40. There is a good discussion of some of the archival material in Claude Courouve, *Les Assemblées de la manchette* (Paris: C. Courouve, 1987), p. 15. Some of the material on this group is published in G.B. Depping (ed.), *Correspondance administrative sous le regne de Louis XIV* (Paris. Imp. Nationale, 1851–1855), vol. 2, pp. 823–24.

41. For the raid of 1706, see APP, Paris, Aa/4/205; in 1715, again for committing sodomy in cabarets, see APP, Paris, Aa/4/626; on sodomites in 1742, see APP, Paris, Aa/7/409; in 1751, for taking money for sodomy, see APP, Paris, Aa/4/730. On Ned Ward see Randolph Trumbach, "The Birth of the Queen: Sodomy and the Emergence of Gender Equality in Modern Culture, 1660-1750," in Martin Duberman, Martha Vicinus and George Chauncey, Jr. (eds.), *Hidden from History: Reclaiming the Gay and Lesbian Past* (New York: New American Library, 1989). Trumbach cites the following records from the period: *The Tryal and Conviction of Several Reputed Sodomites...20th Day of October 1707*, British

Library 515.1.2 (205); Greater London Record Office, MJ/SP September 1707. Ward claims in *The Secret History of Clubs* (London, 1709), pp. 284–300, that they were called "mollies."

42. In 1715, labeled sodomites, see APP, Paris, Aa/4/626. There are in Angélique Lemasson, *Société et criminalité dans le port de Nantes au début du XVIIIᵉ siècle (1699–1723) (d'après les archives de l'Amirauté de Nantes)* (Rennes-Nantes: Matrise, 1989), pp. 66–68, verbal insults about sodomy reported but no arrests for the act.

43. Stockaert or Stocker "est condamné a mort que ses juges se proposent de faire étrangler secretement dans la prison ou il est detenu; de faire assister a cette execution quatre de ses complices seduits par le condamné. . . ." in Archives generales du royaume, Brussels, Conseil privé autri., A124, 576B, April 28, 1781.

44. *Histoire du Princi Apprius, etc. Extraite des fastes du monde, depuis sa creation. Manuscrit Persan trouve dans la bibliotheque de Schah-Hussain, roi de Perse, dethrone par Mamouth en 1722. Traduction Françoise. Par Messire Esprit...* (Constantinople, 1728), pp. 32 and 59. Note that sodomy committed in public, particularly with other criminal behavior, could lead to public and grotesque execution.

45. One Father Ange Reboul, Carmelite, who also rebelled against his superiors, in APP, Paris, Aa/7/759.

46. See Maurice Lever, *Les Bûchers de Sodome* (Paris: Fayard, 1985), ch. 6. I am grateful to Bryant Ragan for this citation.

47. *Les Entretiens de la grille, ou Le Moine au parloir* (Cologne, 1682). There is a copy in the Bibliothèque Nationale, Y2 reserve 3625.

48. *Le Cochon mitré. Dialogue* (n.p., 1689). A copy is in the Bibliothèque Nationale, reserve 826.

49. *Historische print en dicht tafereelen, van Jan Baptist Girar en Juffrou Maris Catharina Cadiere* (n.p., 1735). I am citing the copy in the Private Case of the British Library, 31.K.14, which I think emanates from the Austrian Netherlands. See also the mostly Latin manuscripts of the Dutch art collector, Hadrian Beverland in the British Library and the Bodleian, Oxford; W. Elias, "Het Spinozistisch erotisme van Adriaan Beverland," *Tijdschrift voor de studie van de verlichting* 3–4 (1974), pp. 282–320; and Eric John Dingwall, "Hadrian Beverland: Lord of

Zealand," in his *Very Peculiar People: Portrait Studies in the Queer, the Abnormal and the Uncanny* (London: Rider, 1950), pp. 145–77.

50. Adam Cock, *A Voyage to Lethe; by Capt. Samuel Cock...* (London: J. Conybeare, 1741), p. 9; the copy is in the Bodleian. See also *A New Description of Merryland: Containing a Topographical, Geographical, and Natural History of That Country* (7th ed.; Bath: E. Curll & J. Leake, 1741). This was dedicated ironically to the antioligarchic but pious George Cheyne and it is bound with *Merryland Displayed*.

51. *Harris's List of Covent-Garden Ladies...* (1788) is bound with Harris's List of 1789, pp. iii–x, and see n. 21, above.

52. *Les Bordels de Paris, avec les noms, demeures et prix: Plan salubre et patriotique soumis aux illustres des Etats-Généraux pour en faire un article de la constitution...par MM. Dillon, Sartine, Lenoir, La Troliere* (n.p., L'An Seconde de la Liberté [1790]).

53. *Aphrodisiaque externe, ou Traité du Fouet, et de ses effets sur le physique de l'amour...par Dxxx Medecin* (1788), p. 65. Copy in the Private Case of the British Library, 29 B.87.

54. Ibid., p. 108, for Joseph II, p. 65.

55. *Julie philosophe*, pp. 5, 14–15; on God, p. 16; on the French Revolution, pp. 205–207.

56. Ibid., p. 4.

57. *La Confédération de la Nature, ou l'Art de se reproduire* (London, 1790), pp. 1–5. Copy in the Private Case of the British Library, 30 G.22.

58. *Thérèse philosophe* [1748], p. 120–22. Bodleian copy Vet.B5.e.129.

CHAPTER FIVE: TRUTH AND THE OBSCENE WORD

1. "La chaste Suzanne," *Salon de 1767*, in Diderot, *Oeuvres complètes* (Paris: Hermann, 1990), vol. 16, p. 127.

2. Ibid.

3. This blurring of generic demarcations is still to be found in Sorel's *Francion* (1623). See Jean Marie Goulemot, *Ces Livres qu'on ne lit que d'une main: Lecture et lecteurs de livres pornographiques au XVIIIᵉ siècle* (Aix-en-Provence: Alinéa, 1991),

p. 24. Goulemot's essay situates eighteenth-century pornography against its historical and literary background and studies the narrative strategies through which the pornographic effect is achieved. He uses the words *erotic* and *pornographic* interchangeably, a decision justified in the context of his study (ibid., p. 21). I shall follow the same practice.

4. For instance, it still does not appear in the 1963 edition of *Petit Larousse*.

5. "In primitive times, a certain daily operation, which shall remain unnamed, involved the [left] hand in a perilous exercise which is no longer required, thanks to the progress of civilization and the invention of paper." See the entry for *obscène* in Pierre Larousse, *Grand Dictionnaire du XIXe siècle*.

6. *Le Trésor de la langue française* lists a second, more recent acceptation of the term (and one perhaps more common in English): "That which offends good taste, or shocks on account of its indecorous character, its shamelesness, its vulgarity, or its crudeness." The illustration is a quotation from Roland Barthes that effects a semantic reversal, ascribing obscenity to feeling, and propriety to sex: "Everyone will understand that X has 'huge problems' with his sexuality; but no one will be interested in those Y may have with his sentimentality: love is obscene precisely in that it put the sentimental in place of the sexual." (*A Lover's Discourse*, trans. Richard Howard [New York: Hill & Wang, 1978], p. 178).

7. Diderot, *Oeuvres complètes*, vol. 16, p. 129.

8. Claude Mercier de Compiègne, *La Foutromanie, poème lubrique, suivie de plusieurs autres pièces du même genre* (Sardanapolis: Aux Dépens des Amateurs, 1780), p. 5.

9. Claude Reichler, "La Représentation du corps dans le récit libertin," in François Meureau and Alain-Marc Rieu (eds.), *Eros philosophe* (Paris: Champion, 1984), p. 80.

10. *Vénus en rut* (c. 1784), in *L'Enfer de la Bibliothèque Nationale*: vol. 4, *Oeuvres anonymes du XVIIIe siècle* (Paris: Fayard, 1987), p. 116.

11. As an exception, in Andréa de Nerciat, *Les Aphrodites* (1793), obscene words are reserved for plebeian characters.

12. More than the narrative dimension, Goulemot emphasizes the erotic

effect of the tableau, as being a scene inserted in and, hence, interrupting, the narrative. See Goulemot, *Ces Livres*, pp. 61–62.

13. Goulemot makes this general observation. See ibid., p. 139.

14. Sigmund Freud, *Jokes and their Relation to the Unconscious* (New York: Norton, 1960), pp. 97, 99, 100.

15. Ibid., p. 100.

16. Ibid., pp. 99–100.

17. Joyce McDougall, *Plaidoyer pour une certaine anormalité* (Paris: Gallimard, 1978), p. 97 [trans: *Plea for a Measure of Abnormality* (New York: International Universities Press, 1980) ch. 4.].

18. Ibid. Italics are in the text.

19. See "The Anonymous Spectator," in McDougall, *Plaidoyer*, ch. 1.

20. Ibid., p. 98.

21. See Goulemot, *Ces Livres*, pp. 139–41.

22. For example: *La Messaline française...*, A Tribaldis, de l'imprimerie de Priape (1789); *La Liberté, ou Mlle Raucour...*, A Lèche-Con (1791); André-Robert Andréa de Nerciat, *Le Diable au corps* (1803), said to be written by a "membre extraordinaire de la joyeuse Faculté phallo-coïto-pygo-glottonomique."

23. For example: Vitnègre, Conquonnette, Conquette, Couillette, Foutà-mort, Beauconnin and Timori-Lenfonceur.

24. Goulemot, *Ces Livres*, pp. 85–86.

25. Jean Laplanche and J.-B. Pontalis, *The Language of Psycho-Analysis*, trans. Donald Nicholson-Smith (New York: Norton, 1973), p. 339 (translation modified).

26. The theme of love does appear in *Histoire de Dom Bougre, portier des Chartreux*, which may be considered an exception.

27. Max Horkheimer and Theodor W. Adorno, "Notes and Drafts," in *Dialectic of Enlightenment* (1944; New York: Herder & Herder, 1972), pp. 232–33.

28. Marquis de Sade, *Histoire de Juliette*, in *Oeuvres complètes du marquis de Sade* (Paris: Cercle du Livre Précieux, 1963), vol. 9, p. 148.

29. Nancy Armstrong, "The Pornographic Effect: A Response," *The American Journal of Semiotics* 7 (1990), p. 30.

30. Armstrong also states, however, that "any representation of that which is...outside discourse is of course discourse...rather than the thing itself," so that pornography, with its "announced artificiality, leaves the real body securely in the domain of nature" (ibid., p. 32).

31. Marc Guillaume, "Délivrez-nous du corps," *Traverses* 29 (Oct. 1983), pp. 59–65. I am summarizing pages 59–60, using the author's language. Guillaume seems implicitly to lean on and link together the Sartrian definition of "the contingent" (which Sartre has associated with the experience of "nausea") and the Lacanian concept of "real." The rest of the article examines how contemporary media oppose new kinds of safety devices to the invasion of the "contingent excess."

32. See Freud's "Rat Man" case: "The little boy had flown into a terrible rage and had hurled abuse at his father even while he was under his blows. But as he knew no bad language, he had called him all the names of common objects that he could think of, and had screamed: 'You lamp! you towel! you plate!' and so on." Sigmund Freud, "Notes Upon a Case of Obsessional Neurosis (1909)," in *Three Case Histories* (New York: Collier Books, 1963), pp. 62–63.

33. See Pierre Fédida, "L'Amour muqueux," *Traverses* 29 (Oct. 1983), pp. 95 and 98.

34. See Annie Lelièvre, "La Correction," in *L'Ecrit du temps* 2 (Autumn 1982), p. 147. She writes that "school...is the locus of a relation in which the child, freed from any real entity, experiences the other's body through the variations which s/he inflicts on the signifier.... If the child invests her pleasure in the pleasure of this part object, writing, it is because, from the other's body, this is all s/he has left. Through the institutionalized signs of a body transformed into language, s/he performs the ascesis of renunciation. S/he exhausts the wish for incest through the dreamed figures of appropriation which found the ritual of her writing." Indeed, this might account for some adult conflictual relations to writing, such as writer's block.

35. "It is easy to observe the inclination to self-exposure in young children" (Freud, *Jokes*, p. 98).

36. As an unusual example of this trend, Robert Darnton has emphasized,

in his analysis of *Thérèse philosophe* (1748), a ground-breaking treatment of woman as erotic subject. He shows that a dominant theme in the novel, governing the plot itself, is the idea that woman's health and well-being require that she satisfy her sexual needs and limit or altogether avoid child-bearing. See his *Edition et sédition: L'Univers de la littérature clandestine au XVIIIᵉ siècle* (Paris: Gallimard, 1991), pp. 180–88.

37. Thomas Sebeok, "Fetish," *The American Journal of Semiotics* 6 (1989), p. 62. He is referring to Konrad Lorenz, *Studies in Animal and Human Behaviour* (Cambridge, MA: Harvard University Press, 1971), vol. 2.

38. Goulemot, *Ces Livres*, p. 53.

39. Ibid., pp. 71, 70–72.

40. Ibid., pp. 132–34, 135–36.

41. Ibid., p. 74.

42. Ibid., p. 129.

43. Ibid., p. 153.

CHAPTER SIX: THE LIBERTINE WHORE

1. Here, I am thinking of the typical nineteenth-century picture of the prostitute. There are a number of excellent studies of the representation of prostitutes in nineteenth-century literature and social thought. The best are Charles Bernheimer, *Figures of Ill Repute: Representing Prostitution in Nineteenth-Century France* (Cambridge, MA: Harvard University Press, 1989); and Jann Matlock's forthcoming book, *Scenes of Seduction*, to be published by Columbia University Press.

2. Klaus Sasse, *Die Entdeckung der "courtisane vertueuse" in der französischen Literatur des 18. Jahrhunderts: Restif de la Bretonne une seine Vorganger* (Hamburg: Universität Hamburg, 1967).

3. Restif de la Bretonne, *Le Paysan perverti* (Lausanne: Editions L'Age d'Homme, 1977).

4. Ibid., vol. 2, p. 403.

5. Sometimes the virtuous courtesan was juxtaposed with a truly vicious prostitute, a real bacchante who had none of the "philosophy" so characteris-

tic of the libertine whore. In Nougaret's *Lucette*, both types coexist in the same text. See Pierre-Jean-Baptiste Nougaret, *Lucette, ou Le Progrès de la vertu* (Paris, 1765; reprint ed. Paris: Editions Fayard, 1986).

6. In England, a similar variety of whore texts existed. See Peter Wagner, *Eros Revived: Erotica of the Enlightenment in England and America* (London: Secker & Warburg, 1988), pp. 133–42.

7. On the bawdy in French popular culture see Robert M. Isherwood, *Farce and Fantasy: Popular Entertainment in Eighteenth-Century Paris* (New York: Oxford University Press, 1986).

8. These prostitutes' letters are in some ways similar to the scandal sheets from the capital published by Bachaumont (*Correspondance littéraire*) and Métra (*Correspondance secrète*), which also provided provincials with information about Parisian fashions and fads, and included reports of the sexual shenanigans of leading courtesans.

9. The distinction between prostitute and whore is a fine one, especially in these French novels where *putain*, *fille* and *catin* are used interchangeably. In all of these novels, the heroine is, at least for some period, a bona fide prostitute who accepts money in return for sexual favors. There are other eighteenth-century pornographic texts, such as Andréa de Nerciat's *Félicia* or the classic *Thérèse philosophe*, in which the heroine is a libertine, but not a prostitute.

10. Jean Marie Goulemot in Philippe Ariès and Georges Duby (eds.), History of Private Life: vol. 3, *Passions of the Renaissance*, ed. Roger Chartier et al. (Cambridge: Harvard University Press, 1989). The English male-authored, female-narrated text has been analyzed in Madeleine Kahn, *Narrative Transvestism: Rhetoric and Gender in the Eighteenth-Century English Novel* (Ithaca, NY: Cornell University Press, 1991).

11. *Mademoiselle Javotte: Ouvrage moral écrit par elle-meme* (The Hague: J. Neauluz, 1757; reprint ed. Tchou, 1967), p. 33; the observations of Julia Epstein on *Fanny Hill* are relevant to the French whore texts, see "Fanny's Fanny: Epistolarity, Eroticism and the Transsexual," in Elizabeth C. Goldsmith (ed.), *The Female Voice* (Boston: Northeastern University Press, 1989), p. 148.

12. Jane Gallop, *Intersections* (Ohama: University of Nebraska Press, 1978), p. 33.

13. *Margot la ravaudeuse* (Hamburg, 1750; reprint ed. Paris: Pauvert, 1958), pp. 38–39.

14. *La Sainte Nitouche, ou Histoire galante de la Tourière des Carmélites, suivie de l'histoire de La Duchapt, célèbre marchand de mode* (London, 1748; rev. ed. Paris, 1830), p. 27.

15. *Mademoiselle Javotte*, p. 114; *La Sainte Nitouche*, p. 25.

16. Zéphire, the sweet-hearted whore in Restif de la Bretonne's *Le Paysan et la paysanne pervertie*, is rewarded for her goodness by being raped, beaten and repeatedly abused.

17. *Correspondence d'Eulalie* (Paris: Fayard, 1984), p. 284.

18. *Mademoiselle Javotte*, pp. 108–109.

19. *Le Catéchisme libertin à l'usage des filles de joie et de jeunes demoiselles qui se décident à embraser cette profession* (Paris, 1792), p. 23.

20. *La Cauchoise* (Paris: Imprimerie du Louvre, 1784; rev. ed. Paris: Fayard, 1985), p. 399.

21. *Mademoiselle Javotte*, p. 61.

22. *La Sainte Nitouche*, p. 47.

23. *La Cauchoise*, p. 388.

24. *Mademoiselle Javotte*, p. 48.

25. *Margot la ravaudeuse*, p. 41.

26. *Mademoiselle Javotte*, p. 63.

27. According to Nougaret (*Lucette*, p. 360), syphillis was treated "as a joke."

28. *Margot la ravaudeuse*, pp. 75–76.

29. Ibid., p. 130.

30. *Mademoiselle Javotte*, p. 23.

31. *Margot la ravaudeuse*, p. 25.

32. Ibid., p. 31.

33. *Mademoiselle Javotte*, p. 64.

34. *Margot la ravaudeuse*, p. 82.

35. *La Sainte Nitouche*, p. 25.

36. On *pudeur* and Enlightenment thought see Paul Hoffmann, *La Femme dans la pensée des lumières* (Strasbourg: Associations des publications près les universités de Strasbourg, 1977), pp. 324–34, 359–443.

37. *Mademoiselle Javotte*, p. 23.

38. *La Cauchoise*, p. 432.

39. *Mademoiselle Javotte*, pp. 29–30; and *La Sainte Nitouche*, p. 47.

40. On eighteenth-century materialism's view of women, see Hoffmann, *La Femme dans la pensée*, p. 109.

41. *Mademoiselle Javotte*, p. 47.

42. Ibid., p. 73.

43. *La Cauchoise*, p. 453.

44. *Vénus en rut, ou Vie d'une célèbre libertine* in *Collection d'Enfer de la Bibliothèque Nationale*: vol. 4, *Oeuvres anonymes du XVIIIᵉ siècle* (Paris: Fayard, 1987), p. 161.

45. Obviously, I have been much influenced here by Thomas Laqueur, *Making Sex: Body and Gender from the Greeks to Freud* (Cambridge, MA: Harvard University Press, 1990).

46. I do not deal here with the large pamphlet literature concerning Marie Antoinette which has already been analyzed by Chantal Thomas, among others. See Chantal Thomas, *La Reine scélérate: Marie-Antoinette dans les pamphlets* (Paris: Seuil, 1989). In addition to these pamphlets which deal with the queen there is abundant literature on the nobility and the clergy and their appetite for whores and deviant sexuality. Among these are *Le Bordel apostolique* (1790), *Les Bordels de Thalie* (1793) and *Les Fouteurs, ou Chants des aristocrats* (1792).

47. *Les Délices de Coblentz, ou Anecdotes libertins des émigrés français* (Coblentz, 1792).

48. *Les Derniers soupirs de la garce en pleurs adressés à la ci-devant noblesse* (Branlimes: l'An de la Bienheureuse Fouterie, 1791).

49. Hector Fleischmann has counted forty-nine of these lists that pertain to the Palais-Royal. There are certainly more. Hector Fleischmann, *Les Demoiselles d'amour du Palais Royal* (Paris, 1909).

50. *Nouvelle liste des plus jolies femmes publiques de Paris* (Paris, 1792).

51. Marquis de Sade, *Histoire de Juliette, ou Les Prospérités du vice* (Paris, 1796; Paris: Edition Pauvert, 1987), vol. 1, p. 134.

52. Ibid., pp. 128–29.

53. Ibid., pp. 109–10.

54. Ibid., p. 55.

55. Angela Carter makes this point about Noirceuil's marriage in *The Sadeian Woman: An Exercise in Cultural History* (New York: Pantheon, 1979).

56. Ibid.

CHAPTER SEVEN: EROTIC FANTASY AND MALE LIBERTINISM

1. John Cleland, *Memoirs of a Woman of Pleasure*, ed. Peter Sabor (Oxford, UK: Oxford University Press, 1985), is the standard edition, with a good bibliography of modern studies. John Cleland, *The Woman of Honour*, 3 vols. (London, 1769), is discussed in its political aspect by Raymond K. Whitley, "Rationalizing a Rogue: Themes and Techniques in the Novels of John Cleland" (Ph.D. thesis, Dalhousie University, 1978), ch. 5. There is also some discussion of Cleland's politics in William H. Epstein, *John Cleland: Images of a Life* (New York: Columbia University Press, 1974). Cleland probably wrote a final novel that has been lost, *The Man of Honour* (London, 1771–1772): see James G. Basker, " 'The Wages of Sin': The Later Career of John Cleland," *Etudes Anglaises* 40 (1987), pp. 178–94. Other works are attributed to John Cleland by Roger Lonsdale, "New Attributions to John Cleland," *Review of English Studies* 30 (1979), pp. 268–90. The history of English erotic writing from 1660 to 1800 is surveyed in Roger Thompson, *Unfit for Modest Ears* (Totowa, NJ: Rowman & Littlefield, 1979); and Peter Wagner, *Eros Revived: Erotica of the Enlightenment in England and America* (London: Secher & Warburg, 1988). David Foxon produced some pioneering studies in his *Libertine Literature in England, 1660–1745* (New Hyde Park, NY: University Books, 1965). James G. Turner has published a series of essays tying the more pornographic works to the traditional canonical ones; see his "The Properties of Libertinism," in Robert Maccubbin (ed.), *'Tis Nature's Fault: Unauthorized Sexual Behavior During the Enlightenment* (New York: Cambridge

University Press, 1987), pp. 75–87; "Pope's Libertine Self-Fashioning," *The Eighteenth Century* 29 (1988), pp. 123–44; "The Culture of Priapism," *Review* 10 (1988), pp. 1–34; "Lovelace and the Paradoxes of Libertinism," in Margaret Ann Doody and Peter Sabor (eds.), *Samuel Richardson* (Cambridge, UK: Cambridge University Press, 1989), pp. 70–88, 273–74; "The Libertine Sublime: Love and Death in Restoration England," in Leslie Ellen Brown and Patricia Craddock (eds.), *Studies in Eighteenth-Century Culture* 19 (1989), pp. 99–115; " 'Illustrious Depravity' and the Erotic Sublime," in Paul J. Korshin (ed.), *The Age of Johnson*, 4 vols. (New York: AMS Press, 1989), vol. 2, pp. 1–38; and "Sex and Consequence," *Review* 11 (1989), pp. 133–77.

2. The history of the changes in the eighteenth-century English family can be found in Lawrence Stone, *The Family, Sex and Marriage in England, 1500–1800* (New York: Harper & Row, 1977) and in his *Road to Divorce* (New York: Oxford University Press, 1990); my book, *The Rise of the Egalitarian Family* (New York: Academic Press, 1978); Judith S. Lewis, *In the Family Way* (New Brunswick, NJ: Rutgers University Press, 1986); and John Gillis, *For Better, For Worse* (New York: Oxford University Press, 1985). I have discussed these works in the following essays: See "Europe and Its Families," *Journal of Social History* 13 (1979), pp. 136–43; "Kinship and Marriage in Early Modern France and England," *Annals of Scholarship* 2 (1981), pp. 113–28; "Is There a Modern Sexual Culture in the West; or, Did England Never Change Between 1500 and 1900," *Journal of the History of Sexuality* 1 (1991), pp. 296–309.

3. I have argued the nature of the change in sexual relations in a series of essays. See "Sodomitical Subcultures, Sodomitical Roles, and the Gender Revolution of the Eighteenth Century: The Recent Historiography," in Maccubbin, *'Tis Nature's Fault*, pp. 109–21; "Gender and the Homosexual Role in Modern Western Culture: The Eighteenth and Nineteenth Centuries Compared," in Dennis Altman et al., *Which Homosexuality?* (London: Gay Men's Press, 1989), pp. 149–69; "The Birth of the Queen: Sodomy and the Emergence of Gender Equality in Modern Culture, 1600–1750," in Martin Duberman, Martha Vicinus and George Chauncey, Jr. (eds.), *Hidden from History: Reclaiming the Gay and Lesbian Past* (New York: New American Library, 1989), pp. 129–40, 509–11; "Sod-

omy Transformed: Aristocratic Libertinage, Public Reputation and the Gender Revolution of the Eighteenth Century," *Journal of Homosexuality* 19 (1990), pp. 105–24. Since this is still a new and controversial point, see the end of these notes for a section of references that provides a larger account of the new literature on male homosexual behavior before 1700. The changes for northwestern Europe after 1700 are documented by my essays, mentioned above, and the work cited in note 4, below.

4. For England see my articles listed in note 3, above, and also my "Sodomitical Assaults, Gender Role, and Sexual Development in Eighteenth-Century London," in Kent Gerard and Gert Hekma (eds.), *The Pursuit of Sodomy: Male Homosexuality in Renaissance and Enlightenment Europe* (New York: Harrington Park Press, 1989), pp. 407–29; Polly Morris, "Sodomy and Male Honor: The Case of Somerset, 1740–1850," in ibid., pp. 383–406; and G.S. Rousseau, *Perilous Enlightenment* (Manchester, UK: Manchester University Press, 1991). For the Netherlands, see Theo van der Meer, "The Persecutions of Sodomites in Eighteenth-Century Amsterdam: Changing Perceptions of Sodomy," in Gerard and Hekma, *Pursuit of Sodomy*, pp. 263–307, which is a summary of his *De Wesentlijke Sonde van Sodomie en Andere Vuyligheeden* (Amsterdam: Tabula, 1984). There are other pertinent articles on the Dutch by D.J. Noordam, Jan Oosterhoff, L.J. Boon and Arend H. Huussen in Gerard and Hekma, *Pursuit of Sodomy*. For France, see Michel Rey, "Parisian Homosexuals Create a Lifestyle, 1700–1750: The Police Archives," in Maccubbin, *'Tis Nature's Fault*, pp. 179–91; and idem, "Police and Sodomy in Eighteenth-Century Paris: From Sin to Disorder," in Gerard and Hekma, *Pursuit of Sodomy*, pp. 129–46.

5. See my *Egalitarian Family*; and Stone, *Family, Sex and Marriage*. The history of attitudes toward women in England can be traced in Felicity A. Nussbaum, *The Brink of All We Hate* (Lexington: University Press of Kentucky, 1984); Alice Browne, *The Eighteenth-Century Feminist Mind* (Brighton, UK: Harvester, 1987); and Kathleen Rogers, *Feminism in Eighteenth-Century England* (Brighton, UK: Harvester, 1982).

6. For separation rituals, see my *Egalitarian Family*, pp. 251–85; and my "Sodomitical Assaults," as well as my "Sex, Gender, and Sexual Identity in Mod-

ern Culture: Male Sodomy and Female Prostitution in Enlightenment London," *Journal of the History of Sexuality* 2 (1991), pp. 186–203.

7. Randolph Trumbach, "London's Sapphists: From Three Sexes to Four Genders in the Making of Modern Culture," in Julia Epstein and Kristina Straub (eds.), *Body Guards: The Cultural Politics of Gender Ambiguity* (New York: Routledge, 1991), pp. 112–41; and Theo van der Meer, "Tribades Tried: Female Same-Sex Offenders in Late Eighteenth-Century Amsterdam," *Journal of the History of Sexuality* 1 (1991), pp. 424–45. For the history of the lesbian role in France, see Marie-Jo Bonnet, *Un Choix sans équivoque* (Paris: Denoël, 1981); and Joan DeJean, *Fictions of Sappho, 1546–1937* (Chicago: University of Chicago Press, 1989). It is important to note that both authors presume that there has always been a lesbian identity. There is a useful survey of the variety of patterns of female behavior in Martha Vicinus, " 'They Wonder to which Sex I Belong': The Historical Roots of the Modern Lesbian Identity," in Altman, *Which Homosexuality?*, pp. 171–98. The argument of a pioneering work like Lillian Faderman, *Surpassing the Love of Men* (New York: Morrow, 1981), now stands in considerable need of revision.

8. Corporation of London Record Office: Sessions Roll [hereafter CLRO:SR] (April 1720), Recognisance 82; Mansion House Charge Book, August 17–18, 1729; *The Autobiography of Francis Place (1771–1854)*, ed. Mary Thale (Cambridge, UK: Cambridge University Press, 1972), pp. 57–59.

9. Henry Deacon, *A Compendious Treatise on the Venereal Disease* (London, n.d.), p. 24; Alexander Smith, *The School of Venus*, 2 vols. (London, 1716), vol. 1, p. 192; Lady Cowper's Diary, Hertfordshire Record Office, D/EP/F30, entry for October 12, 1704; Place, *The Autobiography*, p. 51; "The Grosvenor Case," in *Trials for Adultery*, 7 vols. (London, 1780; reprint ed. New York: Garland, 1985), vol. 6, p. 114; James Graham, *Lectures on the Generation, Increase and Improvement of the Human Species* (London [1780]), p. 55.

10. *The History of the Human Heart* (London, 1749), pp. 123–29; *The Midnight Spy* (London, 1766), quoted in Iwan Bloch, *Sexual Life in England* (London: Arco, 1958), p. 327: Bloch is wrong to say that posture girls first appeared in 1750; Edward Ward, *The London Spy* (London, 1709; reprint ed. New York:

Garland, 1985), p. 140; CLRO:SR (December 1704), Recognisance 49; Mansion House Justice Room Minute Book, December 31, 1789.

11. *Aristotle's Masterpiece: or, The Secrets of Generation* (London, 1694), p. 99ff., 172–74. The 1694 edition, the 1710 edition (in a version from 1776) and the 1725 edition (in a 1749 version) were reprinted in a single volume, which I compiled (New York: Garland, 1986). For a good start at the analysis of the various editions, see Roy Porter, "The Secrets of Generation Display'd: *Aristotle's Masterpiece* in Eighteenth-Century England," in Maccubbin, *'Tis Nature's Fault*, pp. 1–21; Place, *The Autobiography*, p. 45.

12. T.G.A. Nelson, "Women of Pleasure," *Eighteenth-Century Life* 11 (1987), pp. 181–98.

13. Randolph Trumbach, "Modern Prostitution and Gender in *Fanny Hill*: Libertine and Domesticated Fantasy," in G.S. Rousseau and Roy Porter (eds.), *Sexual Underworlds of the Enlightenment* (Manchester, UK: Manchester University Press, 1987), pp. 69–85, contrasts prostitution in the novel with what can be found in the actualities of the legal sources. For Cleland's treatment of the clitoris, see Robert Scholes, *Semiotics and Interpretation* (New Haven, CT: Yale University Press, 1982). Other eighteenth-century discussions of the clitoris, especially in *Aristotle's Masterpiece* are considered in Angus McLaren, *Reproductive Rituals* (New York: Methuen, 1984). For the way in which social ideology can reconstruct the gender characteristics of bodies, see Thomas Laqueur, *Making Sex: Body and Gender from the Greeks to Freud* (Cambridge, MA: Harvard University Press, 1990).

14. J.W. Johnson, "Did Lord Rochester Write *Sodom?*" *Papers of the Bibliographical Society of America* 81 (1987), pp. 119–53. For *Sodom*, I use a text prepared by Larry D. Carver in a forthcoming volume edited by Carol Barash and Rachel Weil. Rochester's eighteenth-century reputation can be traced in *Rochester: The Critical Heritage*, ed. David Farley-Hills (New York: Barnes & Noble, 1972).

15. Foxon, *Libertine Literature*, on *Sodom*, see p. 13; for Cleland's prosecution, see pp. 52–63; *The Tryal and Conviction of Several Reputed Sodomites* (London, 1707). For more on *The Tryal*, see Trumbach, "Birth of the Queen," and "Sodomy Transformed"; on two youths, see Cleland, *Memoirs*, pp. 156–60;

on Ayres, see pp. 10–34; Henry Merritt, "A Biographical Note on John Cleland," *Notes and Queries* 28 (1981), pp. 305–306; for Cleland's attitudes toward sex between women, see Trumbach, "London's Sapphists," pp. 124–30.

16. Epstein, *Cleland*, pp. 33–53; Leo Braudy, "*Fanny Hill* and Materialism," *Eighteenth-Century Studies* 4 (1970), pp. 21–40; Whitley, "Rationalizing a Rogue," pp. 430–43, is the better discussion of Cleland's materialism; James Boswell, *Private Papers* (1928–1934), vol. 13, p. 220, cited in Whitley, "Rationalizing a Rogue," p. 504, n. 202; *Complete Works of…the 3rd Earl of Shaftesbury*, ed. Gerd Hemmerich and Wolfram Bends (Stuttgart-Bad Cannstatt, 1981), vol. 1, pt. 2, pp. 378–442; Robert Voitle, *The Third Earl of Shaftesbury, 1671–1713* (Baton Rouge: Louisiana State University Press, 1984), pp. 241–42; Lord Shaftesbury, *Characteristics*, ed. J.M. Robertson and Stanley Green, 2 vols. (New York: Bobbs-Merrill, 1964), vol. 1, pp. 217–18 and vol. 2, pp. 4, 252–53, 255, 269. For Shaftesbury's influence, see Lawrence Klein, "The Third Earl of Shaftesbury and the Progress of Politeness," *Eighteenth-Century Studies* 18 (1984–1985), pp. 186–214; idem, "Liberty, Manners and Politeness in Early Eighteenth-Century England," *Historical Journal* 32 (1989), pp. 583–605.

17. *Nocturnal Revels: or, The History of King's Place and Other Modern Nunneries…By a Monk of the Order of St. Francis*, 2 vols. (London, 1779), vol. 2, p. 77 and *passim*; Stanley Nash, "Prostitution and Charity: The Magdalen Hospital, A Case Study," *Journal of Social History* 17 (1984), pp. 617–28; Trumbach, "Sex, Gender, and Sexual Identity"; John Bender, *Imagining the Penitentiary* (Chicago: University of Chicago Press, 1987); and Nancy Armstrong, *Desire and Domestic Fiction* (New York: Oxford University Press, 1987). There is a popular description of the domesticated brothel in E.J. Burford, *Royal St. James's* (London: Hale, 1988), and a scholarly one in my forthcoming *The Sexual Life of Eighteenth-Century London*.

18. Martin Madan, *Thelypthora: or, A Treatise on Female Ruin*, 3 vols. (London, 1781); and Trumbach, "Sex, Gender, and Sexual Identity."

19. For the Dilettanti, see Cecil Harcourt-Smith, *The Society of Dilettanti, Its Regalia and Pictures* (London: Macmillan, 1932); and Lionel Cust, *History of the Society of Dilettanti* (London: Macmillan, 1914). For the Hell-Fire Club, there

are books of varying value: See L.C. Clark, *The Clubs of the Georgian Rakes* (New York: Columbia University Press, 1942); and D.P. Mannix, *The Hell-Fire Club* (New York: Ballantine, 1959).

20. Betty Kemp, *Sir Francis Dashwood* (London: Macmillan, 1967), pp. 101-104, 116, 137-57; Horace Walpole, *Memoirs of the Reign of George III*, 3 vols., ed. G.F. Russell Barker (London, 1894), vol. 1, pp. 136-38, 248.

21. Kemp, *Dashwood*, pp. 131-36; Walpole, *Memoirs*, vol. 1, p. 138; Raymond Postgate, *'That Devil Wilkes'* (London: Dobson, 1956), pp. 22-23; Charles Churchill, "The Candidate," in *Poetical Works*, ed. Douglas Grant (Oxford, UK: Oxford University Press, 1956), ll. 695-701. Statues of Venus appeared in some eighteenth-century gardens as erotic symbols: The Venus at Stowe was accompanied by obscene paintings and verses, as well as soft couches for lovemaking. For this, see J.G. Turner, "The Sexual Politics of Landscape: Images of Venus in Eighteenth-Century English Poetry and Landscape Gardening," *Studies in Eighteenth-Century Culture* 11 (1982), pp. 343-66.

22. The text is from Adrian Hamilton, *The Infamous "Essay on Woman"* (London: Deutsch, 1972); Eric R. Watson, "John Wilkes and the 'Essay on Woman,' " *Notes and Queries* 9 (1914), pp. 121-23, 143-45, 162-64, 183-85, 203-205, 222-23; Calhoun Winton, "John Wilkes and 'An Essay on Woman,' " in Donald Kay (ed.), *A Provision of Human Nature* (University, AL: University of Alabama Press, 1977), pp. 121-32; and Wagner, *Eros Revived*, pp. 191-200.

23. Hamilton's letter was printed in Richard Payne Knight, *Discourse on the Worship of Priapus* (London, 1786), which is reprinted in Ashley Montagu (ed.), *Sexual Symbolism* (New York: Julian Press, 1957), pp. 13-23. See also Brian Fothergill, *Sir William Hamilton: Envoy Extraordinary* (New York: Harcourt, Brace & World, 1969), pp. 173-74.

24. Peter Funnell, in Michael Clarke and Nicholas Penny (eds.), *The Arrogant Connoisseur: Richard Payne Knight, 1751-1824* (Manchester, UK: Manchester University Press, 1982), ch. 4; and G.S. Rousseau, "The Sorrows of Priapus," in Rousseau and Porter, *Sexual Underworlds*, pp. 101-53.

25. Payne Knight, *Discourse*, in Montagu, *Sexual Symbolism*, pp. 26-27, 30, 53-54, 61-62, 67, 72-73, 75, 81, 84, 86-89, 123, 134-35, 200-207 and 216.

Appendix: Bibliography of European Sodomy before 1700

The history of European sodomy before 1700 is best documented for southern Europe where there were two slightly variant patterns. One was for Italy, where men had sexual relations exclusively with boys, and another for Spain and Portugal, where relations were mainly between men and boys but where there were also a few adult passive effeminate and transvestite males.

For Italy, see Guido Ruggiero, *The Boundaries of Eros* (New York: Oxford University Press, 1985). My review of it can be found in Kent Gerard and Gert Hekma (eds.), *The Pursuit of Sodomy: Male Homosexuality in Renaissance and Enlightenment Europe* (New York: Harrington Park Press, 1989), also published as numbers 1 and 2 of the *Journal of Homosexuality* 16 (1988). See also the very important work on Florence by Michael Rocke in Gerard and Hekma, *Pursuit of Sodomy*, pp. 7–31; idem, "Male Homosexuality and Its Regulation in Late Medieval Florence" (Ph.D. thesis, State University of New York at Binghamton, 1989), which, in revised form, is forthcoming from Oxford University Press.

For Spain and Portugal, see Rafael Carrasco, *Inquisición y represión sexual en Valencia* (Barcelona: Laertes, 1985); Mary Elizabeth Perry, "The Nefarious Sin in Early Modern Seville," in Gerard and Hekma, *Pursuit of Sodomy*, pp. 67–89; E. William Monter, *Frontiers of Heresy* (New York: Cambridge University Press, 1990); Luiz Mott, "Pogoda português: A subcultura *gay* em Portugal nos tempos inquisitoriais," *Ciência e Cultura* 40 (1988), pp. 120–39, an English version of which is forthcoming in the Amsterdam gay and lesbian studies conference proceedings of 1987, which will appear in an issue of the *Journal of Homosexuality* edited by Theo van der Meer; idem, "Justitia et misericordia: A inquisição Portuguesa e a repressão ao nefando pecado de sodomia," in Ad. van der Woude (ed.), *The Role of the State and Public Opinion in Sexual Attitudes and Demographic Behaviour* (Madrid: International Commission of Historical Demography, 1990), pp. 243–58; and idem and Aroldo Assunção, in Gerard and Hekma, *Pursuit of Sodomy*, pp. 91–101. Mott and I considerably disagree in our reading of his evidence; see Trumbach, "Gender and the Homosexual Role," cited in note 3, above. I also disagree with E. William Monter's early essay on sodomy, "Sodomy and Heresy in Early Modern Switzerland," in Salvatore J. Licata and Robert

P. Petersen (eds.), *Historical Perspectives on Homosexuality* (Binghamton, NY: Haworth Press, 1982), pp. 41–55. See Trumbach, "Sodomitical Subcultures," cited in note 3, above. From my point of view, both of these very good historians are misled by twentieth-century presuppositions, drawn from the gay movement in Mott's case and from psychoanalysis in Monter's.

There is less evidence for northern Europe. For France – which, in the eighteenth century, looks more like England and the Netherlands, but which had before 1700 a prosecution record more like southern Europe's – see, Maurice Lever, *Les Bûchers de sodome* (Paris: Fayard, 1985); David Teasley, "The Charge of Sodomy as a Political Weapon in Early Modern France: The Case of Henry III in Catholic League Polemic, 1585-1589," in *The Maryland Historian* 18 (1987), pp. 17-30; and Robert Oresko, "Homosexuality and the Court Elites of Early Modern France," in Gerard and Hekma, *Pursuit of Sodomy*, pp. 105-28. For England, see Alan Bray, *Homosexuality in Renaissance England* (London: Gay Men's Press, 1982). See also the work of three literary historians: Steve Brown, "The Boyhood of Shakespeare's Heroines: Notes on Gender Ambiguity in the Sixteenth Century," *Studies in English Literature* 30 (1990), pp. 243-63; Bruce R. Smith, *Homosexual Desire in Shakespeare's England* (Chicago: University of Chicago Press, 1991); and Gregory W. Bredbeck, *Sodomy and Interpretation* (Ithaca, NY: Cornell University Press, 1991).

For the Netherlands, see Dirk Jaap Noordam, "Sodomy in the Dutch Republic 1600-1725," in Gerard and Hekma, *Pursuit of Sodomy*, pp. 207-28; idem, "Sodomites in the Rural Areas of the Low Countries in the Early Modern Period (15th-19th Centuries)," forthcoming in the Amsterdam conference proceedings to appear in the *Journal of Homosexuality*. The documentation for England and the Netherlands before 1700 is problematic since there were not the waves of prosecutions found in France, Switzerland, Spain, Portugal and Italy; nonetheless, the pattern of sex between men and passive adolescent youths is clear. The movement from a system of sexual relations between males in which domination was organized by age (men with adolescents) to one organized by gender (or relations with passive effeminate males) was a movement from one to the other of the two worldwide patterns of sexual relations between males. These

389

worldwide patterns were identified in Randolph Trumbach, "London's Sodomites: Homosexual Behavior and Western Culture in the Eighteenth Century,"
Journal of Social History 11 (1977), pp. 1–33. They were further analyzed, without a sufficient indication of indebtedness, and with inelegant overelaborations
and doubtful historical contextualizing by David F. Greenberg, *The Construction
of Homosexuality* (Chicago: University of Chicago Press, 1988).

CHAPTER EIGHT: POLITICS AND PORNOGRAPHY

1. Robert Darnton, *Edition et sédition: L'Univers de la littérature clandestine
au XVIIIᵉ siècle* (Paris: Gallimard, 1991).

2. Wijnand W. Mijnhardt, "The Dutch Enlightenment: Humanism, Nation-
alism and Decline," in Margaret C. Jacob and Wijnand W. Mijnhardt (eds.), *The
Dutch Republic in the Eighteenth Century: Decline, Enlightenment and Revolution*
(Ithaca, NY: Cornell University Press, 1992).

3. Steven Marcus, *The Other Victorians: A Study of Sexuality and Pornography in Mid-Nineteenth-Century England* (New York: Basic Books, 1966), see the
conclusion.

4. Only two authors have contributed to the problem of Dutch pornography: Petrus Jacobus Buijnsters, "Libertijnse literatuur in Nederland gedurende
de 18e eeuw?" in Petrus Jacobus Buijnsters (ed.), *Nederlandse literatuur van de
achttiende eeuw* (Utrecht: Hes, 1984), pp. 99–113; and Donald Haks, "Libertinisme en Nederlands verhalend proza, 1650–1700," in Gert Hekma and Herman
Roodenburg (eds.), *Soete minne en helsche boosheit: Seksuele voorstellingen in
Nederland, 1300–1850* (Nijmegen: Sun, 1988), pp. 85–108. Because a specialized
bibliography does not exist, my research has been based on the following: Emma
Dronckers, *Verzameling F.G. Waller: Catalogus van Nederlandsche en vlaamsche
populaire boeken* (The Hague: M. Nijhoff, 1936); M. Buisman, *Populaire prozaschrijvers van 1600–1815: Alfabetische naamlijst* (Amsterdam: Israel, 1960);
Short-title-catalogus van Nederlandstalig populair proza (in het bijzonder: romans)
(Amsterdam: Instituut voor Neerlandistick, 1981); Petrus Jacobus Buijnsters
(ed.), *Populaire prozaschrijvers der XVIIᵉ en XVIIIᵉ eeuw* (Utrecht: Hes, 1981);
and J.L.M. Gieles and A.P.J. Plak, *Bibliografie van het Nederlandstalig narratief*

fictioneel proza, 1670-1700 (Nieuwkoop: De Graaf, 1988).

5. See David Foxon, *Libertine Literature in England, 1660-1745* (New Hyde Park, NY: University Books, 1965). For full bibliographical details of these translations, see Buijnsters, "Libertijnse literatuur," p. 105.

6. John Landwehr, *Romeyn de Hooghe (1645-1708) as Book Illustrator* (Amsterdam: Van Genut, 1970), p. 121. A few years later, de Hooghe was accused by some of his political opponents of having engraved the prints of the Dutch translation of *La Puttana errante* (falsely attributed to Aretino). See also Gerhard Langemeyer, "Aesopus in Europa," in *Bemerkungen zur politischen graphik des Romeyn de Hooghe* (Munster: Landesmuseum für kunst und kulturgeschichte, 1974), pp. 39-40; and Arend H. Huussen, Jr., "Censorship in the Netherlands," in Robert P. Maccubbin and Martha Hamilton-Phillips (eds.), *The Age of William III and Mary II: Power, Politics and Patronage, 1688-1702* (Williamsburg, VA: College of William & Mary English Department, 1989), p. 349.

7. Haks, "Libertinisme," pp. 90-96.

8. *Het Amsterdamsch hoerdom* (Amsterdam, 1681; reprint eds. 1684, 1756, 1765, 1782); *D'openhertige juffrouw of d'ontdekte geveinsdheid* (Leiden, 1679; reprint eds. 1699, 1725, 1744, 1769, 1774, 1790); *De hedendaagsche Haagsche en Amsterdamse zalet-juffers* (Amsterdam, 1696, reprint eds. 1696, 1699). See M. Buisman, *Populaire prozaschrijvers.*

9. Roland Mortier, "Libertinage littéraire et tensions sociales dans la littérature de l'ancien régime: De la 'Picara' a la 'fille de joie,' " *Revue de Littérature Comparée* (1972), pp. 35-45; Hendrik van Gorp, *Inleiding tot de picareske verhaalkunst* (Groningen: Wolters-Noordhof, 1978), pp. 57-60; and see Haks, "Libertinisme," pp. 94-95.

10. See *De Amsterdamsche lichtmis of Zoldaat van Fortuin* [The Amsterdam rake] (Amsterdam, 1731); *De Middelburgsche Avanturier: Of het leven van een Burger Persoon* [The Middelburg adventurer] (Amsterdam, 1760) and its predecessors; Buisman, *Populaire prozaschrijvers*, pp. 22-24; *De Belydenis van een lichtmis* [Confessions of a rake] (n.p., 1770); and Buijnsters, "Libertijnse Literatuur," pp. 107-108.

11. Buijnsters, "Libertijnse Literatuur," p. 99.

12. B. Ivker, "Towards a Definition of Libertinism in Eighteenth-Century French Fiction," *Studies on Voltaire and the Eighteenth Century* 73 (1970), pp. 221–39.

13. Truusje Goedings, "De 'vrijerijboeken' en 'pareltjes' van Simon Eikelenberg (1663-1738): Iets over de erotische belangstelling van een 17de-eeuwer," *De Boekenwereld* 1 (1984), pp. 47–57, and *De Boekenwereld* 2 (1985-1986), pp. 80–92.

14. Arend H. Huussen, "Freedom of the Press and Censorship in the Netherlands, 1780-1810," in A.C. Duke and C.A. Tamse (eds.), *Too Mighty to be Free: Censorship and the Press in Britain and the Netherlands* (Zutphen: de Walburg Pers, 1987), p. 113.

15. Willem Pieter Cornelis Knuttel, *Catalogus van de pamflettenverzameling berustende in de Koninklÿke Bibliotheek*, 9 vols. (The Hague, 1889-1920). I cite the pamphlet under no. 20674.

16. Darnton, *Edition et sédition*, pp. v, 13–16. For a discussion of the modern French usage of *pornographie*, see Lynn Hunt's introduction.

17. Tom Schalken, *Pornografie en strafrecht: Beschouwingen over het pornografiebegrip en zijn juridische hanteerbaarheid* (Arnhem: Gouda Quint, 1972), pp. 7–10.

18. Wijnand W. Mijnhardt, "De geschiedschrijving over de ideeëngeschiedenis van de 17e- en 18e-eeuwse Republiek," in Wijnand W. Mijnhardt (ed.), *Kantelend geschiedbeeld: Nederlandse historiografie sinds 1945* (Utrecht & Antwerp: Het Spectrum, 1983), pp. 165–68; and Ernst Heinrich Kossmann, "Freedom in Seventeenth-Century Dutch Thought and Practice," in Jonathan I. Israel (ed.), *The Anglo-Dutch Moment: Essays on the Glorious Revolution and Its World Impact* (Cambridge, UK: Cambridge University Press, 1991), pp. 281–98. See also *Too Mighty to be Free*, in particular the contributions of Simon Groenveld and Arend H. Huussen.

19. Willem Pieter Cornelis Knuttel, *Verboden boeken in de republiek der Verenigde Nederlanden: Beredeneerde catalogus* (The Hague: M. Nijhoff, 1914). I cite the pamphlet listed under no. 67.

20. I owe this reference to Han Brouwer, who is preparing a Ph.D on the subject.

21. Wijnand W. Mijnhardt, "The Dutch Enlightenment"; and N.C.F. van Sas (eds.), "Opiniepers en politieke cultuur," in F. Grijzenhout, Wijnand W. Mijnhardt and N.C.F. van Sas, *Voor vaderland en vrijheid: De revolutie van de patriotten* (Amsterdam: Bataafsche Leeuw, 1987), pp. 114–21.

22. Peter Wagner, *Eros Revived: Erotica of the Enlightenment in England and America* (London: Secker & Warburg, 1988), pp. 47–112.

23. D.J. Noordam, "Lust, last en plezier: Vier eeuwen seksualiteit in Nederland," in *Een kind onder het hart: Verloskunde, volksgeloof, gezin, seksualiteit en moraal vroeger en nu* (Amsterdam: Meulenhoff, 1987), pp. 146–48.

24. W.Th.M. Frijhoff, "Seksualiteit en erotiek in de achttiende eeuw," *Documentatieblad Werkgroep Achttiende Eeuw* 17 (1985), p. 203.

25. Noordam, "Lust, last en plezier," pp. 128–29.

26. J. de Brune de Jonge, *Wetsteen der vernuften oft bequaam middel om van alle voorvallende zaken aardighlik te leeren spreken* (Amsterdam, 1644), see preface, "Aen den Leser."

27. See Th.J. Meijer, "Brieven uit de studentenkerker," *Leids Jaarboekje* 63 (1971), pp. 43–64.

28. See Herman Roodenburg, " 'Venus Minsieke Gasthuis': Over seksuele attitudes in de achttiende-eeuwse Republiek," in J. Bremmer (ed.), *Van Sappho tot de Sade: Momenten in de geschiedenis van de seksualiteit* (Amsterdam: Wereldbibliotheek, 1988), pp. 80–99.

29. E. de Jongh, "Erotica in vogelperspectief: De dubbelzinnigheid van een reeks 17de-eeuwse genrevoorstellingen," *Simiolus* 1 (1968-1969), pp. 22–72.

30. Haks, "Libertinisme," p. 86.

31. Leendert F. Groenendijk, *De nadere reformatie van het gezin: De visie van Petrus Wittewrongel op de christelijke huishouding* (Dordrecht: Vandentol, 1984), pp. 82–83.

32. P.J.H. Kapteyn, *Taboe, ontwikkelingen in macht en moraal speciaal in Nederland* (Amsterdam: De Arbeiderspers, 1980), p. 71; and Lotte C. van der Pol, "Van speelhuis naar bordeel: Veranderingen in de organisatie van de prostitutie in Amsterdam in de tweede helft van de achttiende eeuw," *Documentatieblad Werkgroep Achttiende Eeuw* 17 (1985), pp. 157–72.

33. Mirjam Westen, "Over het naakt in de Noordnederlandse kunst in de periode 1770-1830," *De Negentiende Eeuw* 10 (1986), pp. 219-20.

34. Walter Gobbers, *Jean-Jeacques Rousseau in Holland: Een onderzoek naar de invloed van de mens en het werk (1760-1810)* (Gent: Secretariaat van de Koninklijke Vlaämse Academie voor taal en Letterkunde, 1963), pp. 71-74.

35. The interrogation of the Jewish peddler Matthijs Modechai Cohen in 1768, apprehended while in possession of condoms, dildos, copies of *L'Ecole des filles* and prints from *Dom Bougre*, revealed the existence of such an underground circuit. Archives Court of Holland, Algemeen Rijksarchief, the Hague, Criminele sententies, Inv. no. 5665. The failed prosecution of the Rotterdam distributor Julien in 1772 indicated the existence of a similar network reaching into the southern Netherlands (ibid., Inv. no. 5500.10).

36. This practice applies, for example, to *Het Amsterdamsch hoerdom*, which was published anonymously in 1756 and after.

37. For a more extensive discussion of this problem, see my essays "The Dutch Enlightenment" and "Dutch Culture in the Age of William and Mary: Cosmopolitan or Provincial?" in Dale Hoak and Mordechai Feingold (eds.), *The Glorious Revolution* (Berkeley: University of California Press, 1992).

38. W. van den Berg, "Sara Burgerhart en haar derde stem," *Documentatieblad Werkgroep Achttiende Eeuw* 13 (1981), pp. 151-208.

39. A highlight of these new sexual education manuals was Gerrit Warnars, *Alexis en Gualthur of de wijze om jongelingen tegen ontucht te beveiligen: Een boek ter bevordering van zedelijk en huiselijk geluk* [The means to protect the youth from immorality: A contribution to moral and domestic happiness] (Amsterdam, 1801).

CHAPTER NINE: PORNOGRAPHY AND THE FRENCH REVOLUTION

1. In 1792-1793, Sade held various minor posts in his ward (*section*) of Paris. On Sade's revolutionary career, see Gilbert Lély, *The Marquis de Sade: A Biography*, trans. Alec Brown (New York: Grove Press, 1961), pp. 310-57.

2. See my discussion in the introduction, pp. 9-45. The essential source is Etienne-Gabriel Peignot, *Dictionnaire critique, littéraire, et bibliographique des*

principaux livres condamnés au feu, supprimés ou censurés, 2 vols. (Paris, 1806).

3. Donald Thomas, *A Long Time Burning: The History of Literary Censorship in England* (New York: Praeger, 1969), p. 78, quoting a justice at Queen's Bench in 1707.

4. Ibid., pp. 113 and 189.

5. Ibid., p. 189.

6. Ibid., pp. 179 and 186.

7. Peter Wagner, *Eros Revived: Erotica of the Enlightenment in England and America* (London: Secker & Warburg, 1988), p. 6.

8. Robert Darnton, "The High Enlightenment and the Low-Life of Literature," in *The Literary Underground of the Old Regime* (Cambridge, MA: Harvard University Press, 1982), pp. 1–40, especially p. 29.

9. Sarah Maza, "The Diamond Necklace Affair Revisited (1785–1786): The Case of the Missing Queen," in Lynn Hunt (ed.), *Eroticism and the Body Politic* (Baltimore, MD: Johns Hopkins University Press, 1991), pp. 63–89.

10. Chantal Thomas, *La Reine scélérate: Marie-Antoinette dans les pamphlets* (Paris: Seuil, 1989). See also Lynn Hunt, "The Many Bodies of Marie Antoinette: The Problem of the Feminine in the French Revolution," in Hunt (ed.), *Eroticism*, pp. 108–30.

11. Jeffrey Merrick, "Sexual Politics and Public Order in Late Eighteenth-Century France," *Journal of the History of Sexuality* 1 (1990), pp. 68–84.

12. Edward A. Tiryakian, "From Underground to Convention: Sexual Anomie as an Antecedent to the French Revolution," *Social Theory* 5 (1984), pp. 289–307, quote p. 302; the quote from Restif is on p. 301.

13. *Chronique Arétine, ou Recherches pour servir à l'histoire des moeurs du XVIIIe siècle* (Caprée, 1789).

14. *L'Autrichienne en goguettes, ou L'Orgie royale, opéra proverbe, 1789: Composé par un Garde-du-Corps, et publié depuis la liberté de la presse, et mis en musique par la Reine* (n.p., 1789). For an analysis of the differences between pre- and post-1789 pamphlets about the queen, see Hunt, "The Many Bodies."

15. *Apparution de Thérèse philosophe à Saint-Cloud, ou Le Triomphe de la volupté. Dédié à la Reine* (Saint-Cloud: Chez la Mère des Grâces, 1790).

16. *Les Enfans de Sodome à l'Assemblée nationale, ou Députation de l'ordre de la manchette* (Paris, 1790).

17. *Fredaines lubriques de J— F— Maury, prêtre indigne de l'Eglise catholique* (n.p., 1790). Jean-Siffrein Maury (1746-1817) was a clerical deputy to the Estates General known for his opposition to the nationalization of church property and the Civil Constitution of the Clergy. He emigrated in late 1791.

18. For a general overview emphasizing the contrast between aristocratic degeneracy and republican health, see Antoine de Baecque, "Pamphlets: Libel and Political Mythology," in Robert Darnton and Daniel Roche (eds.), *Revolution in Print: The Press in France, 1775-1800* (Berkeley: University of California Press, 1989), pp. 165-76; and idem, "Dégénérescence et régénération: Le Livre licencieux juge la Révolution française," in Daniel Roche and Roger Chartier (eds.), *Mélanges de la Bibliothèque de la Sorbonne*: vol. 9, *Livre et Révolution* (Paris: Aux Amateurs de Livres, 1989), pp. 123-32. My own view is that de Baecque may have overemphasized the prevalence of this theme.

19. *Les Travaux d'Hercule, ou La Rocambole de la fouterie, Par un Emule de Piron, Grécourt et Gervais* (Paris: L'An Deuxième de la Liberté [1790]).

20. I am taking issue with the view implied by Darnton, "The High Enlightenment," especially p. 33.

21. The attribution is mentioned in *Dictionnaire des oeuvres érotiques: Domaine français* (Paris: Mercure de France, 1971), p. 147.

22. Antoine de Baecque, "The 'Livres remplis d'horreur': Pornographic Literature and Politics at the Beginning of the French Revolution," in Peter Wagner (ed.), *Erotica and the Enlightenment* (Frankfurt, 1991), p. 152.

23. For a brief discussion of legislative efforts, see Jean-Jacques Pauvert, *Estampes érotiques révolutionnaires: La Révolution française et l'obscénité* (Paris: Henri Veyrier, 1989), especially pp. 18-40. See also Alma Söderhjelm, *Le Régime de la presse pendant la Révolution française*, 2 vols. (Geneva: Slatkine Reprints, 1971). For the particular discussion and the text of the law, see M.J. Mavidal and M.E. Laurent (eds.), *Archives parlementaires de 1787 à 1870*, first series, 1787-1799, vol. 28 (Paris, 1887), p. 28.

24. Söderhjelm, *Le Régime de la presse*, vol. 1, pp. 154-92.

25. For information on peddlers, see ibid. but especially de Baecque, "The 'Livres remplis d'horreur,' " pp. 123–65.

26. Pauvert, *Estampes érotiques révolutionnaires*; and Antoine de Baecque, *La Caricature révolutionnaire* (Paris: Presses du CNRS, 1988), pp. 30–31, 37, 236–37.

27. Based on the inventory of the confiscation of *libelles*, in APP, Paris, Aa.

28. As quoted in the *Journal du soir des frères Chaignieau* of February 23, 1799, in Alphonse Aulard, *Paris pendant la réaction thermidorienne et sous le Directoire*, vol. 5, *Du 3 thermidor an VI au 19 brumaire an VIII / 21 juillet 1798 – 10 novembre 1799* (Paris, 1902), p. 397.

29. Louis-Sébastien Mercier, *Le Nouveau Paris* (Paris, an 7 [1799]), vol. 3, pp. 178–79.

30. On the attempts to suppress political journals, see Söderhjelm, *Le Régime de la presse*, vol. 2.

31. Pascal Pia, *Les Livres de l'Enfer: Bibliographie critique des ouvrages érotiques dans leurs différentes éditions du XVIe siècle à nos jours*, 2 vols. (Paris: C. Cloulet & A. Faure, 1978). Pia's catalog is alphabetical, not chronological. I singled out all the works published during the revolutionary decade for my comparisons.

32. To determine the content of those works that I had not read myself, I used the *Dictionnaire des oeuvres érotiques*. It lists some but not all of the works given in the Pia catalog for the Bibliothèque Nationale.

33. These figures are tabulated from the information given in Angus Martin, Vivienne G. Mylne and Richard Frautschi, *Bibliographie du genre romanesque français, 1751–1800* (London: Mansell, 1977).

34. De Baecque, "The 'Livres remplis d'horreur,' " pp. 123–65. For more details, see also, the discussion in idem, "Le Corps de la Révolution: La souveraineté, le récit et le rituel politiques étudiés à travers leurs représentations corporelle (de l'ancien régime à la Révolution française)," 2 vols. (Ph.D. thesis, Université de Paris I, 1992).

35. For an analysis of this print – "Grand Débandement de l'armée anti-constitutionelle" – see Vivian Cameron, "Political Exposures: Sexuality and Caricature in the French Revolution," in Hunt (ed.), *Eroticism*, pp. 90–107. The engraving, first advertised in February 1792, showed various aristocratic women

displaying their bare bottoms to the Austrian army. They are led by Théroigne de Méricourt, noted democrat, who shows her "République" (public thing, pudendum) to the army, which is caught in a pose of virtual Freudian sexual fright at the sight. The Jacobins and sans-culottes hide behind the row of bare women's bottoms, presenting pikes with dangling hams and sausages. In this print, however, satire is much more evident than pornographic intent.

36. On the production of royalist caricatures, see Claude Langlois, *La Caricature contre-révolutionnaire* (Paris: Presses du CNRS, 1988).

37. The fanciful publication data reads "A Cythere et dans tous les bordels de Paris, 1790."

38. The social circuit for scurrilous gossip is described by the author of *Portefeuille d'un talon rouge*: "a vile courtier weaves the stories in the shadows of the court, another courtier puts them into verse and couplets, and their valets pass them around even as far as the marketplaces. From the markets they are passed on to the artisan who, in his turn, reports them to the lords who had fabricated them in the first place and who, without wasting a minute, whisper to their friends in the tones of the most consummate hypocrisy, 'have you read them?'" reprint ed. (Paris: Bibliothèque des Curieux, 1911), p. 22. This reprint is based on the edition dated 178–, De l'Imprimerie du Comte de Paradès.

39. De Baecque, "The 'Livres remplis d'horreur.'"

40. These engravings have been reproduced in Pauvert, *Estampes érotiques*. The originals are in the reserve of the Cabinet des Estampes, Bibliothèque Nationale.

41. Boyer de Nîmes [Jacques Marie Boyer], *Histoire des caricatures de la révolte des Français*, 2 vols. (Paris: De l'Imprimerie du Journal du Peuple, 1792), vol. 1, p. 10 and vol. 2, p. 6. In his work, Boyer provides copies of many engravings, some of which verge on the pornographic, and he discusses the outpouring of pornographic literature and engravings even though he does not name them by title.

42. De Baecque, "The 'Livres remplis d'horreur,'" pp. 134–37.

43. Boyer, *Histoire*, vol. 2, p. 9.

44. I am indebted to Hans-Ulrich Gumbrecht for suggestions along these lines.

45. (n.p., n.d.).

46. *Le Cadran des plaisirs de la cour, ou Les Aventures du petit page Chérubin. Pour servir de suite à la vie de Marie-Antoinette, ci-devant Reine de France. Suivi de la confession de Mademoiselle Sapho* (Paris: Chez les Marchands de Nouveautés, n.d.).

47. *Les Roup—tes des Calotins* (n.p., n.d.).

48. *Dom-Bougre*.

49. (Paris: De L'Imprimerie de la Delaunay, connoisseuse, si jamais il en fut, 1791).

50. (London, 1790).

51. *Julie philosophe, ou Le Bon patriote. Histoire à peu près véritable, d'une Citoyenne active qui a été tour-à-tour agent et victime dans les dernières révolutions de la Hollande, du Brabant et de la France*, 2 vols. (n.p., 1791).

52. Ibid., vol. 2, p. 221.

53. De Baecque, "The 'Livres remplis d'horreur,' " pp. 129–30.

54. See my argument in *The Family Romance of the French Revolution* (Berkeley, CA: University of California Press, 1992).

55. For a much more nuanced view than the one on which I elaborate here, see Lucienne Frappier-Mazur, *Sade et l'écriture de l'orgie* (Paris: Nathan, 1991), especially pp. 29–85.

56. I have analyzed this work at greater length in *The Family Romance*, pp. 124–50. For a suggestive but different analysis of Sade, see Frances Ferguson, "Sade and the Pornographic Legacy," *Representations* 36 (1991), pp. 1–21.

57. This is evident from the index to Alphonse Aulard, *Paris pendant la réaction thermidorienne et sous le Directoire: Recueil de documents pour l'histoire de l'esprit public à Paris*, 5 vols. (Paris, 1898–1902); and idem, *Paris sous le Consulat: Recueil de documents pour l'histoire de l'esprit public à Paris*, 4 vols. (Paris, 1903–1909).

58. *Paris, littéraire* (Hamburg, an 7).

59. *L'Anti-Justine, ou Les Délices de l'amour, par M. Linguet, Avocat au et en Parlement* (Paris: Palais-Royal, 1798), p. 3.

60. Guillaume Apollinaire, *Les Maîtres de l'Amour: L'Oeuvre du chevalier*

Andréa de Nerciat, 2 vols. (Paris: Bibliothèque des Curieux, 1910), vol. 1, p. 33, from letter of May 1797 from Sabatier de Castres to Napoleon Bonaparte.

61. For the publishing history, see Martin, Mylne and Frautschi, *Bibliographie du genre romanesque français*.

62. Pia, *Les Livres de l'Enfer*, vol. 1, pp. 247–48.

63. Louis Perceau, *Bibliographie du roman érotique au XIXe siècle*, 2 vols. (Paris: G. Fourdrinier, 1930), vol. 1, p. 27.

64. *Félicia*, 4 vols. (Paris, 1782), vol. 1, p. 2.

65. *Monrose, ou Le Libertin par fatalité*, 2 vols. (n.p., 1792).

66. *Le Diable au corps, oeuvre posthume du très recommandable Docteur Cazzoné, membre extraordinaire de la joyeuse Faculté Phallo-coiro-pygo-glottonomique*, 2 vols. (Paris, 1803), vol. 1, pp. i and 134.

67. *Les Aphrodites, ou Fragments thali-priapiques pour servir à l'histoire du plaisir*, 4 vols. (1793; reprint ed. 1864), vol. 1, pp. 21–22 and vol. 4, pp. 181–85.

68. André-Robert Andréa de Nerciat, *Mon Noviciat, ou Les Joies de Lolotte*, 2 vols. (n.p., 1792–1864), vol. 1, p. 14.

69. *Le Diable au corps*, vol. 1, pp. i and 176.

70. For a discussion of the "child" novel, see Hunt, *The Family Romance*, pp. 171–81.

71. On nineteenth-century pornography see Annie Stora-Lamarre, *L'Enfer de la IIIe République: Censeurs et pornographes (1881–1914)* (Paris: Imago, 1990), pp. 22–44.

Contributors

JOAN DEJEAN is Trustee Professor of French at the University of Pennsylvania. She is the author of *Fictions of Sappho* and *Tender Geographies: Women and the Origins of the Novel in France*.

PAULA FINDLEN teaches in the Department of History and the Program in the History and Philosophy of Science at the University of California, Davis. She is the author of *Possessing Nature: Museums, Collecting and Scientific Culture in Early Modern Italy*.

LUCIENNE FRAPPIER-MAZUR, Professor of French at the University of Pennsylvania, is the author of *L'Expression métaphorique dans "La Comédie humaine"* and *Sade et l'écriture de l'orgie*. She has published numerous articles on novelistic representation in the nineteenth century and is pursuing her research on representations of the body in the French novel.

LYNN HUNT is Annenberg Professor of History at the University of Pennsylvania. She is the author of various books on the French Revolution and on the new cultural history.

MARGARET C. JACOB is Professor of History in the University at the New School for Social Research. She is the author of several books on the cultural contexts of science and the Enlightenment.

WIJNAND W. MIJNHARDT is Professor of Cultural History at the University of Utrecht. He is the author of a major history of eighteenth-century Dutch sociability. Together with Margaret Jacob he edited *The Dutch Republic in the Eighteenth Century: Decline, Enlightenment, and Revolution*. He is currently completing a book on publishing and reading in the Netherlands between 1780 and 1850.

KATHRYN NORBERG is Associate Professor in the Department of History at the University of California, Los Angeles and Director of the UCLA Center for the Study of Women. She is the author of *Rich and Poor in Grenoble, 1600–1814* and is finishing a book on the history of prostitution and its representations in France between 1600 and 1814.

RANDOLPH TRUMBACH is Professor of History at Baruch College, City University of New York. He has written *The Rise of the Egalitarian Family* and a recent series of ten articles on homosexuality and prostitution, preliminaries to a two-volume study of sexual life in eighteenth-century London.

RACHEL WEIL is Assistant Professor of History at Cornell University. She is working on a book about the relationship between gender ideology and political discourse in late Stuart England.

Index

403

This edition designed by Bruce Mau
with Nigel Smith and Alison Hahn
Type composed by Archetype
Printed and bound Smythe-sewn by Maple-Vail
using Sebago acid-free paper